The Lakeside Classics

Absaraka
Home of the Crows

The Lakeside Classics

Absaraka

(*Ab-sa-ra-ka*)

Home of the Crows

BY

MRS. MARGARET I. CARRINGTON

EDITED BY

MILO MILTON QUAIFE

CHICAGO

The Lakeside Press

R. R. DONNELLEY & SONS CO.

Christmas, 1950

Publishers' Preface

———

THE last volume of The Lakeside Classics dealing with Indian warfare was "Army Life in Dakota" by De Trobriand. That volume, published in 1941, had been selected and edited before Pearl Harbor. This year's volume, too, another tale of Indian warfare, was selected and edited before there was any thought that long before its publication date all branches of our armed forces would be engaged in hostilities in far off Korea and before there was any thought that members of our own organization would have been called up for military service. Fortunately these events have not prevented publication of this forty-eighth volume of The Lakeside Classics.

The publishers are presenting "Absaraka" to their readers in the confident hope that this narrative of an isolated expedition of our army will hold their interest. The area in which it operated is to the west of the country in which the events described by De Trobriand took place.

The circumstances in which that expedition was sent forth and many of the difficulties which it faced with great courage will be best understood by a reading of the editor's historical introduction, the first paragraph of which alone gives food for serious thought.

Again we express our thanks to The Newberry Library for making its copy of the original edition available and to Dr. Quaife for his scholarly introduction and notes.

A continuing satisfactory volume of work, the absence of interruption in operations, and the gratifying interest and cooperation of all its employees have made it possible for the company to give its major attention to satisfying the needs of its customers and to the problems of orderly production. Continued emphasis has been placed on research and the improvement and development of processes, and such items as lighting and the general health of the employees continue to be stressed as improvements are made in plant layout.

Again we extend to our patrons and other good friends best wishes for a Merry Christmas and for the New Year.

THE PUBLISHERS.

Christmas, 1950.

Contents

xi

Contents

xii

Contents

Contents

Illustrations

———

XV

Historical Introduction

Historical Introduction

―――

A T the close of every war triumphant America proceeds, with indecent haste and incredible folly, to destroy her armed forces. So it was in 1783, when the Revolutionary army was disbanded and the ships of the first American navy were sold or given away. So it was in 1945 when the most powerful army the world has yet known was disbanded almost before the echoes of its victorious gunfire had ceased to reverberate. So, too, it was in 1865 when the Grand Army of the Republic was so completely obliterated that a few thousand savages of the western Plains could challenge victoriously the armed might of the United States.

In such a background is laid the narrative of *Absaraka*, a tale of remarkable courage of an isolated detachment of soldiery, and of shocking blundering and inefficiency on the part of the higher command. Fundamentally, the narrative constitutes but one chapter in the 400-year story of the white conquest of the American continent. The European new-comers of 1492 and later found the red race in possession, living for the most part in the stone age state of culture. The white men coveted, and proceeded to possess the continent, a procedure which the native occupants resisted to the extent of their ability.

The ensuing four-century-long struggle was therefore inevitable. It ended, appropriately enough, at Wounded Knee, South Dakota on December 29, 1890, when the last battle between Indian warriors and the United States Army was fought. Thenceforward the red race would accept such largess as its white conquerors saw fit to accord.

For the more immediate background of *Absaraka* we may turn to the Fort Laramie Treaty of 1851. From time without record the Plains and mountain tribes—Crow, Sioux, Arapahoe, Cheyenne, Shoshone and others—had fought each other for possession of the rich hunting grounds lying eastward of the Rockies and the Big Horns. More recently white emigrants to Oregon and California had been thronging across the Plains, and Indian raids upon them had become commonplace. To protect the emigrants from such attacks, and to establish peace between the warring Indian tribes were the objectives of the Fort Laramie Treaty.

The Council which ensued was one of the largest and most colorful gatherings of its kind in American history.[1] The outcome of its debates was the negotiation of an agreement establishing lasting peace between the several tribes and with the United States. The white government was given permission to establish roads and military posts in the Indian country and boundaries were fixed for the several tribes, with freedom to all to hunt and fish in the general Indian domain. In consideration of the concessions granted by the Indians they were promised $50,000 worth of goods annually for fifty years, and suitable penalties for violations of the treaty were agreed upon.

The hopes for peace proved largely illusory. The Senate made material changes in the terms of the treaty as it had been negotiated, and although some Indian spokesmen assented to them, the obligation to maintain a permanent peace was quickly forgotten.

Until the early sixties, however, a relative degree of freedom from violence was achieved. Then, with the national attention and energies centered upon the Civil War, warfare with the Sioux and certain other tribes began in earnest. Egged on by Con-

---

[1] In Chapter XVI of *Broken Hand. The Life Story of Thomas Fitzpatrick, Chief of the Mountain Men*, Leroy R. Hafen and W. J. Ghent present a vivid narrative of the proceedings attending the council.

federate agents and animated by resentment over the increasing pressure of white settlement, the Sioux struck blindly against the whites in Minnesota and along the Platte frontier. Punitive expeditions invaded their Dakota homeland in 1863 and 1864, and in 1865 one led by General Connor invaded the Powder River country of Wyoming. Meanwhile, detachments of Iowa and Ohio soldiery endeavored more or less vainly to safeguard the emigrants over the Oregon and Overland trails.

The discovery of gold in Montana and the resultant rush of fortune-seekers into that area intensified the conflict. The new El Dorado was well-nigh inaccessible to immigrants from the East, and to provide them a more direct route John M. Bozeman pioneered the Bozeman Trail leading northward from Julesburg, Colorado, through the Powder River country to the upper Yellowstone, and thence westward to Virginia City.

The Bozeman Trail bisected the choicest remaining hunting grounds of the Sioux, lying between the Black Hills and the Big Horns. Although the Crow tribe claimed ownership of this region, the Sioux had long been engaged in wresting control of it, and their aggression had been intensified by the pressure upon them exerted by the advancing tide of settlement in Minnesota and Iowa. In an effort to restore peace, a Peace Commission, appointed by President Johnson, convened another council at Fort Laramie in the summer of 1866.

Foremost spokesman of the Peace Commission policy was the U.S. Indian Department, which throughout most of the history of the Republic had been an agency of the War Department. Transferred to the Department of the Interior, it had become a vigorous critic of practically all army policies toward the Indians, and by 1866 its spokesmen were urging that the military be reduced to the status of a mere police force under the control of the civilian agency. Conversely the highest officers of the army were united in demanding that the entire control of Indians be intrusted to it, and that the Indian Department with its great array of agents, traders, and other appendages be abolished. Both civilian and military agencies were agreed that the state of divided control of the Indians by independent and mutually antagonistic governmental departments was chiefly responsible for the existing state of warfare and violence.

More striking illustration of the truth of this contention than the Fort Laramie Council of 1866 and the Carrington expedition into Absaraka afforded could scarcely be asked or desired. While the Peace Commissioners were proceeding on their way to Fort Laramie, Major General Pope, commander of the Department of the Missouri, on March 10, 1866 issued General Orders No. 33 for the dispatch of the Carrington expedition. General J. B. Sanborn, who as special commissioner on July 8, 1867 reported the results of his investigation of the Fetterman Massacre, stated that the order was issued "with the express understanding" that the Bozeman Road was to be opened through the Indian country by compact or treaty with the Indians occupying it, "and not by conquest and the exercise of arbitrary power on the part of the Government."[2]

While the Council was in the midst of its sessions, however, Colonel Carrington's army, 700 strong, appeared on the scene, en route to establish three forts (one of them, Fort Reno, to be relocated) in the midst of the Indian country. Although some of the Indians still yielded to the blandishments of the Commissioners, Red Cloud and other chiefs angrily denounced the proceedings as a fraud and withdrawing from the Council

[2] For Sanborn's report, see U.S. Serial 1308, Senate Exec Doc. 13, pp. 60–74; reprinted in part by Mrs. Carrington, *Absaraka, post*, Appendix I.

proclaimed their intention to resist by force any advance of the army beyond Powder River.

In the warfare that followed Red Cloud and his followers were cast in the role of defenders of their homeland against hostile invasion, and Colonel Carrington and his men were simple soldiers performing the task they had been ordered to execute. For two years the red men were triumphant. They contemptuously ignored another Peace Commission, dispatched in 1867, and a year later at Fort Laramie they consented to deal with still another only upon terms dictated by themselves. The resultant Fort Laramie Treaty of 1868 recognized all of the country north of the North Platte and east of the Big Horns as unceded Indian territory wherein no white might settle. The Bozeman Road was closed and the forts established to guard it were abandoned; and all of later-day South Dakota west of the Missouri was erected as a Sioux reservation.

Relative peace now brooded over the northern Plains for several years until the discovery of gold in the Black Hills brought a tide of fortune seekers into that region and precipitated the warfare of the middle seventies. With this, however, we have no present occasion to deal. It remains only to characterize the Carrington expedition and its principal actors.

Henry B. Carrington, civilization's leader in the invasion of Absaraka, had a long and moderately distinguished career. A native of Connecticut, where he was born in 1824, his ancestral inheritance included successive generations of Yale men. It included also a predisposition to army life and to tuberculosis. One greatgrandfather (Yale, 1745) served as chaplain in General Amherst's army which compelled the surrender of Canada in 1759. A grandfather, James Carrington, was for twenty-five years a partner of Eli Whitney, superintending the manufacture of arms for the Government and serving as inspector at the Springfield and Harper's Ferry arsenals. Colonel Carrington himself would probably have entered West Point but for the tuberculosis which plagued so much of his life. Instead, he graduated from Yale in 1845, taught school and studied law, and in 1848 on the advice of an uncle that a midwestern climate might prove beneficial to him, located at Columbus, Ohio.

At Columbus, despite physical ills[3], he entered upon a successful legal and civic

[3] His striking manuscript narrative of his battle with "Phthisis Pulmonaris," written out in his eighty-fifth

career. In 1850 he established a partnership
with Governor William Dennison which continued until the outbreak of the Civil War.

Active in both religion and politics, Carrington aided in organizing the Republican
Party in Ohio, and in 1857 was appointed
adjutant general of the State by Governor
Chase. In this capacity he escorted the
Prince of Wales from Cincinnati to Columbus in 1860 and President Lincoln from
Indianapolis to Columbus in 1861. Of more
importance to his future career was the action of Governor Dennison, his long-time
legal partner, to whose energy and foresight
the prominent role played by Ohio's soldiery
in the opening stage of the Civil War was
chiefly due. Regarding the Ohio River as an
unsafe line of defense for his State, he favored
strengthening the loyal forces in Kentucky
and Virginia. President Lincoln vetoed the
former, but the Governor appointed George
B. McClellan, until then a mere captain,

year for his physician, is among the Carrington Papers
in the Ohio State Archeological and Historical Society
Library Building at Columbus. Although the Carringtons were commonly a long-lived race, his maternal
grandfather (Yale, 1785) was a victim of tuberculosis,
as were his mother's brother and sister. Colonel Carrington conquered the disease, but the effects upon him
of the struggle were lifelong, and two of his sons who
attained maturity died from it.

Major General of Ohio troops and nine regiments organized by Carrington were poured into western Virginia. The early successes achieved by McClellan in this area captured the attention of the nation and catapulted him to the position of general-in-chief of the United States Army on November 1, 1861.

Carrington, meanwhile, had been commissioned colonel of the Eighteenth U.S. Infantry and assigned to command the regular army camp at Columbus. Soon afterward, upon request of Governor Morton of Indiana, he was ordered to Indianapolis to organize the soldiery of that state. There, he superintended the enrollment of more than 100,000 Indiana soldiers and vigorously combatted the projects of the Sons of Liberty and other disloyal elements. In doing so he incurred opposition, and toward the end of the war he rejoined his regiment, which he had largely recruited at Columbus. He was still in active service when in the autumn of 1865 he was assigned to the command of Fort Kearney, Nebraska, the most important military station between Leavenworth and Fort Laramie.

For Colonel Carrington the assignment proved to be exceedingly unfortunate. His regiment had been decimated of its veteran soldiers by the expiration of Civil War enlistments and its ranks were chiefly composed of new recruits. The dispute between the Army and the Indian Department over the policy to be pursued toward the hostile tribes merely reflected the broader confusion of the public mind on the subject. Throughout the populous East, far remote from the frontier and its problems, the "brutality" of the Army toward Indians was vociferously condemned; on the frontier itself the Indian Office policy was the subject of like condemnation. To make matters worse, the Army higher command itself—in particular General Cooke, commander of the Department of the Platte and Carrington's immediate superior—displayed but a faint conception of the realities of the situation which faced the expedition.

So the little army moved westward, defective in numbers, in horses, in discipline, and in arms and ammunition. Yet between midsummer and the advent of winter three army posts were built from materials hewed out of the forest and dug from the ground. Fort Philip Kearney, the principal one, was characterized by General Hazen as the best stockade post he had ever seen, save for one Hudson's Bay Company post. The amount of labor entailed in constructing it and in discharging the multitude of other cares which devolved upon the commandant was prodigious. And practically all the time the fort was kept in a state of siege by hostile warriors who invested it so closely that no man's life was safe if separated a dozen rods from his fellows.[4]

Added to the other difficulties of the hard pressed commandant was the violation of his orders by his subordinate officers. To this, and to the misconduct of many of the mounted men the two disasters of December 6 and 21 were immediately due. On the first date noted an attack was made on the wood train which, as usual corralled and awaited rescuers from the fort. Colonel Carrington sent a small party of cavalry under Captain Fetterman to attack the Indians in front, while with every horse available he led in person a detachment of mounted infantry to gain their rear and thus entrap them. His plan was defeated by the disgraceful retreat of some of the cavalry, and by Lieutenant

[4] From July 26 to December 21, 1866, hostile demonstrations were made in front of Fort Kearney 51 times. In the same period 96 officers and soldiers and 58 civilians were killed, and "nearly every train and person that attempted to pass over the Montana Road" was attacked. Report of General Sanborn, July 8, 1867. The figures cited include the 81 victims of the Fetterman Massacre of December 21.

Bingham's misconduct, for which he paid with the sacrifice of his life.

Although Captain Fetterman had witnessed, and professed his inability to account for, Lieutenant Bingham's misconduct, his own disobedience of orders, clearly and repeatedly given, was directly responsible for the terrible slaughter of December 21. Again the wood train had been attacked and a detachment of troops, 78 in number, was promptly started for its relief.[5] Captain Powell was at first assigned the command, but Fetterman, who was a brevet lieutenant colonel, claimed and was given it by virtue of his superior rank. Under orders to relieve the train and "under no circumstances" to cross Lodge Trail Ridge, Captain Fetterman led his followers in another direction, in pursuit of the Indians, and quickly disappeared from sight of the fort over Lodge Trail Ridge. There, surrounded by a large number of warriors, the entire command was slaughtered in a few minutes time. Their work finished, the Indians withdrew. The supporting detachment of soldiers which had been promptly dispatched returned to the fort at nightfall,

[5] Captain Brown and two civilians attached themselves to the party without orders, raising its number to 81.

bringing in wagons the naked and obscenely mutilated bodies of forty-nine men. The thirty-two remaining were brought in by Colonel Carrington himself the following day, and all but one or two were buried in one common grave. Only a handful of the victims had been shot, the great majority having been dispatched by arrows and lances.

After the holocaust come the futile investigations. Although all of Colonel Carrington's appeals for men and munitions had failed to make an impression upon General Cooke, he now made indecent haste to fix upon Carrington the unwelcome role of scapegoat. Relieved of his command, he was ordered to make a midwinter march, in weather of terrible severity, to Fort Caspar, and on arrival there was informed that his destination had been changed to Fort McPherson in Nebraska.

There an investigation into the causes of the Fetterman Massacre was conducted in the spring of 1867. Without awaiting its outcome—even without awaiting the receipt of Colonel Carrington's official report, the process of smearing his name, with which the present-day generation is unhappily familiar, was set in motion.

"Colonel Carrington is very plausible—an energetic, industrious man in garrison,"

wrote Cooke on December 27, when as yet
he had only the bare news that the massacre
had occurred, "but it is too evident that he
has not maintained discipline and that his
officers have no confidence in him. Some of
his acts officially reported, such as shelling
woods when Indians had appeared on a previous day may have, by this time settled
his appreciation by Indians."

Although the General's precise meaning
is somewhat cloudy, his eagerness to casti-
gate Colonel Carrington is clear—an eagerness further displayed three weeks later,
when, on January 14, 1867, although he
still lacked data on which to base a "version"
of the massacre, he proceeded nevertheless
to invent one.[6]

[6] Senate Executive Document 13, U.S. Serial 1308,
p. 29. This document is a 128-page compilation made
by the Secretary of the Interior, in response to a Senate
resolution of July 8, 1867, on the subject of the current
Indian hostilities. Although the Senate Resolution of
January 30, 1867 called upon the Secretaries of War
and the Interior for "all official reports, papers and
other facts" in the possession of their respective departments concerning the causes of the Fetterman
Massacre, the documents submitted did not include
Colonel Carrington's reports upon it and upon the
skirmish of December 6. They did include, however,
Captain Fetterman's report upon the December 6
affair, from which General Cooke derived the conclusions, sharply critical of Colonel Carrington, stated in

his "version" of the massacre of December 21. Commenting upon this, in his defense before the investigating commission at Fort McPherson, Colonel Carrington stated that the sub-report of Fetterman "made to my adjutant on my order" had been supplied to the Senate and printed, although his own report had not been. "That report [of Fetterman] was a schedule and duly marked and inclosed in my official report of that skirmish and mailed to the department headquarters. The pamphlet [Senate Document] does not include my report of that skirmish, neither do I know that it was ever forwarded from the department headquarters." Senate Exec. Doc. 33, U.S. Serial 2504, p. 37. This statement, made in 1867, first saw public light in 1887. Colonel Carrington's implication that the report had never been forwarded finds proof in the statement of General Grant to the Secretary of War that he was forwarding "all official reports, papers and other facts" in the possession of the Department. This definitely fixes upon General Cooke the withholding of Colonel Carrington's report from his own superiors. In 1890, now old and crippled, he made a belated explanation and apology to Colonel Carrington: "The country was greatly excited, and the government very urgent so I endorsed the papers for transmission by one of my staff. I do not remember which. I can do nothing more now than to express my deep pain at what transpired. My memory recalls nothing of the details, except that it was hurried off to General Sherman, and you must take my regrets as sincere, and my congratulations that in the end you were fully vindicated." Hebard and Brininstool, *The Bozeman Trail*, I, 340–41. Like most other death-bed repentances this one accomplished nothing toward undoing the terrible wrong that had been done.

The Commissioner of Indian Affairs provided, as might have been anticipated, an even more remarkable version of the massacre than did General Cooke. He ridiculed the idea that 300 Indians had attacked the wood train on December 6. "There were, perhaps, five or six men with the train and if 300 Indians had really attacked them, it is not doubted that one or more of them would have been killed. But the report was made of an attack by 300 Indians; this led to a sortie from the fort; and even then, it appears, the Indians did not wish to fight, as they retreated, and no soldier was killed until several Indians had been dispatched by our soldiers. It seems that then some Indians hovered around the fort till the 21st, the day of the fatal disaster. To say that they came to the fort to challenge the force at that point to a fight is simply absurd . . .

"Now, I understand this was the fact: These Indians, being in absolute want of guns and ammunition to make their winter hunt, were on a friendly visit to the post, desiring to communicate with the commanding officer to get the order refusing them guns and ammunition rescinded so that they might be enabled to procure their winter supply of buffalo . . . Although I regret the unfortunate death of so many brave soldiers, yet there can be no doubt that it is owing to the foolish and rash management of the officer in command of that fort."[7]

Although the Senate twice demanded from the Secretaries of War and Interior "all the official reports, papers and other facts in their possession" concerning the Fetterman Massacre, Colonel Carrington's own report was not transmitted to it, nor was his extended defense at the investigation conducted at Fort McPherson. Finally in 1887, when most of the actors, red and white alike, were dead or forgotten, in response to another Senate Resolution (its

[7] Concerning the "friendly" Indian theory, Colonel Carrington's report of September 25, 1866, may be noted: On the 21st. a large force had surrounded the hay party, under escort of 40 infantry soldiers. The next day the hay party was again attacked by nearly 300 warriors, who withdrew upon the approach of a party of mounted soldiers from the fort. The next day (September 23) Contractor Chandler's party was raided and 94 head of cattle driven off. A detachment of mounted soldiers and 15 miners pursued the Indians a dozen miles, fought and killed half a dozen of them (one, a white man) and recovered all the stock. Meanwhile "along the line" the week had been marked by the killing of Contractor Grull and his two companions, and by a descent upon Fort C. F. Smith. "They [the Sioux] pretended friendship but getting no presents and not being admitted at the fort, they scalped a white man within sight of the garrison." U.S. Serial 2504, Doc. 33, p. 25.

COLONEL CARRINGTON IN CIVIL WAR UNIFORM
From original photograph
owned by Miss Madge Sullivant, Columbus, Ohio.

third demand for information concerning the Fetterman Massacre) Colonel Carrington's defense of his conduct as submitted to the special committee of investigation at Fort McPherson twenty years earlier was published.[8] The resolution demanding it was introduced by Senator Dawes of Massachusetts, and since Carrington was now a resident of that state and still smarting under the mistreatment to which he had been subjected, it may reasonably be inferred that he was indirectly responsible for its introduction.

Long before this, however, the Interior Department had supplied the Senate with one convincing exculpation of Colonel Carrington's conduct, the report of General San-

---

[8] U.S. Serial 2504, Senate Exec. Doc. 33, 50th Cong., 1st Sess. The document, titled "History of Indian Operations on the Plains," runs to more than fifty printed pages. In transmitting it to the Senate, the Secretary of the Interior commented that it contained "146 long type-written pages." In an old-age letter (June 21, 1908) to E. O. Randall of the Ohio State Archeological and Historical Society, Carrington stated that the document had been found after twenty years "among waste material in a government cellar" and published "upon third demand" by the Senate. See also Hebard and Brininstool, *The Bozeman Trail*, I 339–42 for letter of Carrington, June 6, 1902, reciting circumstances of suppression of his report and its publication, by permission of General Sherman, in the second edition of *Absaraka*.

born's investigation of the causes of the Fetterman Massacre. Sanborn was a member of the Peace Commission of 1867. His report, dated at Washington, July 8, 1867 was transmitted to the Senate along with other documents and printed in Senate Executive Document 13, 40th Congress, 1st session. The more pertinent portion of Sanborn's report was reprinted by Mrs. Carrington as Appendix I of *Absaraka* and constitutes perhaps the clearest account of the massacre ever published. Although General Sanborn refrained from fixing the responsibility of persons "more remotely connected with the massacre" its implications are clear. "In a nutshell," it concluded, the difficulty was that the commanding officer of the district (Carrington) was furnished no more troops or supplies for a state of war than had been provided him for a state of profound peace. "In regions where all was peace, as at Laramie in November, twelve companies were stationed, while in regions where all was war, as at Philip Kearney, there were only five companies allowed."

The ill-health which dogged Colonel Carrington throughout his life was accentuated by the consequences of a wound accidentally received from his own revolver during the Absaraka expedition and at his own request he was retired from active service, and for ten years served as Professor of Military Science at Wabash College. He subsequently removed to Hyde Park, Massachusetts, where the remainder of his life was spent. On several occasions he performed special governmental services in connection with the Indians, and for the rest became a prolific writer on patriotic and military themes, Mrs. Carrington having died in 1870, the following year he married Frances Courtney Grummond, widow of Lieutenant George W. Grummond, who was slain in the Fetterman Massacre. She was a native of Tennessee and an author in her own right. Her last book, *My Army Life and the Fort Phil. Kearney Massacre* devoted, perhaps unwisely, to a recounting of the events more capably celebrated in *Absaraka*, was published a short time before her death, which occurred in 1911. Colonel Carrington himself died at the age of eighty-eight, October 26, 1912.

Margaret Irvin McDowell Sullivant, the author of *Absaraka*, belonged to a family of much distinction in Ohio and elsewhere. Her grandfather, Lucas S. Sullivant, was the founder of Franklinton (now Columbus) in 1797, and members of her family have ever since been prominent there. His eldest son, William S. Sullivant, born in the tiny settlement in 1803, became a distinguished scientist, whose fame is world-wide. Another son, Joseph (father of Mrs. Carrington) was likewise a scientist of note, one of the founders of Ohio State University, which has named in his honor the Joseph Sullivant Medal, awarded each five years to the University's most outstanding son or daughter.

Joseph Sullivant married Margaret Irvin McDowell, who was born in 1810, the daughter of Colonel Joseph McDowell of Danville, Kentucky. His brother, Abraham, was the father of General Irvin McDowell of Civil War fame, who was thus a first cousin of Mrs. Carrington's mother. Through other McDowell connections she was more or less closely related to the families of Justice John Marshall, President James Madison, James G. Birney, Abolitionist Presidential candidate, Dr. Ephraim McDowell of Kentucky, first surgeon in the world to perform the operation of ovariotomy, and John McDowell, founder of the McDowell Medical College at St. Louis.[9]

[9] For these family relationships see Joseph Sullivant, *A Genealogical and Family Memorial* (Columbus, 1874), Margaret Sullivant Carrington was the eldest child of the author, yet curiously he misdates the year of her death, although she had died but four years earlier.

Historical Introduction

Margaret was born at Danville, Kentucky May 10, 1831 and while still an infant was orphaned by the death of her mother. In 1851 she married Colonel Carrington, then an aspiring young lawyer of Columbus. In the family memorial volume penned by her father, this picture of her is given: "Of fine form and size, she was commanding in presence, gentle and dignified in deportment. Modest and retiring by nature, refined and cultivated in taste, yet firm and dignified when requisite, she was altogether of a high type of womanhood, and loved and respected by relations and friends."

Her domestic career was marked by a succession of tragedies which might well have broken the spirit of any woman. No less than five of her children, born in the years between 1852 and 1864, died before reaching a third birthday. Yet she conquered her grief and continued to entertain a lively interest in her contemporary world of affairs. Indicative of the confusion in official circles over the Indian situation is the fact that Margaret and the other army wives accompanied the Absaraka expedition upon the advice of General Sherman that it would be a pleasant excursion for the officers' families. When she underwent the experiences depicted in *Absaraka* she was still scarcely of middle age. In further pursuance of General Sherman's advice she kept a journal, which afforded the basis for her subsequent book. Despite the trials she had undergone she must have retained an abundant degree of energy to enable her to produce it in so short a time. The return from Absaraka occupied the midwinter of 1866–67 and the detention and investigation at Fort McPherson consumed the ensuing spring. *Absaraka* was published at Philadelphia in 1868. Its contents disclose that the author supplemented her own first-hand knowledge by the accumulation of considerable additional information. The Union Pacific Railroad was now rapidly being pushed across the Plains to its dramatic junction with the Central Pacific at Promontory, and interest in western migration was at high tide. These facts no doubt determined to some extent the contents of *Absaraka*. In addition to recounting the ill-fated military expedition of 1866, it comprises, to a considerable extent, the features of an emigrant guide. Chiefly, however, it struck an heroic blow in defense of Colonel Carrington's reputation at a time when he was the devoted object of combined official and popular vilification.

Mrs. Carrington did not long enjoy her literary fame. She died at Crawfordsville,

May 11, 1870, but one day over thirty-nine
years of age. Her remains rest beside four
of her children in beautiful Green Lawn
Cemetery at Columbus, not far from Lot
Number 1 in which an impressive array of
members of the Sullivant clan are interred.

The reopening of the Sioux wars in the
seventies and the subsequent westward tide
of settlement served to create continuing interest in Mrs. Carrington's book. The Custer Massacre of 1876 was merely a second
enactment, on a somewhat larger scale, of
the Fetterman Massacre ten years earlier.
Following his retirement from the army,
Colonel Carrington entered upon an active
literary career, in the course of which he
thoroughly exploited Mrs. Carrington's narrative. A second edition, which seems to
have been merely a reprint of the first, was
issued in 1869, a year before her death. A
third edition, issued in 1878, some time after
the Custer Massacre, was entitled *Absaraka,
Land of Massacre; being the Experience of
an Officer's Wife on the Plains. With an
Outline of Indian Operations and Conferences
from 1865–1878.* By Col. Carrington, Re-
vised, Enlarged and Illustrated with Maps,
Cuts, Indian Portraits, etc. Other editions,
slightly changed as to title and material supplied by Colonel Carrington, followed until

the seventh in 1896. By this time several new states had been carved out of the former Indian domain, and warfare with the Sioux had become but a memory.

An interesting circumstance provided still another book on the subject-matter of *Absaraka*, published in 1910. In Mrs. Carrington's narrative the terrible plight and heroic conduct of the young wife of Lieutenant George Grummond, who perished in the Fetterman Massacre, are feelingly related. Mrs. Grummond (accompanied by her dead husband) made the long journey back to her Tennessee home in the winter of 1867, where she presently lost all contact with the Carringtons, who, meanwhile, settled at Crawfordsville.

On a visit to Cincinnati in 1868, Mrs. Grummond encountered and read Mrs. Carrington's *Absaraka* and learned that Colonel Carrington had been assigned to Wabash College. Two years later she read an announcement of the death of a Mrs. Carrington and wrote a letter to the Colonel asking if it was his wife who had died. The correspondence that ensued eventuated in their marriage in April, 1871.

Forty years of life together followed. Toward its close the townsmen of Sheridan, Wyoming, staged an historical celebration on July 3-4 1908, which Colonel and Mrs. Carrington were invited to attend as guests of the city. They accepted, and apparently this circumstance gave rise to the book published by Mrs. Carrington two years later entitled *My Army Life and the Fort Phil. Kearney Massacre. With an account of the celebration of "Wyoming Opened."*

Part IV of the book, sub-titled "After Many Days," is devoted to a 97-page account of the incidents attending the celebration. The earlier portion of the volume is chiefly a restatement of the contents of *Absaraka*. Apparently this was a final effort to capitalize on the name and fame of the narrative written by the author's predecessor. To the present Editor the wisdom of publishing the volume seems questionable.

Our present edition of *Absaraka* is reprinted from the first edition (1868). In editing it we have introduced numerous typographical changes and have corrected a few misprints or other errors. We have also provided the historical introduction and explanatory foot notes. We have retained only the concluding portion of Mrs. Carrington's Appendix II, which was chiefly devoted to a sketch of the Eighteenth U.S. Infantry Regiment; and have supplied, as Appendix III, Colonel Carrington's official and long-suppressed reports of the actions of December 6 and December 21, which he put into his defense before the army board of investigation at Fort McPherson in 1867, and which were published twenty years later as U.S. Serial Document 2504, entitled "Indian Operations on the Plains."

For much information cordially supplied I am indebted to Miss Madge Sullivant of Columbus, granddaughter of Joseph Sullivant and niece of Margaret Sullivant Carrington, the author of *Absaraka*. Dr. James H. Rodabaugh, editor of the State Archeological and Historical Society of Ohio, and other members of the Society's staff afforded me every facility in consulting the Carrington Papers and other records in the library of that institution. Dr. Stanley Pargellis, Librarian of the Newberry Library, Chicago, facilitated the task of both Editor and Publisher by permitting the photostating of the Library's copy of the original edition of *Absaraka*. I have only to regret that circumstances prevented me from utilizing the permission accorded by the Publisher to traverse the route of Colonel Carrington in 1866–67 from Fort Kearney, Nebraska, to Fort Philip Kearney, Wyoming, and back.

M. M. QUAIFE

Detroit,—1950

AB-SA-RA-KA

HOME OF THE CROWS:

BEING THE

EXPERIENCE OF AN OFFICER'S WIFE

ON

THE PLAINS,

AND

MARKING THE VICISSITUDES OF PERIL AND PLEASURE
DURING THE OCCUPATION OF THE NEW ROUTE TO VIRGINIA
CITY, MONTANA, 1866-7, AND THE INDIAN HOSTILITY THERETO;

WITH

OUTLINES OF THE NATURAL FEATURES AND RESOURCES OF THE
LAND, TABLES OF DISTANCES, MAPS, AND OTHER AIDS TO
THE TRAVELER; GATHERED FROM OBSERVATION
AND OTHER RELIABLE SOURCES.

PHILADELPHIA:

J. B. LIPPINCOTT & CO.

1868.

Dedication

———

WITH acknowledgments to LIEUTEN-ANT-GENERAL SHERMAN, whose suggestions at Fort Kearney, in the spring of 1866, were adopted, in preserving a daily record of the events of a peculiarly eventful journey, and whose vigorous policy is as promising of the final settlement of Indian troubles and the quick completion of the Union Pacific Railroad as his March to the Sea was signal in crushing the last hope of armed rebellion, this narrative is respectfully dedicated.

M. I. C.

Prologue

———

THE importunity of friends who have
been interested in the journal of a
summer's trip and a winter's experience on the Plains, and which, as a matter of
taste, now assumes the more easy flow of
Narrative, has overruled the first refusal to
permit its use in more available form for
their leisurely reading. Gathering many of
its details from officers of the posts, from
Major James Bridger and others, and so
gathering as each day's experience unfolded
events of interest, there is no assumption of
anything further than to express the facts so
recorded just as they were impressed upon
the judgment or fancy.

If, on the one hand, the recital of military
preparations or movements be so inartificial
as to excite the smile of the critic, or if the
natural tendency to adopt the idioms and
style which, every way and forever, surround
the wife of an officer, shall seem so con-
strained as to repel the lady reader, it can
only be said that we wrote, when we wrote,
just as the surroundings inspired or compelled us.

In this change from the form of a journal we have adhered to its record, and preserved the integrity of the original, so as to reproduce our life as it was lived and give incidents as they transpired.

While nearly one-half of the Indian demonstrations were under our own eye, the authentic reports of others were of equal value to history; and the narrative differs little from what would be the written experience of others, except that we availed ourselves more fully of classes of facts and sources of knowledge equally open to all, and so cherished their record, as in earlier life we garnered up details of a first visit to Mammoth Cave or the Falls of Niagara.

If our statistics and statements as to Indian councils, usages, or raids, or the record of labor, casualties, and incidents, savor much of routine, yet through incidental form we have gathered historical facts, and thus do we present our life and the exact history of the first year of the military occupation of Absaraka.

And again; if there be a savor of whining because the soldiers were so few and support was unfurnished, it will not be taken as criticism to offend anybody, since everybody knows how small was the army, and how incapable of immediate expansion to meet the issues of the Northwestern frontier at the close of the war.

So, then, our friends will accept this response to their wishes, and at least gather instruction for their guidance when they undertake their first visit to Absaraka, Home of the Crows.

Absaraka
Home of the Crows

MRS. MARGARET I. CARRINGTON
From original photograph
owned by Miss Madge Sullivant, Columbus, Ohio.

Absaraka

Chapter 1

ABSARAKA, HOME OF THE CROWS

ABSARAKA, in the language of the Crow Indians, translated, Home of the Crows, was once the field of their proudest successes.

The fertile basins of the Yellowstone, Big Horn, and Tongue Rivers were enlivened by the presence of their many villages; and in the early days of Bridger and Beckwourth, the Crow Indians accumulated considerable wealth by a prolific trade in pelts and dressed furs, which those veteran trappers and frontiersmen delivered for them at St. Louis and other border depots for Indian commerce.

Partially girt in by the Big Horn and Panther Mountains, yet roaming at will, they were masters of a region of country which has no peer in its exhaustless game resources, and is rarely surpassed in its production of wild fruits, grasses, and cereals; while its natural scenery, made up of snowy crests, pine-clad slopes and summits, crystal waters, and luxuriant vales, certainly has no rival in our great sisterhood of States.

The Snake Indians, who roamed farther north and west, and who had even crossed lances with the Piegans and Bloods, on the confines of British America, were unable, man for man, to match their more numerous and more adventurous rivals, the Crows, and at last, in 1856, joined friendly hands with them, or at least observed a fair neutrality in the later conflicts of the Crows with their hereditary and deadly enemies, the Sioux and Northern Cheyennes.

When the Cheyennes of the Black Hills of eastern Dakota divided their bands,[1] and one portion went to the Red River country, while another portion left the old home, with nearly half of the remaining families, for Powder River and Tongue River valleys, the Oglala Sioux at last found allies to support their operations against the Crows. With a portion of the Arapahoes, Blackfeet, and Gros

[1] Following the building of Bent's Fort on the upper Arkansas in 1832, a large portion of the Cheyenne tribe, then living on the upper Platte River, removed southward to the Arkansas. The remainder of the Cheyennes continued to reside about the headwaters of the North Platte and the Yellowstone. The separation of the tribe was made permanent by the Fort Laramie Treaty of 1851 and the two groups were subsequently known as the Northern Cheyennes and the Southern Cheyennes.

Ventres of the Prairie, popularly known as the Big Bellies, they prosecuted the war with vigor and unrelenting hatred. Breaking into the long-coveted region about which they had been testing their valor for years in fruitless forays and uncertain adventures, the Sioux, aided by their new friends, succeeded in occupying the choice valleys of the lower Big Horn and Tongue Rivers, and still held them in comparative independence when the expedition of 1866, sent to open the new route to Virginia City, forced them to accept the challenge of the white man for the future possession of their stolen dwelling-place.

The Crows fell back of the Yellowstone, though still operating eastward as far as the west bank of Big Horn River; and a few attempted something like local improvement, imitating the Flat Heads, who, though few of numbers, were not the less energetic, and seemed to be really desirous of gaining some affinity with the ideas and civilization of the whites.

With all these changes and the continued aggression of the Sioux, the Crows maintained their passion for their old and their favorite home. It had its peculiar virtues. At once grand and beautiful, prolific in game beyond all precedent, susceptible of culture and the development of vast mineral wealth, while offering a new avenue for travel to Montana nearly five hundred miles shorter than that by Salt Lake City, how can it be deemed strange that they looked upon that redundancy of game, that exceeding fertility, and that natural forage, as wonderfully adapted for their perpetual home and abiding-place!

The white man had given it no distinctive name, and had scarcely trespassed upon its soil. Farther west, he had occupied the Madison and Jefferson branches and the head waters of the Missouri. Flourishing towns and cities had been located, and the Indians, who had so long been driven westward, were now crowded back upon the Yellowstone and Big Horn; so that the Crows must soon renew their active antagonism with their old plunderers, or seek other fields or methods of life.

This great hunting sphere, though nameless, had a natural independence both of Montana and Dakota, while attached in part to each. All that lies east of Black Foot and Clark's Passes had its special relation to the territory extending as far as Powder River. Somebody had indeed ventured to style this country Wyoming, a name which might do very well for a county of Pennsylvania, but had the least claim for application to the stolen land of the Crows.

These same Crow Indians, in addition to their natural title to the land, maintain, to this day, the proud claim never to have killed a white man but in self-defense. All their intercourse in 1866, and their relations in 1867, combine to show the integrity of their friendship and the truth of their protestations.

Their very enemies concede to them the rightful title to the territory so long struggled for. At a formal council held at Fort Philip Kearney in July, 1866, between Colonel Carrington and certain Cheyenne chiefs, who were then in close relations with Red Cloud and other Oglala Sioux, but desirous of breaking loose from the tie, that they might receive protection from the whites, the following question was addressed to Black Horse:

"Why do the Sioux and Cheyennes claim the land which belongs to the Crows?"

Black Horse, The Wolf that Lies Down, Red Arm, and Dull Knife promptly answered:

"The Sioux helped us. We stole the hunting-grounds of the Crows because they were the best. The white man is along the great waters, and we wanted more room. We fight the Crows, because they will not take half and give us peace with the other half."

Absaraka is therefore in fact, as the Crows have fondly named that whole region (absurdly styled Wyoming by some), the Home of the Crows.

Bound to it by sacred legends; endeared as it is by years of occupation and wasting conflicts for its repossession; pressed by the whites from the west, and now approached from the east, yet restricted to the use of the Upper Yellowstone and west bank of the Big Horn Rivers, the Crows still maintain their rightful title, and ask of the white man that he acknowledge it.

No less firmly do they maintain inviolate their solemn faith once pledged to the white man, and they look to his advent, in sufficient numbers, as the signal of their own deliverance and the destruction of their old enemies the Sioux.

Ready to co-operate with the whites—kindly disposed toward the new road—beginning to appreciate the fate of the red man who shall oppose the progress of civilization and frontier settlement, they regard with something like hope the strong arm of that progress, and stand ready to perpetuate their own life by a just conformity to its reasonable demands.

There is another fact which appeals strongly to other sentiments than those that favor simple justice.

Among all the tribes of the Northwest, the Crow Indian stands first in manliness and physical perfection.

While they alone have the title to negotiate the right of way for the new Virginia City road, independently of its occupation by the Sioux and their allies, they also have pride of race and nation. They can be trusted as friends within its boundaries whenever they are treated with the consideration they deserve. Would white men do more?

The Crows lost possession by robbery. Their enemies have become the white man's enemy. Their enemies have ignored treaty obligations, have despised all terms of compromise or honorable warfare, and defy the Crows and white man alike.

To the Crow, therefore, should be tendered support and friendship. Whatever the result as to the possession of the soil, it is as wicked to give it to the Sioux, for fear of his enmity, as it is to rob the Crows, if they wish to retain or jointly enjoy it.[2]

[2] Mrs. Carrington wrote as a partisan of the Crows, and her knowledge of the past Indian history of the region was somewhat defective. The Crows were themselves a Siouan Tribe who had separated from their

Above all, the land should bear its true name, and thus give to posterity some index to its past history and the issues and struggles which have preceded its use by the white man. Let it be known, whether as Territory, State, or Indian Reservation, as Absaraka, Home of the Crows.

Herein, honor is rendered to noble red men, for such these are! Herein, justice is done to the Crow nation, which has hardly been less honorable and true to their friendship than the Narragansetts, the Delawares, and the Pawnees. Herein, shall be established a memorial name that will connect with the last supremacy of the red man a

compatriots on the upper Missouri River probably sometime during the eighteenth century. Lewis and Clark in 1804 found them living on the Big Horn. In 1862 they were still in this general vicinity, adjoining the Rocky Mountains along the upper Big Horn, Powder, and Wind rivers, and along the Yellowstone as far down as its mouth. Their history as far as known to white chroniclers was one of continual warfare with the surrounding tribes. By the mid-nineteenth century the Sioux, themselves under white pressure from the eastward, were crowding hard upon the Crow country in the same way the latter had crowded out its former possessors. Although the Crows as a nation were commonly at peace with the United States their record of individual pilfering of lone settlers and travelers was by no means enviable.

tribute to those who were truly worthy; and past injustice shall be partially atoned for, in giving to the Crow Indians this perpetual recognition in the land of Absaraka, the Home of the Crows.

Chapter 2

ABSARAKA DESCRIBED

THIS land of the largest liberty for the red man and the chase is as varied in surface and general features as it is attractive to the various tribes that have contended for its possession.

Nearly all maps, and even the experience of Major James Bridger, the chief guide of the expedition of 1866, and that of Mr. Brannan, an assistant guide, who was with General Connor in 1865, so far as he advanced in the valley of Tongue River, fail to furnish such data as to afford an adequate judgment of this region and its capacity for future development.

All guides and scouts very naturally fix their attention upon points where water and grazing can be found by emigrants *in transitu;* but they do not as often generalize the result of these varied adventures, and fix the relations of diverse soils and geographical features to the purposes of advancing civilization and general settlement.

And yet, as the army and people have been released from the engrossing interests of a great domestic war, and the failure of

the Laramie Treaty of 1866, with its immediate succession of hostilities to every foot
of progress over the route claimed to have
been guaranteed by that treaty, has turned
the attention of the national Congress and
the national army to this new field of fight,
it will be found that no portion of the public
domain, heretofore almost *terra incognita*,
will challenge a greater public favor when
its elements of value are known.

Not that it will prove a paradise for mere
adventurers who aspire after good and sudden riches at the expense of the substantial
development of the lands they traverse and
prospect; but this idea is founded upon the
basis of actual settlement, and the ultimate
adoption of Absaraka into the great family
of American States.

And yet, it is true that even the adventurer will find a field of promise. Every creek,
from Clear Fork to the upper Yellowstone,
gives gold color, and there is no doubt that
patient, well-directed labor will realize fair
returns. Certain it is, that but for the Indian
hostilities—engendered partly by bad faith
exercised toward some of their bands; partly
by excessive intimacy, degrading to both the
white and red man, and resulting in the ultimate vengeance of the latter when he learns
the drift of such intimacy; partly by failure

13

to support the Indians who deserve support; and especially by failure to punish those who were incorrigibly wicked and ugly—the new route, so short, and in the main so fruitful in supplies for the emigrant, would become a favorite with all travelers to eastern and lower Montana.

Of course it has its supposed rivals. Salt Lake City, so beautiful in location, with its shaded avenues, its ever-flowing fountains, and lavish soil, cannot cheerfully spare from its markets the long trains which have made the circuit by its route; and everybody who owns a light-draught steamer will willingly transport from St. Louis, Nebraska City, or Omaha, as many passengers as the capacity of his cabin or the stage of river moisture will permit; but the mathematical difficulty of making the hypothenuse of an acute angled triangle greater than the sum of the sides is a never-failing embarrassment to either party, and the question of distance remains as nature established it.

The honest stranger who seeks a home in lower Montana, and a short reliable route to Bozeman City, the Gallatin Valley, and Jefferson City, and the agricultural or mineral districts of that region, desires more definite information of the land to which his thoughts turn; and not only the people of Nebraska,

Iowa, Minnesota, Illinois, and Indiana, but those of more eastern States, are pushing their trains across the Plains, looking in vain, as they have long looked, for some definite details of the route they are to traverse.

It is not always convenient, each day, for the emigrant to depend upon some transient ranchero or squatter for information as to the next grass, timber, or water along the route; and it is therefore of practical value for the traveler to have a definite outline of the country before furnishing such details as specify the route, with its history, resources, and supplies.

The geographical outline of Absaraka is special and full of interest.

The general course of the Big Horn Mountains is from southeast to northwest, until it reaches the Big Horn River, when the direction changes westward; but the Big Horn Mountains proper die out before reaching the Upper Yellowstone River and Clark's and Blackfoot Passes, yet only a short distance from the former.

At the lower or southeastern terminus, the range doubles back upon itself to the southwest, in form not unlike a big horn or cornucopia, and gives significance to its name, although the big horn of the mountain sheep is credited as source of the title.

Of course it is presumed that the reader has gained some knowledge of the course of the Platte, and entertains at least general ideas of the routes to Salt Lake City by way of Denver, Fort Bridger, or Forts Laramie and Caspar.

While this narrative will embrace directions for the traveler, even from the South Platte, and especially after the journey leaves the line of the Union Pacific Railroad, with all the definiteness needed for daily practical use, it does not require, in this general description of Absaraka, that those elements should be noticed at present.

Omitting, therefore, all branches of the Big Cheyenne, and all tributaries of either Fork of the Platte, the general survey begins with Powder River.

Powder River, which is a muddy stream, comes from the southern side of the Big Horn Mountains and a southwestern source, and therefore is not a part of the great aggregate of bright channels that combine to feed the Missouri River from the Big Horn range proper. True it is, that it may be held responsible for their subsequent discoloration, and it does help the Missouri to no little portion of that final burden of deposit and gravity which so unfavorably appeals to the first taste of the traveler from the East; but this is its mission, and simply vindicates its own character, as do similar currents in the aggregate of the great flow of human life.

The Big Horn range of the Rocky Mountains possesses two distinct and marked features. There is, first, a central or backbone range, which culminates in perpetual snow, where Cloud Peak grandly rises as the chief of all its proud summits, falling off slowly and patiently toward the southern valleys that are soon confronted by similar ranges of the Wind River Mountains beyond.

The second range is north of the first, and after clearly leaving the loftier sweep, it presents nearly a perpendicular face to the north, except where the earnest torrents have cut deep gorges, and thus forced their way to the main tributaries of the Missouri.

Between these ranges, and varying in breadth from twelve to twenty-five miles, are fine hunting-grounds, abounding in noble orchards, wild fruits and grasses, as well as the choicest game for the huntsman. This special tract is hardly a true plateau, as are the more uniform offsets of the *Tierre Calientes* of the Mexican ranges; but with all its vicinity to perpetual snow, there are gentle slopes which possess peculiar loveliness and many elements of future value. With this general outline in mind, let the

17

traveler start from Fort Reno on Powder River.

He is in the midst of a sterile country, a sage desert. Before him rise the snow-clad mountains, but he has weary miles to travel before he gets the real value of their benignant expenditure of clear cold water upon the vales below.

A march of twenty-six miles brings him to Crazy Woman's Fork. This river, ever flowing, is also ever muddy, having received its largest contingent of supply from the same yellow source as Powder River. Six miles northwest, and following the sweep of the Big Horn northern range, and some six to eight miles outside its general base, a new country opens. Sage brush and cactus, which for nearly two hundred miles have so largely monopolized the soil, rapidly disappear. The change is beautiful as it is sudden. One narrow divide only is crossed, and the transition is like the quick turn of the kaleidoscope, which retains indeed the outline, but supplies new combinations and new tints for every object the light illuminates.

Twenty-three miles from Crazy Woman's Fork, the bright, noisy, and transparent waters, and the rich valley of Clear Fork are reached: so swift that mules and horses have difficulty in crossing; so clear that every fish

18

and pebble is well defined; and so cool that ice in midsummer is no object of desire, this same Clear Fork introduces the series of natural charms that have endeared the country to the savage, and will in the future have equal beauty for those who seek homes in a new and hitherto undeveloped land.

Clear Fork is a genuine flow from the Big Horn Mountains, and is a type of many others no less constant, pure, and valuable. It is partly snow derived, and partly the sum of innumerable springs.

Rock Creek comes next, with far less pretension, but similar in character.

After passing Lake De Smet, the great nursing haunt for ducks, wild geese, and brant, and which bears the name of Father De Smet, who, as a Catholic priest, has ministered to the spiritual and social wants of the northwestern tribes for many years, and only fourteen miles from Clear Fork, the traveler comes suddenly upon the two Piney Forks of Clear Fork of Powder River.

Here exhaustless supplies of pine and all affiliated trees gather about the mountain sides and crawl down even to the islands of the larger Fork, where access is easy and convenient; while the abundant game, the local supremacy of the situation and its relations to the predominating lodge trails of the country, have made this immediate region the theater of active Indian hostilities from the time of its first occupation.

Peno Creek, Goose Creek, Tongue River, Rotten Grass Creek, Little Big Horn, and Big Horn Rivers succeed, each with bright tributaries; and so, stream succeeds stream as far as the great mountain gates through which the traveler enters the rich Gallatin Valley and finds himself in Montana proper.

Nearly parallel, but distant from twelve to twenty-five miles northward from the Big Horn range, are *Mauvais Terres*, or Bad Lands, whose conical hills and irregular outlines present all the desolate features of old volcanic debris; and when seen from some commanding point, appear to be hopelessly barren of good, either to man or beast.

And yet, all the rivers above named, and many others, boldly cut their way through these obstructions, and gather upon their borders rich fringes of vegetation and many elements of future development and profit.

The valleys of these streams greatly vary in width and scope; that of the Big Horn ranging from fifteen to twenty miles, and that of Tongue River covering nearly twice that area after it receives the contributions of Goose Creek and its other mountain feeders.

Absaraka Described

The region of country embraced within this outline, including the Upper Yellowstone and all east of Black Foot and Clark Passes, grasps more area of land than most of the large States or Territories; and with all its natural connections with Montana and Dakota, possesses an individual status that must eventually give it independence of each.

Chapter 3

THE NATURAL HISTORY AND CLIMATE
OF ABSARAKA

THE agricultural features of Absaraka have had incidental notice, but not sufficiently to advise a stranger of their real merit.

Wild wheat and oats abound in all the main valleys: both are grateful to stock, and sustain them well. The grasses are very heavy, so that in the summer of 1866 they were almost too resistant for easy use of machinery, and so thick that a horse could not be trotted rapidly in the bottom lands of Goose Creek and Tongue River.

Grasshoppers now and then made a visit, coming in clouds, like the drifting smoke of a prairie fire; but they failed to destroy the great grass region. Still they are no insignificant enemy, and a literal statement of their dense masses, put in the most guarded manner, would seem like the tale of a Munchausen or Gulliver. They cover a blade of grass until it bends to the earth. They cover horse and rider, ruthlessly dashing at every exposed part of the face or breast. They pass over with a rush, like the night roar of the cascades of the Pineys; and they shield the eye so that you can look the sun in the face as though a light flirt of snow had crossed its disk. And yet they are so subject to the mastery of the mountain winds, whose currents are as constant as they are fickle, that they quickly change their place of labor and again renew it in other fields of freshness and beauty.

The soil of the valleys is, in the main, a rich, deep loam, well adapted for vegetables, and in that climate for cereals; but alternate late and early frosts seem combined to refuse to corn a fair chance with other grain, while on the other hand barley, so grateful to mules, could seek no better region for its best development.

While rain, other than the dripping skirts of some mountain shower, is rare as diamonds, the numberless dashing streams, tributary to the great flows, present such ready means of irrigation that small labor and expense would apply them to all desired uses. Besides this, the deep snows of the winter season long leave the effects of their fertilizing agency, and when the autumn has turned all general vegetation from green to brown, the side hills will still be spotted with verdant places, where the lingering snow had last struggled, as if to contend with the summer's sun for mastery of the grass it had gifted with such precocious life and protracted vigor.

Of wild fruit there is great variety. Raspberries, strawberries, gooseberries, red currants, plums, cherries, and rock grapes are among the number. The cottonwood trees are often festooned with the vine of the hop, which here gives forth its product in such profusion and perfection, as will find no rival in the cultivated acres of eastern New York.

The pine and hemlock, the spruce and balsam, the cottonwood and ash, and willow are some of the trees which are ready of access and ample in supply for the demands of generations.

The climate is invigorating and healthful. There is no dew; and sickness is so rare, that for days in succession, during the constant labor and exposure of 1866, no soldiers attended the stated daily sick call, and the hospital itself was monopolized by cases of surgery only.

The summer temperature rarely exceeds ninety, and the nights are always cool and refreshing. Few take cold; and from July 15th, 1866, to January 15th, 1867, the barometer changed from fair, or very dry, only at the advent of winds sweeping from the snow mountains, and at one storm of mixed rain and snow, near the date of the autumnal equinox.

The field of natural history is rich beyond all precedent. The vicinity of Piney Forks and Tongue River is in the very heart of the game country. It is, as between several tribes, a semi-neutral and general hunting-ground. It is a great thoroughfare for migration to and from the Arkansas, and the hills in front and rear of Fort Philip Kearney are seamed and scarred by countless trails, where the Indian ponies have dragged lodge poles in their periodical or other changes of habitation and hunting.

The antipathy of the Indian to its occupation by the white man is very intense and bitter. The rattle of the mower, the whistle of the steam saw-mill, the felling of timber, the quick rise of stockade and substantial warehouses and quarters, are such sure signs of permanent possession, that they lose no opportunity to steal or kill when they can do so with comparative impunity. Yet the game still clings to its favorite haunts, and the Indian must press upon the steps of the white man or lose all hope of future independence. Herds of elk proudly stand with erect antlers, as if charmed by the morning music of garrison guard parade, or as if curious to understand this strange inroad upon their long secluded parks of pleasure. The mountain sheep look down from the beetling crags that skirt the perpendicular northern face of the Big Horn Mountains, and yield to no rival their claims to excellence for food. The black and white tail deer and the antelope are ever present; while the hare and the rabbit, the sage hen and prairie chicken, are nearly trodden down before they yield to the intrusion of the stranger. Brant, wild geese and ducks multiply and people the waters of Lake De Smet, and are found in nearly the same profusion all along the streams under the Big Horn Mountains; while the grizzly and cinnamon bear, not unseldom give up their lives and their rich material for the table, when, in the pursuit of wild plums and other fruit, they are crossed by the hunter and are dropped by his rifle. Last, and largest, and numberless, the buffalo, with tens of thousands in a herd, sweep back and forth, filling the valleys as far as the eye can reach, and adding their weight and numbers to the other substantial claims of the red man to entitle this same Absaraka, "Their last and best hunting-grounds."

The Big Horn River and its branches, as well as the streams beyond, are plentifully supplied with trout, the mountain pike, and other valuable fish, and thus complete the complement of supplies with which the country is so generously provided.

Innumerable wolves do indeed pierce the night air with their howls; but like the beaver, whose dams encumber all the smaller streams, and the otter, they are forced to yield their winter covering for those nice coats and caps, those mitts and blankets and leggings, which make men glad when zero is often reached, or the mercury calmly congeals in the bulb.

And yet, with the intervals of extreme cold and protracted snow, there is comparatively little suffering, unless from scurvy, when antiscorbutics are scarce, or men are careless, and rheumatism attends peculiar exposure. The dry snows, when in real earnest, penetrate every crevice, and drift about every obstruction. Valleys and gulches are filled, and travel is tedious or in abeyance; but the winter has its pleasures no less than the summer, and but for the hostility of the red man the upper garrisons of that line would hardly exchange their posts for any other on the frontier.

The mineral field imparts some of its peculiar contributions to the stores of Absaraka. Gold color is given in nearly all the streams, as already once indicated. Whether the sources of those streams will ever equal Montana precedents, must remain for the hard labor or good chance of the adventurer, or the skill and patience of some enterprising savant, to determine. The Black Hills, east of Fort Reno, have indications that promise rich returns of labor, and the lower Powder River has been left unoccupied by miners only because of the hostility of Buffalo Tongue and other Indians who infest its valley. The few excursions of a geological and scientific character, made in 1866, were almost always restricted in range and results by the exposure involved, and the absolute impossibility of procuring escort from small and hard worked commands. Small samples of lead and silver were found, but these and gold will have to be worked for. Neither will often be stumbled upon by treasure seekers; neither will they roll their offerings to the feet of idlers to solicit the appropriation of their pounds and ounces.

Coal is exhaustless. It can be found all along the route from Powder River to the Upper Yellowstone, and the red buttes which dot the country for miles northward are grand repositories of the same article. Lignite and the lower grades of wood coal are the prevailing type; but a vein was opened close to Fort Philip Kearney, soon after its establishment, in 1866, which was advantageously used in welding of iron, and will prove no less valuable for winter fires.

Limestone is attainable from the mountains, although somewhat difficult of transportation at present. Clay is abundant, and of such quality as to make a firm plaster coating upon simple exposure to the sun.

While the discoloration of the red buttes has been traced to the presence of iron, and it is also found in many of the sands, no ores have yet been exposed, nor have indications been made of its presence in any available supply. All other building materials are plentiful, and the tall pines furnish clear lumber of any required length or breadth, without a knot or blemish to mar their uniformity or beauty. Where some Indian fire has spread and struck a forest, so as to benumb its growth, the house builder finds his sound dry timber, which readily takes the plane and a handsome finish, and the perfection of its seasoning in that dry atmosphere is a work of short duration.

The magnetic variation at Fort Phil Kearney is 19° 20′, and its altitude over six thousand feet above the level of the sea; while half as high again above it rises Cloud Peak,[3] completing the landscape and crowning all with its purity and beauty.

[3] An understatement. The Wyoming State *Guide* gives the height of Cloud Peak as 13165 feet.

Chapter 4

ORGANIZATION OF THE EXPEDITION TO ABSARAKA

FORT KEARNEY, Nebraska, was the rendezvous where the first expedition was organized for the permanent occupation of Absaraka.[4] With little positive in-

[4] Widespread confusion has long existed among writers over the names of Fort Kearny and Fort Philip Kearny. The first Fort Kearny, Nebraska, was established by Colonel Stephen W. Kearny in 1846 on the site of present-day Nebraska City. Called Camp Kearny for a short time, it was officially named Fort Kearny, in honor of its founder, by War Department General Order No. 66, issued December 30, 1847.

The advancing frontier quickly left no reason for maintaining a garrison at Fort Kearny, and in the spring of 1848 the second Fort Kearny was established at Grand Island on the Platte. It quickly became the most important military center between Fort Leavenworth and Fort Laramie, and a notable way station for all travelers over the Oregon-California Road. Before long a postoffice was established, and in this connection some one at Washington fixed upon it the spelling "Kearney", and this became the accepted spelling of the town of Kearney which subsequently developed.

To Fort Kearny came Colonel Carrington as commandant in the winter of 1865–66. His stay was brief, however, for in the spring the War Department determined to safeguard the Bozeman Road connecting the Oregon Road with the Montana gold-mining centers by regarrisoning Fort Reno on Powder River and establishing new posts at Piney Fork of Clear Fork of the Powder and at the crossing of the Big Horn.

The task was assigned to Colonel Carrington's command at Fort Kearny, and his performance of it is the subject of Mrs. Carrington's *Absaraka*. Although it was at first intended to name the new posts Fort Reno and Fort Ransom, by General Order No. 7, Department of the Platte, issued June 28, 1866, the post about to be established on Piney Fork was named Fort Philip Kearny and the one on the Big Horn, Fort C. F. Smith. See U.S. Serial 2504, Exec. Doc. No. 33, p. 55.

Despite the fact that both Colonel Stephen W. Kearny and General Philip Kearny were two of the best-known officers in the U.S. Army, confusion early arose over the spelling of the two forts named for them. It is obvious that the last syllable of "Kearny" might readily be spelled with an *e*, and this error was perpetrated, as we have already seen, in the naming of Kearney Post Office. As a consequence of the Fetterman disaster Colonel Carrington was subjected to an investigation by court martial in the spring of 1867, and his long and able defense of his conduct introduced a large number of contemporary letters, reports to superiors, etc., in all of which the name of the fort is correctly spelled, "Philip Kearny".

However, this defense was not published until 1887 (U.S. Serial 2504, Exec. Doc. No. 13). Meanwhile, by Senate Resolution of July 8, 1867 Secretary of Interior Browning was required to transmit to the Senate all the information in his possession concerning the current Indian war. His lengthy report, like the defense of Colonel Carrington, included many orders and other military and Indian Office communications, in all of which the name "Kearny" was spelled with a second *e*.

Browning's report was promptly published (U.S. Serial 1308, Exec. Doc. No. 13) and since the public formation of the country to be occupied, we had the assurance that it was a precious region to the Indian; the most direct route for emigration to Montana; and then, there was the pressure of public opinion at the West in favor of the early establishment of the route, under the sanction of military authority, and its corresponding guarantees of troops and the support of connected posts.

interest in the Fetterman Massacre was intense it must have been widely read and commented upon. Unless we are prepared to believe that all of the officials whose reports and orders are included in the Browning report (among them such men as Generals Grant and Sherman and Secretary of War Stanton), many of whom were old-time friends of General Kearny, were unable to spell his name correctly we must assume that the erroneous spelling was the work of some copy reader in the Government Printing Office, intent upon achieving uniformity and himself ignorant of the correct spelling.

However this may be, the confusion noted earlier was intensified, to befuddle writers down to the present moment. In such standard works as Miss Wellman's "History of Fort Kearny" (*Nebraska Hist. Publications*, Vol. XXI) and the Scribner *Dictionary of American History*, edited by James Truslow Adams, the correct spelling of "Kearny" is followed. In many other works (among others, Mrs. Carrington's *Absaraka* and Hebard and Brininstool's *The Bozeman Trail*) it is not. In making the present reprint of *Absaraka*, to maintain uniformity and to avoid confusing the reader with variant spellings, the publisher has deemed it desirable to conform to the spelling adopted by the publisher of the original edition.

Organization of the Expedition

Maps were consulted in vain for something definite in the way of description, and everybody's book which said anything about the Indian of the Rocky Mountains was eagerly read and carefully digested, from the adventures of Lewis and Clark to the last newspaper correspondent from the Plains.

Then we had the foreshadowings of the long-heralded Laramie council to be held in May, when all the Indians of the disputed region were to assemble, and where, after the inevitable smoking and talking, a solemn peace was to be established and ratified, and a genuine right of way was to be secured to the modern land of Ophir.

Then began preparations for the march. Reports were conflicting as to whether the climate belonged truly to the frigid or temperate zone; whether the land was prolific in vegetation, or barren and worthless.

A winter's march from Fort Leavenworth to Fort Kearney in 1865, when the mercury was twelve degrees below zero and two feet of snow was first to be shoveled aside before a tent could be pitched—when the prairie winds penetrated every garment, and drifting snows often blinded any advance—was deemed a sufficient experience to decide the ladies to undertake the journey and risk the issues of a Rocky Mountain winter.

It was a little drawback to the perfection of plans for housekeeping that the only post on a line of more than seven hundred miles was to be abandoned, and that all the posts in the new command were to be built far from civilization and supplies, and in time for winter use; but seeming banishment did not discourage, after the purpose was settled to go on.

The general plan had been outlined by General Pope,[5] who had large experience in Indian affairs, and had in view the exact relations of the new route to advancing emigration, the quickest communication with Montana, and the probability of a peaceful occupation through the agency of the Laramie Council.

[5] General John Pope graduated from West Point in 1842 and served in the army until he was retired for age with the rank of major general in 1886. Both before and after the Civil War he served extensively on the frontier. His victories in the West in the early period of the Civil War led to his appointment by President Lincoln to succeed General McClellan as commander of the Army of the Potomac. Defeated by Lee and Jackson in the second Bull Run campaign (July–August, 1862), he was soon relieved of his command. From 1870 to 1883 he commanded the Department of the Missouri, and from the latter date until his retirement in 1886 the Department of California. Although his Civil War career ended in humiliation, his long service on the western frontier was distinctly creditable.

Organization of the Expedition

Northwest of Fort Laramie, one hundred and sixty-seven miles distant, was Fort Reno, formerly Fort Connor, named after General Connor, who marched to Tongue River in 1865, and returned safely, after meeting ample opposition to discourage a farther advance. This was to be moved about forty miles west, to be rebuilt for a four-company post, and two additional forts were to be constructed—one on or near the Big Horn River, and the second on or near the Upper Yellowstone.[6] To this duty the 2d Battalion of the 18th U. S. Infantry had been assigned, under the command of Colonel Carrington of that regiment, who was also designated as District Commander, with headquarters at the new Fort Reno. The battalion numbered at that time just about two hundred and twenty men, many of whom were veterans having less than a year to serve, but, with the band and clerks, making an aggregate of nearly two

[6] Fort Reno had been established by General Connor at the Bozeman Trail crossing of Powder River on August 19, 1865 and named for that officer. It was rebuilt by Colonel Carrington in 1866 and at the same time Fort Philip Kearney at the forks of the Big and Little Piney and Fort C. F. Smith at the Big Horn crossing of the Bozeman Trail were established. All three forts were abandoned by the government at the behest of the Sioux in 1868.

hundred and sixty who were preparing for the trip.

General Dodge,[7] who then commanded the United States forces in Kansas and the territories, and whose map is the only intelligible map of that country, actively interested himself in the expected movement, and within a week after he received application for a steam saw-mill, had purchased and started it on its journey. The Interior Department furnished maps. The Smithsonian gave its contributions. Professors Silliman and Dana, of Yale College, supplied standard English and American works upon the various departments of natural science; while transit, level, and other instruments for surveys, observations, and such other duty as would aid in the exploration and development of a new country were also provided.

A strange medley was that outfit, and its catalogue, to which something was constantly added, opened our eyes to a clearer view of

[7] General Grenville M. Dodge, notable builder of the Union Pacific and other railroads. The Union Pacific was completed in May, 1869, when for the first time the iron rail spanned the continent. In a single year under Dodge's driving energy 568 miles of road were located, built, and equipped. The incident cited by Mrs. Carrington affords a characteristic illustration of his terrific efficiency.

the fact that we were to live a pioneer life, and begin a new career at the very foundation of border experience.

Tools of all kinds were of course to be gathered together. Thus, there were mowing machines, and shingle and brick machines, doors, sash, glass, nails, locks, and every conceivable article that can enter into housebuilding. Future blacksmiths, wheelwrights, painters, harnessmakers, and carpenters, who were to be hunted up out of the command, had to be provided with the implements of their craft. All contingencies had to be anticipated, so that the day of arrival in the new country should be the day of commencement, and there should then be no delay to wait for anything from the United States.

Meanwhile, the Laramie contributors to the public press were swelling the numbers of the Indians who already were or soon would be at the conference, some estimating the number as high as twenty and even thirty thousand. Certainly there were indications that the Indians were really intending to visit that post and deliberate upon surrender of the coveted route.

The death of the young daughter of Spotted Tail, and her burial at Laramie with religious rites and many complimentary

services, had brought that chief[8] into closer
relations of friendship, and messengers had
been sent far and wide to bid Cheyennes and
Arapahoes, as well as Sioux, to the grave
discussion.

The contingency that the Indians who occupied the territory in question might stay

[8] Spotted Tail was not an hereditary chief, but he had
attained the office by force of personality and aggressive
character. On August 19, 1854 near Fort Laramie
Lieutenant John L. Grattan and twenty-nine soldiers
were slain in a battle with 1000 or more Sioux warriors.
An emigrant's cow had been killed by the Sioux, and
Grattan had entered the Sioux camp to demand the surrender of the guilty warrior. Although Addison E.
Sheldon, Nebraska State Historian, represents that the
ensuing fight (the first battle between the Sioux and
United States soldiers) was wholly caused by Grattan's
folly and unreason, General William S. Harney a year
later led a punitive expedition against the Sioux and in
the battle of Ash Hollow on September 4, 1855 killed
eighty-six of their warriors. Soon afterward he built a
sod fort at the mouth of Ash Hollow and named it Fort
Grattan. Spotted Tail and two others who had partici-
pated in the killing of Grattan's detachment now came
into Fort Laramie, singing their death songs and offering themselves as scapegoats for their tribe. Spotted
Tail was subsequently freed, however, to resume his
chieftainship. He was killed near the Rosebud Agency
in South Dakota by Crow Dog, a fellow tribesman, on
August 5, 1881. On the Grattan battle and its disastrous consequences, see Addison E. Sheldon, *Nebraska,
the Land and the People*, I, 133–35. A vivid account of
the remarkable career and funeral of Ao-ho-appa,
daughter of Spotted Tail, is given by Eugene F. Ware,
The Indian War of 1864, (Topeka, 1911) 565–82.

away, and then fight the expedition, was so remote in the assurance of a treaty, that it was hardly considered, except that it induced a request for a short delay, until the arrival of recruits who were already enlisted and on the way from New York.

The band donned additional equipments, and drilled with the Spencer carbine, and these same arms afterward proved of infinite value; while the afternoon and evening music of the band lightened the labor and sweetened the privations of our partial exile.

While still waiting for recruits, General Sherman visited the post, entering into the spirit and plans of the expedition with his usual energy and skill.[9] At his suggestion some of the ladies began their daily journal

[9] By order of June 27, 1865 the entire United States had been divided into five military districts, and General Sherman had been appointed to command the Second (later called the District of the Missouri) with headquarters at St. Louis. He was actively interested in promoting the construction of the Pacific Railroad and on his recommendation the President, on March 5, 1866 created the Department of the Platte, with General Philip St. George Cooke as commander, to afford protection in particular to the workers on the Union Pacific. Meanwhile General Sherman himself reconnoitered the area, traversing it from north to south and from east to west in order to insure the best possible disposition and employment of the troops. The visit to Fort Laramie was evidently one incident of the General's oversight of his command.

of events, and thus laid the basis for the conversion of one into this narrative for the eyes of friends who could not share the trip.

On the 13th of May the recruits arrived, and were distributed among the companies to learn to be soldiers.[10] With them came the 3d Battalion, Company F of the 1st Battalion, and recruits for the whole regiment, thus swelling the marching command to nearly two thousand men. But the routes to Salt Lake City were to be guarded, both the direct mail line and the northern road by Forts Laramie and Caspar, so that the eight companies of the 2d Battalion remained as the fixed detail for the Mountain District.

There was no cavalry, but as the outgoing volunteer regiments were to leave their horses at Laramie, and we were to have two hundred to mount infantry until cavalry could be furnished, the interesting experiment of determining how many could ride a horse was initiated. Fortunately, two volunteer cavalry regiments passed by, on the way home for muster-out, and the two

[10] The report of the Senate investigating committee on the Fetterman massacre, made in 1867, stated that of the total force of about 700 men assigned to Colonel Carrington 500 were raw recruits. Colonel Carrington himself distinguished them as "220 soldiers and 500 recruits."

hundred horses were procured at once. This was doubly agreeable to officers and men, as it transpired that, on arrival at Laramie, the volunteers had preferred to ride to the Missouri River on horseback rather than to walk, and there were not horses enough to replace a few that died on the road. As memory reverts back, it now seems fortunate in another aspect, as otherwise there would have been no horses for couriers or pickets, and the expedition might have experienced even more difficulties than it did encounter in communicating with the United States and the positions occupied. So cavalry was improvised. Men got upon the horses, and the majority actually made the first trip to water without being dismounted. Some men were embarrassed when the long Springfield rifle was put on the horse with them, but both man and horse soon learned how it was to be done.

At length all things were declared ready. Rocking chairs and sewing chairs, churns and washing machines, with a bountiful supply of canned fruits, were duly stored inside or outside of army wagons; while turkeys and chickens, and one brace of swine added a specially domestic cast to some of the establishments prepared for the journey. Thanks to a defective flue, which set fire to our house, burning it, with all the contents of the attic, a few days before we left—some best chairs, bedsteads, and mattresses (all properly packed), with a half hundred beef tongues, some potatoes and selected groceries, were prematurely consumed; but as this was only an incident very possible in army life, the fun of the affair made up for its losses.

The last thing done looked a little warlike: the magazine was opened and all the ammunition that could be spared from the fort was drawn out and loaded in wagons; but its comparatively meager supply gave little annoyance, as Laramie would be expected to furnish the deficit in case any further fighting material should be required in the way of powder and lead. Then we had the news that a battalion of the 13th Infantry had been ordered to build a new post at the foot of the northern Black Hills, while two companies were to keep open the road thence to Fort Reno, thus giving fair assurance that the Indians of that location and Powder River Valley would be watched and held to their own theater of action in case the Laramie Council should fail to establish a peace on the Plains.

The expedition had the following organization: District Commander, Colonel H. B.

Carrington, 18th U. S. Infantry; Assistant Adjutant-General, Brevt. Captain Frederick Phisterer, Adjutant 18th U. S. Infantry; Chief Quartermaster, Lieutenant Frederick H. Brown, Quartermaster 18th U. S. Infantry; Chief Surgeon, Brevt. Major S. M. Horton, Assistant Surgeon U. S. A.; Acting Assistant Surgeons, Dr. H. M. Matthews, Dr. B. N. McCleary, and Dr. H. Baalan; Battalion Commander, Brevt. Major H. Haymond, 2d Battalion; Mounted Infantry, Captain T. Ten Eyck, 18th U. S. Infantry; Battalion Adjutant, Brevt. Captain Wm. H. Bisbee, 2d Battalion. The additional officers were Captain and Brevt. Lieutenant Colonel N. C. Kinney, Captain J. L. Proctor, Captain T. B. Burrowes, Lieutenant J. J. Adair, Lieutenant Thaddeus P. Kirtland, Lieutenant Isaac D'Isay.

As chief guide, Major James Bridger had been selected, assisted by H. Williams, who had been a guide to several expeditions to the Republican during the winter of 1865–6; and thus organized, the command was ready.

Chapter 5

FEW days on the plains are more bright and promising, notwithstanding such a cloud of dust as the plains only can supply, than was the nineteenth day of May, A.D. 1866.

Two hundred and twenty six-mule teams, besides ambulances, were the outfit, and the band of over thirty pieces regaled us with just the right music, until the column passed Kearney City, popularly known to travelers as "Dobey (Adobe) Town."[11]

[11] In Chapter VI, Mrs. Carrington describes Valley City in the brief period of its glory when General Carrington was serving as commandant of Fort Kearney. It was situated two miles west of the fort, just outside the 10-mile-square military reservation, which was bordered on its eastern side by evanescent Valley City, for which see *post*, note 15. Mrs. Carrington's prophecy of a future period of prosperity for Kearney City has never been realized. As a center of trade and entertainment located conveniently outside the military reservation, "Dobeytown" acquired an evil reputation for lawlessness, which quite possibly grew in the old timers'

Departure from Fort Kearney

The march was along the Platte River, whose quicksands and fickle currents have been the bane of travelers since Lewis and Clark abused it and Colonel Bonneville crossed it. Alkaline and muddy,—sometimes disappearing under the sandy bed, so that a footman can cross from shore to shore without seeing water, and again flowing even with its banks; sometimes surfeiting the south channel, under the pressure of a strong north wind, and again, within the same sun, rolling back so as to foil the calculations of some traveler who crossed in the morning, expecting an equally safe crossing at night,

memories with the passing of the years. One of them relates that at one time the place contained six families and fourteen saloons. Nearby in a cottonwood thicket adjoining the stage road was a house whose character is briefly suggested by its name, Dirty Woman's Ranch, given it probably by the travelers who found lodging there. General Sherman visited Fort Kearney during Colonel Carrington's period of command and the two, accompanied by a party of officers and their ladies, rode out to view the country. While passing through Dobeytown they were hissed by some of the inmates. Soon afterward, the reminiscer relates, Sherman avenged the insult by ordering the abandonment of Fort Kearney. Another chronicler records that quantities of "the meanest whisky on earth" were dispensed at Dobeytown, whose cemetery was larger than the living community. However inaccurate these old-age memories may be they at least serve to suggest that Dobeytown was no Sunday School resort.

45

it has no disputant to oppose its claim to be the most unaccountably contrary and ridiculous river the world ever saw.

But in our course along the Platte in 1866, we had, such as it was, all the water we wished. One day was much like another day, with the same march at the earliest dawn, the same adventures with rattlesnakes, the same pursuit of wild flowers, the same inopportune thunderstorms, the same routine of guard mounting at sunset, the same evening music from the band, and the same sound slumber. Recurring Sabbaths gave us our only intervals of rest; and the fact that at Fort Reno we overtook trains which started before us, but marched daily, is a substantial testimony, concurrent with all intelligent experience, that the observance of the Lord's day is indispensable alike to man and beast. On such occasions Lieutenants Adair, Kirtland, and D'Isay, occasionally joined by Mr. Phisterer, tenor, helped to make something like true melody from the sweet Sabbath Bell sent us by the Sabbath school of Rev. Mr. Dimmick, of Omaha, before our departure from Kearney.

Fort McPherson,[12] then consisting of shabby log-cabins, but now a beautiful and well-

[12] Fort McPherson, originally called Fort Cottonwood, was established in October, 1863 at the mouth of

Cottonwood Canon, where the trading settlement of Cottonwood Springs had developed. The site was on the south side of the Platte in Lincoln County, Nebraska, several miles eastward from present-day North Platte city. The fort was built of logs obtained from trees in the immediate vicinity and was first occupied by a detachment of troops belonging to the Seventh Iowa Cavalry. It was the scene of activities of two notable scouts, Buffalo Bill Cody and Major Frank North, the latter the organizer of a battalion of Pawnee Indians which performed much useful service in the warfare of the period against the Sioux. Buffalo Bill has left this description of their appearance on review: "They had been furnished full cavalry uniforms, and on parade some of them had their Navy overcoats on (in summer); other their large black hats with all the brass accouterments attached. Some of them wore pantaloons and others only wore breech cloths. Others wore regulation pantaloons, but no shirts, and were bareheaded. Others again, had the seat of their pantaloons cut out, leaving only leggings. Some wore brass spurs, but had neither boots nor moccasins. With all this melange of oddity, they understood the drill well for Indians. The commands, of course, were given in their own language by Major North, who could talk it as well as any full-blooded Pawnee."

It was at Fort McPherson that Ned Buntline (real name Edward Z. Judson) encountered Buffalo Bill and started him on his career to popular fame and showmanship. The fort was abandoned in 1887. Both it and the settlement have long since vanished, and the military reserve, save for the cemetery, is divided up for farm land. Where "once sounded the bugle call, and where the stars and stripes were seen flying between the rising and setting sun," wrote the county historian of 1920, "now is heard the rattle of agricultural implements and the dinnerbell of husbandmen who till the soil ... Crops

47

built post, was passed on the 24th of May, the only halt being to seek additional ammunition and take along an idle saw-mill not needed at that post. On the 29th we camped near the Old California Crossing, and received a call from Colonel Otis and some gentlemen of the Peace Commission, who, with agreeable presents for the red men, were on their way to the Laramie council. About dark the news was brought that nearly three hundred Indians had crossed the Platte near by for a hunt on the Republican, having permission to be absent from Laramie until other bands came in and the commission should formally assemble.

Old Little Dog, whose son burned Julesburg in 1864, came into camp and made

grow on the site of the old fort, while the trader, the Indian and his squaw, the trooper and buffalo are faintly remembered by old residents of the 'Kingdom of Lincoln'." The old fort cemetery is preserved as a national cemetery, to which the remains of soldiers from a score of western forts have been consigned, besides bodies of civilians, Pawnee scouts, and World War I soldiers. Among others interred here are the bodies of Lieutenant John L. Grattan and his detachment of twenty-nine soldiers who were slaughtered in an engagement with several hundred Sioux warriors a few miles below Fort Laramie on August 19, 1854. Captain Eugene F. Ware's *The Indian War of 1864* supplies an interesting account of the building of Fort Cottonwood.

complaint that some one of our soldiers had
entered his lodge and stolen his rifle. After a
somewhat curious observation of the performance of the band and special admiration
of the bell chimes, and upon being assured
that his gun should be found and returned
to him, he sprang upon the bare back of his
pony with all the elasticity of youth and
more than the skill of our mounted infantry,
and galloped swiftly away. He had the appearance of being very old, but his agility
and address in his intercourse with that pony
were decidedly suggestive of the probable
skill and activity of the young warriors of
his nation.

Fort Sedgwick, near the so-called city of
Julesburg, was reached on the 30th of
May.[13] This city, though burned by Little

[13] Jules Bené (Beni, Benoit) established a ranch on the
south side of the South Platte about a mile east of the
mouth of Lodge Pole Creek sometime in the fifties. An
order was issued in May, 1864 to establish Camp Rankin
here. Actual construction of the buildings from sod cut
from the nearby prairie was begun in September, 1864
by Company F, Seventh Iowa Cavalry, and the place
was renamed Fort Sedgwick, in honor of Major General
Sedgwick who had been killed in the battle of Spottsyl-
vania Court House a few months earlier. Sod structures
deteriorate rapidly, and General Sherman, who visited
the fort in August, 1866, stated that it looked "like
hovels in which a negro would not go." Despite this, and
the enormous difficulties of maintenance occasioned by

Dog, had been rebuilt, so as to number nearly a dozen houses and stores, and a year
later, in 1867, another Julesburg, of canvas
and portable frame buildings, dwellings,
shops, hotels, refectories, and recreatories,
had sprung up on the north side of the river,
as an accompaniment to the progress of the

scarcity of wood and other supplies, he decided that
Fort Sedgwick must be maintained.

Jules Bené was a rough character around whom
legends readily developed. He is reputed to have been
tortured to death and his ear cut off and utilized as a
watch charm by Jack Slade, who in his turn was hung
by vigilantes at Virginia City. Julesburg was a station
on the Pony Express and the Overland Stage routes,
and in June, 1867 construction headquarters of the
Union Pacific Railroad were removed here from North
Platte, Nebraska. The railroad built its station on the
north side of the river and some three miles east of Old
Julesburg, which now fell into decay. Eventually a
third and a fourth town, the last one located half a
dozen miles east of Old Julesburg, were built.

On January 7, 1865, 1000 or more Cheyenne and other
warriors, embittered by the Chivington Massacre of
November 29, 1864, appeared before Fort Sedgwick.
In the ensuing battle 14 of the soldiers and 56 of the
warriors were killed. Three weeks later, on February 2,
about 1500 Cheyenne and Arapahoe warriors burned
the stage headquarters and other buildings of Julesburg
and began an attack upon Fort Sedgwick, which was
abandoned when a force of several hundred Iowa and
Nebraska cavalry opportunely appeared on the scene.
A detailed and interesting account of these several
activities is given by Ware in *The Indian War of 1864.*

Union Pacific Railroad, boasting its three thousand inhabitants, all of them determined to remain there until they could do as well or better elsewhere farther on. The water and soil of the new location were not equal to those of the Wabash, Scioto, or Connecticut River valleys: but, on the other hand, in neither of these old-fashioned regions could a wall tent rent at one hundred dollars per day; neither could a piece of canvas, sufficiently large to cover a billiard table, command its thousand dollars per week.

But in 1866 we stopped three days, out of respect for the Platte. This delay was somewhat relieved by shopping calls upon the post sutler, Mr. Adams, nephew of Mr. Stanton, Secretary of War, while the troops were drawing supplies or caulking and fitting out a large flatboat, which, procured from Denver, was at the fort, nearly half a mile from the element for which its inventor had designed it.

After caulking, this apparatus had to be conveyed to the water; a double cable had to be sprung across the river, and science was summoned to do its best to adapt its heavy draught to the quicksands, shoals, and currents of the ubiquitous Platte. Two hundred men made quick work, and when the science of the learned was appalled at the magnitude of the undertaking, the common sense and practical skill of Captain Ten Eyck, an old surveyor and lumberman, solved all problems and crossed the craft safely. Twenty yoke of cattle drew the first cable over, when mules struggled in vain to start it; and Mrs. Lieutenant Bisbee and Jean were the first family passengers after the ferry was actually established. But the natural contrariness of the Platte, although so signally rebuked by the passage of a real boat, and permitting its current to aid in its flight, was never more conspicuously developed than when it really seemed to understand that the object of that boat was to get wagons, teams, and stores to the north bank in safety, and thereby circumvent its ugly temper. Although the river had been examined for miles to see if there was not some available ford, before shipcraft and navigation were resorted to, no sooner did that boat attempt its mission in real earnest with prospect of success than this identical Platte River fell more than a foot. Then could be seen navigation under difficulties. New eddies, spiteful currents, and outcropping bars, with desperate quicksands and the constantly varying depth of water, in turn caught it, and stopped it, and turned it, until the gallant crew actually leaped overboard. Then, partly kept out of the river bottom by a grasp upon the gunwale, and partly kept in progress by hand-over-hand along the cable, those intrepid mariners crossed that boat once again in less than four hours by the watch.

The prospect of spending until the autumn fall of water in completing the transit, aroused a fresh spirit of enterprise and developed new expedients. The slight fall of water had been carefully gauged, and, unknown to the water sprite who was plainly in league with the Sioux of Absaraka, and therefore opposed to our further advance, a great array of timber was procured; wagons were unloaded; false beds or frames were prepared; half loads replaced full loads, and a bold push was made to defy all elements of evil. To be sure, the lead mules would be swimming, the middle team pulling, the wheel team floundering, and the wagon would be rolling in quicksand; but the expedient of double teams always left some one or more span on the earth's surface, to pull on or push on the others. It was crossing the Platte in more ways than one; for we did it in very spite of that natural forlornness of disposition which so undeniably approximates the natural depravity of man. Enough to say that the Platte was crossed.

53

A few mules got their ears under water, to drown from innate stubbornness. A few harnesses were cut to save others. Some riders had to tow the lead team with ropes; and enough whipping was applied for a week of ordinary travel. Water would melt sugar and cake the flour, and now and then a stray knapsack or haversack floated down the current; but, the Platte was crossed!

Before the consummation of this achievement, which the innovations of the railroad will prevent us from renewing, there was a social entertainment in camp not to be forgotten.

It was the last reunion of the officers of the 18th Infantry.[14] The bill before Congress proposing to add two companies to each battalion, and thus make of each a new regiment, was already *fait accomplit*; and a regiment that alone had filled its twenty-

[14] Organization of the Eighteenth U.S. Infantry was begun at Columbus in July, 1861 and its three battalions were filled during the ensuing year. To January 1, 1866 the regiment had mustered 4,773 men, approximately one-half of them from Ohio. It served throughout the Civil War in the western arena, and a year following its close the regiment's three battalions were separated to constitute three distinct regiments. In November, 1865 Colonel Carrington was sent to Fort Kearney in charge of the Second Battalion and from here, in the spring of 1866 the expedition to Wyoming was launched.

four companies within a year after its organization in 1861, and which had received into its ranks over five thousand men, was finally to separate and prepare for new relations and new titles.

The young officers, full of regrets, but as full of life and devotion to the general comfort as ever, arranged a farewell concert of "Iron-clad Minstrels", under the supervision of Majors Van Voast and Burt. Hospital tents were unloaded and united in one grand pavilion. Camp stools and chairs from baggage wagons, or the fort, were brought into requisition, and a grand concert was the result.

It is an old army fashion to enliven the monotony of frontier life by extemporized opera, charades, readings, and the miniature drama; and the illustrations on this occasion were excellent. The string band gave us a splendid orchestra, and the violins and violoncello, the clarionets and the flute, the French horns and the trumpet, the trombone and the tuba, alternately supplied the solo, or replenished the chorus, as the bones and banjo called for their interference. Faces only were unfamiliar; and the fifteen or twenty sergeants and soldiers, who, with fine voices, perfect harmony, and the usual *bon-mots* of Ethiopian minstrelsy, entertained the lovers of, now and then, a little sport, did as full justice to their music as they had effectually transformed themselves from Caucasian to African by the pervasive laws of burnt cork.

Then came the parting at the Colonel's tent. A part of the command were to march two days longer with headquarters, while others were to leave the next morning for other fields of duty.

Captain Neill, Mrs. Neill, and Miss Bella had already occupied post headquarters at Fort Sedgwick. Captain Kellogg, Mrs. Kellogg, and little Harry, who, with Harry and Jimmy Carrington, had raced ponies daily on the march from Kearney, were also detached with Lieutenant Wilcox and two companies, and practical separation began.

Army life alone has these peculiar separations. Bound closely in social intimacies, separated from the affinities of active life in the States, the fleeting friendships of garrison or camp life are full of fraternal endearments, both in sickness and health, that go very far, when gentlemen are gentlemen and ladies are ladies, to atone for banishment and public service far from the courtesies and amenities of civil life. Hence, when tender relations are established and congenial spirits meet, it is painful to sunder those ties. Then the *esprit de corps* of families becomes hardly less sacred than that which unites officers when the ideal of army pride is attained, and each regards the honor of another as dear as his own, and jealousies and backbitings sink to the level of their own intrinsic meanness. Exceptions only prove how essential is such a law for social life in the army, and those who violate its behests, alone are degraded and suffer. No caste of rank invades their social life, neither does the parade-ground entrench upon the parlor; yet the proprieties and courtesies of good society everywhere affirm their prerogatives and give delightsomeness to the relations of all.

So pleasant was the parting at Sedgwick, even with its sadness; and long will that evening recall to the old 18th its participation on that occasion when so long a good-by was begun.

Two days of marching from Fort Sedgwick brought us to Louis' ranch at the upper crossing of Lodge Pole Creek. Now, the Union Pacific Railroad has passed that point, and from Cheyenne begins its borings for the waters of the Pacific. The South Platte was left at Sedgwick. The first day's march is seventeen miles to Lodge Pole Creek, and the second is eighteen miles to

Louis' ranch. Here we spent another social evening with those of the third battalion under Major Lewis, a true man and perfect soldier, whose destination was Camp Douglass, by way of Lodge Pole Creek Cañon, and so on to the pleasant land of Deseret and Salt Lake City. Here also we parted with Mrs. McClintick and Mrs. Burt and their husbands, and Mrs. Burt's sister, Miss Reynolds, thus still more reducing our coterie of ladies, and still further separating us from the associations of the march and old times at home.

Chapter 6

UP to Louis' ranch all styles of being,
and the very routes of travel have
changed. This very Pacific Railroad,
with its swift pulse, drives everything along,
and its chief engineer, General Dodge, seems
to attempt the annihilation of time and
space, with the same indefatigable spirit as
that with which he won the thanks of everybody at old Kearney in aiding their efficient
outfit for the Plains; and Superintendent
Duvant is tireless as he is successful. But
the change from 1865, and even from 1866,
when our narrative gathers its chief contributions, is marked. Then, no railroad
stretched its hard arms after the traveler or
emigrant; and the report of its coming was
like the prophecies of some madmen who
think that New York City will soon travel
westward, to absorb the prerogatives and
location of Rocky Mountain custom and
commerce.

Before this railroad began its journey,
travelers from Leavenworth varied their

days' marches, as few will be able to do again. There was first a rough ride to the Nine Mile Station, with its uncomfortable stone house. Then came, in turn, the crossing of the Atchison and Pike's Peak Railroad; Kinnekuck, on the Big Grasshopper, beyond Grenada, where the Kickapoo Indians were buying and begging; Big Muddy; Ash Point; Big Blue, with Simpson's capital Yankee Store of notions; Rock Creek; Big Sandy; Little Blue River, with its perpetual Indian alarms and occasional depredations; Little Blue Station; Spring Creek; Pawnee Ranch; Sand Hill Station; and Valley City, or Dog Town, only nine miles from Fort Kearney.[15]

Valley City was then ambitious and enterprising; but, in 1867, our friend Haney was the sole resident; and Hook, the old caterer

[15] In this paragraph Mrs. Carrington has sketched the highway from Fort Leavenworth in Kansas, to Fort Kearney, Nebraska, a distance of 350 miles. Valley City, long since defunct, was made the county seat of newly-created Kearney County by legislative act of January 10, 1860. That spring, one observer reports, it consisted of five hovels. A year later there were 250 inhabitants and half a dozen stores. It was located eight miles eastward of Fort Kearney, on the border of the military reservation. Its decline was as rapid as its rise had been, a victim of the advent of the Pacific Railroad.

Various items of information about several of the places mentioned by Mrs. Carrington have been gleaned for Fort Kearney, had gone farther west to establish his fortunes in some larger field of usefulness and profit. We saw him at McPherson, in June, when on his winding way, and the papers say he is mayor or alderman in the proud city—Cheyenne.

In those days, Kearney City was a busy mart of trade, and future south side railroads will restore its business. Plattsmouth and Nebraska City sent many an outfit of loaded wagons. Ox-teams and mule-teams, and teams with horses, and horses with saddles, brought many new visitors, who lunched, bartered, and journeyed on. Here, Piper and Robinson, Brown and Linnell, Michel, Thomas, Dr. Brashure, Talbot, the veteran officer, and a host of others devoted their time to the well-being of all who lingered at their doors; but it was after Kearney was passed, that the glory of legitimate ranching began. McLean and the genial Sydenham, our Fort Kearney postmaster; Gallagher;

from Vol. 19 of the *Nebraska State Historical Publications*, and from Ware, *The Indian War of 1864*.

Little Blue Station was four miles northwest of present-day Oak, Nuckolls County, Nebraska. Near here occurred an indecisive battle with Indians on August 15, 1864. Pawnee Ranch was established in 1859 in the southwestern corner of Clay County, 26 miles west of Little Blue Station and 54 miles southeast of Fort Kearney.

Pat Mallalley; Dan Smith; Gilman, a man of business, straightforward and worthy, and Coles, were a few who ministered to our comfort on the way to McPherson. Then came Fitch's, Burke's, Morrow's, Baker's, Brown's, Beauvais, and Valentine's, all accommodating and excellent. We stop to speak of Jack Morrow, the prince of ranchmen, and the king of good fellows. He is a ranchman indeed! Fortune has showered her favors about his life's journey and prosperity dwelleth within his walls. Keen in business, generous, and hail fellow, his career, on the South Platte, has become temporarily restricted; but, with his indomitable spirit, no sooner did that Union Pacific Railroad shoot by his ranch, on the northern shore, than he moved ranch and all across its quicksands and waters, and went on his usual course as if nothing new had come along. A two-story frame, one of the best on the Plains, went down, over, and up again, as if the genii of Aladdin's lamp had been assigned to special duty in his behalf, and Jack was himself again.[16]

[16] Ware, *The Indian War of 1864*, supplies information concerning several of the ranchmen noted by Mrs. Carrington. "Fitches" was probably Thomas French, at whose ranch Ware's company of the Seventh Iowa Cavalry, enroute to establish Fort Cottonwood, stopped

But ranchmen are westward bound. Soon, they will be known no more forever! The Pacific will stop them on this continent, and further than that, the future historian must write of their struggles and their triumphs. It would be just like Jack Morrow to go to Alaska, run a ferry across Bering Straits, and

for the night of October 9, 1863. The place was "a new cedar ranch with sod inclosure for stock," and French, who was reported to be a Confederate deserter, was endeavoring to monopolize the adjoining river bottom grass land. The detachment reached it on the second day's march from Fort Kearney, supposedly a distance of fifty miles. Gilman's ranch was fifteen miles east of Fort Cottonwood. It was owned by two brothers, J. K. and Jud. Gilman. Ware characterizes them as capable, intelligent men "who would make good citizens anywhere" and supplies interesting data concerning their establishment.

Although Jack Morrow may have been "a king of good fellows," his character otherwise was far from sacrosanct. Ware describes him as "a tall, raw-boned, dangerous-looking man, wearing a mustache, and a goatee on his under lip." Aggressive and prosperous, he was reported to be a killer, and was addicted to stupendous drinking spells which were celebrated from Denver to Fort Kearney and even to Omaha. His ranch on the South Platte was two miles west of Fort Cottonwood. Before locating there he had conducted an establishment at Fort Kearney, where he figured actively in the fraudulent congressional election of 1859. He died at Omaha, July 14, 1876.

Beauvais' ranch was about 25 miles east of Julesburg at the Old California Crossing of the South Platte.

open a ranch for Americans and Russians
who choose that route of travel from America to Europe. A tribute to the memory of
ranchmen and a record of their styles and
methods on the Plains is simple justice to the
history of the nineteenth century. Already
they are not as they were! Nebraska, one of
the latest and one of the best of new States
when its development shall ripen, has entertained and profited some of their best, as
well as those not so ambitious or genteel.

From Fort Leavenworth to Fort Kearney,
from Kearney to McPherson, from McPherson to Sedgwick, nearly all ranches have
been abandoned, or the occupants only linger
for the protection of their lives and property.
They have had their comforts and discom-
forts, and among them we met some of the
best and bravest and the biggest hearted
men of any race or people.

To some, who have never tarried at a
ranch, it will not come amiss to introduce a
few samples which our experience impressed
upon the memory.

Ranches alike provide for man and beast,
and are arranged for their special care and
protection. A large yard is surrounded by a
stockade paling, with stabling, feed troughs,
and hayricks, with here and there loop-holes
for the rifle. In places of imminent peril from
Indian attacks, such as Valentine's, Baker's,

or Lewis's, the wall of the upper stories and every angle of house or stable has its outlets for firing upon an approaching foe. The log or adobe house, which provides for the master as well as the corral provides for his beast, is often small; but, like an eastern omnibus or street car, is unlimited in accommodations for all who seek its shelter.

Let the readers of this narrative enter with us into a few sample ranches of our actual and literal experience, for illustration of their social capacity and things as they were, and let them envy the life of an officer's wife on the Plains.

Just at dark, one bitter November afternoon in 1865, when drifting snows obscured all advance, we struck a ranch. It had but one story, was long and narrow, and was divided into three apartments, each having a front window and door. Two Atchison coaches, respectively bound east and west, with the California and Salt Lake City mails, were in front, looking as if they had stood there for six months, through accumulating snow; and yet they were only waiting for their drivers and forlorn passengers to thaw and feed, and for the stock to do the same. Room number one, as well as room number two, had a substantial earth floor. The former, about ten by twelve feet square, had quite a plain plank counter, and upon shelves behind could be seen the names of Mr. Drake, Mr. Kelly, Log Cabin, Bourbon, and others equally euphonious, designed to represent certain bottled products, which for a considerable sum of money were susceptible of transfer on proper demand. Some were labeled Gin, which never saw juniper; some were labeled Rye, which never knew that cereal; and some were simply labeled Whisky, which were modest high wines and water, with very little of the water, at least, so said those gentlemen who tried experiments of analysis for scientific purposes. Nutmegs, peppermint, navy tobacco, clay pipes, salaratus, baking powder, bologna, and ready-made clothing, with rows of canned fruits, furnished a large part of the invoice of the shelves; while black snake whips, tin cups, camp kettles, and frying-pans hung in profusion overhead. This room was well patronized, and in a half frozen state we rushed for its brilliant candlelight, waiting for further notice of our future disposition. Being introduced to room number two, we found passengers, stage drivers and the teamsters of a passing train, apparently surfeited with supplies drawn from room number one, and huddled about a table, where two big platters of bacon and cabbage, with tin cups smoking with coffee, were being disposed of as supper. The conversation of the party (for the wife of the host had been sent to the States) related mainly to a recent Indian depredation on the Little Blue, and what each one would have done if he had been there at the eventful crisis. The language had a medley of positive terms which in New England would be called profane; and the prospect ahead drove us to inquiries as to the shelter of room number three. But, finding that ourself and children and Mrs. Neill and daughter could not agreeably share its board floor with ten or twelve characters whose social habits seemed only adapted to room number one, we threw ourselves upon the courtesy of Adjutant Phisterer and Quartermaster Brown, who soon had the snow shoveled aside, our tents pitched, a piece of the corral carefully chopped for the camp stove, and all arrangements made for hot coffee, and a good wrapping up, either to sleep or freeze. We slept, and survived!

Another ranch was approached, when the storm compelled a full day's stop. The mules could not, or would not go on, and the drivers could neither see nor drive. The upsetting of our ambulance, and being borne by strong men a half mile through drifts is still painfully remembered, as well as the wonderful fact that while our head was nearly broken, our basket of eggs accomplished the upset without injury. Fortunately a ranch

with its usual palisade and stabling was near.
The kind lady proprietress gave us her own
family room; only reserving one-half for herself, her husband, and children, by the inter-
position of a small suspended comfort, while
ample ventilation was insured between the
unchinked logs, where no comfort was. To
our jests, and especially the whimsicalities of
Quartermaster Brown, an inveterate pun-
ster, always full of good cheer, who hazarded
the rather profane jest that, "in his opinion,
it would be hard work for the Angel Gabriel
to make his trumpet reach that country,"
the old lady replied: "Well, you are the jol-
liest set of folks I ever saw out here: don't
see how in mercy you can laugh, and go on
so!" When Mrs. Neill asked if there were
Indians about, another, with more heroism,
replied that "she had heard so much about
Indians, and been half scared out of her
senses so many times, that she had jest about
made up her mind that she wouldn't believe
nothing more, until she was skulped!" Mrs.
Neill, with quick discernment, took a lounge
near the fireplace, while the Colonel and
Lieutenants Phisterer and Brown took to a
shed near by: but during the night the California coach came down, and its half-frozen
passengers rushed for the fire. The lounge
was the first object of seizure; alas, for Mrs.
Neill, who was only relieved from her dis-

comfort, by loss of rest and the banishment of strangers, until she was able to escape, and share with us the family room, par excellence, of the house. Our bill was four dollars each!

A third ranch had its front store-room and its kitchen. Voices of men, who were ranged on the earth, like rows of pins, disturbed sleep, and the kitchen stove nearly burned our blankets, while its steaming incense no less shocked our senses; but we actually slept, everybody was good natured, and some fresh pork and new eggs for breakfast, with a cup of our own coffee, sent us on our way rejoicing.

Louis' ranch, near the present Sydney Station, is quite a fort, and the outhouses and stables are advanced like bastions, so that enfilading fire can be had in all directions.[17]

Such were some of the ranches of 1865.

[17] Sidney is the county seat of Cheyenne County, Nebraska. Sidney Station (Fort Sidney) was established near here, Dec. 13, 1867 as a substation of Fort Sedgwick. It became an independent post Nov. 28, 1870 and was abandoned June 1, 1874. Dennis Farrell, who opened a ranch twenty-two miles northwest of Julesburg about 1866 relates that about fifteen miles beyond his place was another ranch kept by Louis Rouillet and Jim Pringle, and that they subsequently removed to Sidney Station "a few miles up the valley." Evidently this was the Louis of Mrs. Carrington's narrative. See Nebraska State Hist. Society *Collections*, XVII, 226 and 247–58. Farrell's narrative provides an interesting description of his ranch and his ranching experiences.

Chapter 7

ON the sixth day of June we continued our march. The first day was a severe and trying one, and will always be disagreeable to emigrants with loaded trains until Yankee skill shall perfect what has already been begun in the search after water. The ridge or divide which is first crossed is fully twenty-eight miles to the first water or timber. On the summit there is evidence of Anglo Saxon pluck, which was evidently designed to be the accompaniment of a future central ranch. About midway between Lodge Pole Creek and Mud Springs a well had been begun, nearly twenty feet across and two hundred feet deep, without reaching water. The road across the divide is smooth and broad; but our first trip was in the hottest part of June, with the mercury at 101° above zero, and the infantry suffered intensely. Buffalo gnats flitted wickedly about, attacking neck and ears and every other accessible or exposed part of the body, and a sirocco-like wind drove the dust in our way as if determined either to petrify or melt us.

The command halted for ten minutes every hour, and officers and men alike put handkerchiefs on the head and neck to secure all the protection possible; yet there was no alternative but to undergo and go on. The ambulances soon filled with the lame and sunstruck, and every vacant space in the wagons was similarly occupied. No trees relieved the dismal monotony, and every halt brought into requisition the services of our patient surgeons. The tedious day at length spent itself, and we encamped at Mud Springs, just in time to receive the full benefit of a thunder-storm and small tornado, which grappled sternly with our canvas, and for a time threatened to unroof as well as drown us. At Mud Springs are both wood and water, but neither are abundant. In midsummer, the dry sandy bed of the stream shows only here and there a few small pools; but the shovel will soon start it, and any train will find a full supply by patient labor for an hour. It is always possible to procure buffalo chips enough to boil coffee and supply fuel for a camp oven, so that scarcity of timber in the immediate vicinity of water is not a serious embarrassment until snows cover the ground. Most trains wisely take some wood from camp to camp, and a little more permanency to this indispensable station on the route will insure supplies for sale to trains. A few log cabins that have been the quarters of a mail guard and relay of mules, with a sergeant's party in charge, duly represent the dignity of the United States; but no one will voluntarily remain longer than to secure rest from the fatigue of the long journey of the previous day.

The march of June 7th was only ten miles to Pumpkin Creek, which flows past Court House Rock.[18] This stream is ever flowing, and abundance of timber can be found in the cañon near by. The rock itself is mainly composed of sand, hard pan, and clay, so that it is easily chopped with the hatchet, and thus steps are made for those who have the nerve and patience to climb to its top,

[18] This formation is in Merrill County, Nebraska, some half dozen miles southwest of Bridgeport at the eastern terminus of the Wildcat Hills. Many early explorers and travelers on the Oregon Trail have, like Mrs. Carrington, left descriptions of it. Around it and around nearby Jail Rock numerous legends cling. Hundreds of Pioneers of Gold Rush and early Oregon days carved their names, along with other data, on the Rock, a practice which is still kept up by gasoline-age tourists, although the Nebraska State *Guide* affirms that the Rock weathers so easily that a single storm has been known to change its contour.

nearly six hundred feet above the water of the creek. A few of our party accomplished the feat, Adjutant Phisterer taking the lead. The ascent is quite easy, but peculiar. The notches receive the toes and about half the foot, and the hands grasp the gaps above to support the body and keep its gravity within the line of danger. The return trip is not so pleasant, as the heels take the place of the toes and the back rests upon the bluff itself, just as the body was inclined forward during the ascent. The view from the summit is very fine; and far off to the northwest loom up the equally singular proportions of Chimney Rock.[19] Centuries of exposure have evidently wrought their changes upon the great face of Court House Rock, and constant waste is now so rapidly changing its propor-

[19] Like Court House Rock, Chimney Rock, near the eastern border of Morrill County, attracted the attention and comments of all early-day travelers. The descriptions which have been left of it by different chroniclers vary greatly, whether owing to the changes produced by the processes of erosion or to some other reason. The Nebraska State *Guide* of 1939 gives the height of the shaft at the center of the rock as approximately 500 feet, and suggests that early-day observers (of whom Mrs. Carrington was one) may have been generous in their estimates. However, the illustration of the Rock which it supplies shows a markedly more needle-like formation than does Mrs. Carrington's illustration, published seventy years earlier.

tions that, even in 1867, it had lost some of that boldness of definition which in 1866, and for years before, had made it such a noted landmark to the traveler.

The old road and the telegraph route deflect to the right about six miles before reach-

COURT HOUSE ROCK—FROM THE EAST

ing the rock: but the present route saves nearly five miles of distance and is more readily made, although somewhat more rolling and sandy.

The above sketch of Court House Rock will preserve its outline and present character; but, like all other odd and wild things in that region, it will soon become the prey of innovation and the mastery of Time.

The mounted infantry pitched their tents in the basin of the cañon, a short distance from the beautiful grove of cottonwood that lies at the very base of the rock, and the novel

CHIMNEY ROCK—FROM THE EAST

scenery made an afternoon pass pleasantly.

Twelve miles farther on we find Brown's ranch on the North Platte, and five miles more brings the traveler to Chimney Rock. While substantially the same in material as Court House Rock, it derives its name from a singular shaft which springs from the apex

75

of a true cone, and is nearly three hundred and eighty feet high. It stands about five hundred feet from the bluff of which it was once a portion, and close to the level at which the cone leaves the general surface of the plain there is a stratum of true limestone, six feet in depth, interspersed with fossils indicating its origin, and closely resembling that of the quarries of central Ohio. Chimney Rock is fast gathering about it the debris of waste, and will soon lose the bold outline and marked symmetry of its present proportions. It is now much more beautiful than when Fremont visited it, and is worn to such a fine delineation that it seems that the first summer's storm or winter's blast must topple it from its base and destroy it utterly.

Fifteen miles farther on we passed Terry's ranch, opposite Fortification Rocks, and approached Scott's Bluffs.[20] These are also of mixed clay and sand, plentifully supplied

[20] Scott's Bluffs, rising 750 feet above the river plain was the first considerable height encountered by westward bound Oregon Trail emigrants. Mitchell Pass, followed by the Carrington party, which cuts midway through the Bluffs, was excavated for wagon use in the early fifties. Prior to this time emigrants used the pass alluded to by Mrs. Carrington several miles farther south which is known as Robidou Pass, named for Basil Robidou, who established a trading post at its western end about the year 1848.

with fossils, and throw a spur across the Platte Basin so as to compel the traveler to leave the river and make a long detour to the south, or to pass through the bluffs themselves. This passage is by a tortuous gorge where wagons can seldom pass each other; and at times the drifting snows or sands almost obscure the high walls and battlements that rise several hundred feet on either side. Cedar trees climb to their very summit and crop out in every cañon; and although these seem to the unpracticed eye like little shrubs clinging to the cliffs, the enterprising visitor who climbs to their nestling-place finds them to be full-grown trees of large diameter and proportionate height.

Scott's Bluffs is reputed to have been named for a traveler of this name who sometime during the early half of the nineteenth century became sick and in consequence was abandoned by his associates, who were descending the Platte on their return to civilization. The following year some members of the party, returning to the same area, came upon a skeleton which by certain clues they identified as the remains of Scott. The bones were found sixty miles east of the point where he had been deserted, and unable to walk, he had evidently crawled this entire distance before expiring. Tradition identifies the place where the skeleton was found with Hiram Scott Spring, at the point of the bluff on its eastern side. Relics still found about the spring indicate that it was formerly a stopping place for Gold Seekers and Oregon Trail travelers.

Fortification Rocks were so named in 1866; and at sunset the terraces and bastions, the pinnacles and turrets are quite a good embodiment of one's natural idea of old-time fortifications on a grand and comprehensive scale.

Almost immediately after leaving the Bluffs, and at the foot of the descent, after the gorge is passed, we find Fort Mitchell.[21] This is a sub-post of Laramie of peculiar style and compactness. The walls of the quarters are also the outlines of the fort itself, and the four sides of the rectangle are respectively the quarters of officers, soldiers, and horses, and the warehouse of supplies. Windows open into the little court or parade-ground; and bed-rooms, as well as all other apartments, are loop-holed for defense.

June 12th. We marched twenty-one miles to Cold Spring or Cold Creek, which is a

[21] Fort Mitchell was established as Camp Shuman in September, 1864. It was subsequently renamed Fort Mitchell in honor of General Robert B. Mitchell who in 1865 was charged with the defense of the Overland Trail from Omaha to South Pass against Indian attacks. The site was a few miles east of the Wyoming-Nebraska line, midway between present-day Gering and Haig. The latter town was named for a cattleman brother of British General Haig of World War I fame. An original drawing of Fort Mitchell is reproduced in Grace R. Hebard and E. A. Brininstool, *The Bozeman Trail*, I, 74. The fort was a telegraph station, and in 1866 was garrisoned by 60 soldiers.

beautiful stream, thirty feet wide, emptying into the south channel of the North Platte.

As the Ottawa and St. Lawrence, or the Missouri and Mississippi retain their distinctive characteristics for many miles after their nominal union, so when Cold Creek strikes the south arm of the North Platte, it does not mingle with its muddy current, but each occupies its own half of the swollen stream, and so runs on its race.

A novel incident, valuable to mention for the information of other travelers, occurred shortly before sunset, which resulted in a bountiful supply of fine fresh fish for all who desired them. Sergeant Barnes took up the idea that he would fish at the junction of the two streams, and actually hooked a fine mountain pike. The news soon spread, and the soldiers gathered from all directions. For want of proper tackle a seine was extemporized. Gunny sacks were sewn together, mule shoes were fastened to the bottom for dead weight, and quartermaster's hay forks were borrowed to guide the net. Then a strong party waded in neck deep, and with one end of this seine held firmly to shore, made a half circle with the remainder, bringing it all back to land. To the great amazement of spectators and actors, just where the eddies, at the meeting of the two rivers, struggled to keep by themselves, there was a fine school of pike. A few hauls soon landed over a hundred, varying in weight from one to four pounds. Their hard white meat was excellent, and made amends for the ridiculous stupidity of the fish and the simplicity of their method of capture. They evidently were unaccustomed to visits from the white man, or could not see his approach through the turbid waters of their neighbor Platte until too late for escape.

Up to this time we had invariably found sufficient grass for all stock, and the Platte was always at hand for water.

The next day the troops forded this beautiful creek about half a mile from its mouth, and after eighteen miles' march we encamped above Jules Coffee's ranch, four miles east of Laramie. Here two of our best sergeants were drowned, being carried away by the current while bathing.

Just about sunset, Standing Elk—a fine specimen of the Brulè Sioux, and who, in company with Spotted Tail, Two Strike, and Swift Bear, again visited us at McPherson in 1867—called to pay his respects, receive a present of tobacco, and have a talk. He asked us where we were going, and was very frankly told the destination of the command. He then told us that a treaty was being talked about at Laramie with a great many Indians, some of whom belonged in the country to which we were going; but that the fighting men of those bands had not come in, and would not; but that we would have to fight them, as they would not sell their hunting-grounds to the white men for a road. He exhibited all indications of sincere friendship, and said that he and Spotted Tail would sign the treaty and would always be friends. His pledge, thus given for both, and renewed at Fort McPherson in June, 1867, and often afterward, was fully redeemed, and our first interview with the Indians of the Northwest was both the assurance of the friendship of some, and the bitter animosity and opposition of many. It was proof that the careful marching, guarding of trains, and precautions against annoyance or intercourse with Indians had been judicious, and was equally suggestive of like prudence as the expedition advanced. Thus far, with the exception of Little Dog's rifle, which had been duly returned, not an Indian had suffered from injury at the hands of the command, and those who had visited the various camps had been kindly treated, and parted as friends.

Chapter 8

FORT Laramie was the center of important interests to the people of the West
in June, 1866, and subsequent events
show how important were the negotiations
then begun, and how disastrous and costly
have been the consequences of that false
security as to the animus and purposes of the
Indians of the Northwest which pervaded
the country until the beginning of the year
1867.

The Peace Commission was in session. It
was accredited from the highest sources and
had in charge great interests. The proposed
general peace with the Sioux, the Arapahoes,
and the Cheyennes, and their anticipated
surrender of the right of way to Virginia
City, by Powder River and along the Big Horn
Mountains—our very route—were matters
of personal interest, independent of the difficulties that would be in the way of successfully building new forts and fighting Indians
with a command that was barely sufficient

to do its expected work on the basis of a permanent and reliable peace.

General Cooke had closed a published circular with the emphatic and cheering assurance that "there must be peace," and from leaving Fort Kearney all pains had been taken to avoid collision with Indian hunting parties who were on their way to Laramie, or who were moving to and fro in anticipation of such a visit when the council was really ready.

Our trains were habitually formed in a hollow square or corral, upon reaching camping grounds, to insure the safety of stock at night, while pickets and mounted parties carefully guarded all animals on herd as soon as they were turned loose. The strictest discipline was enforced, and nothing was left undone that the energy and ambition of the officers could accomplish to instruct new recruits and prepare them for the labor and possible conflicts that the future might unfold.

No bartering with Indians was permitted under any circumstances; but all Indians who really wished an interview had the privilege of visiting headquarters, and there received kind attention and some little gifts, like tobacco or old garments, but never arms, powder, or whisky.

Our camp near Laramie was therefore located close enough for business, but far enough away to prevent the mingling of the troops and Indians for any purposes—thus avoiding the possibility of collisions growing out of trades in furs, beads, and other articles, in which the Indian is generally the unlucky one, and often exhibits his disappointment by becoming revengeful and wicked.

The next day, June 14th, wagons were sent to the fort for one hundred thousand rounds of rifle ammunition, and to perfect the arrangement for supplies for the upper posts to be built in the new district. Unfortunately there happened to be at the fort not a single thousand rounds for infantry arms such as are used in the army; so it was assumed that we should have a happy journey, a happy peace, and a happy future. Twenty-six wagons of additional provisions were ready, with the single drawback that drivers had to be furnished from the command; but this nice economy had the effect, practically, to put that number of soldiers *hors de combat*, in case of any trouble requiring soldiers, and thus disposed of some of the best of our men. Major Bridger told us that he had seen kegs of powder distributed to the Indians and carried away on their ponies; but this gave no concern, as there was none for us.

The next day came shopping, which busied our little coterie of ladies, and it certainly had claims to novelty in its associations and incidents.

The long counter of Messrs. Bullock and Ward was a scene of seeming confusion not surpassed in any popular, overcrowded store of Omaha itself. Indians, dressed and half dressed and undressed; squaws, dressed to the same degree of completeness as their noble lords; papooses, absolutely nude, slightly not nude, or wrapped in calico, buckskin, or furs, mingled with soldiers of the garrison, teamsters, emigrants, speculators, half-breeds, and interpreters. Here, cups of rice, sugar, coffee, or flour were being emptied into the looped-up skirts or blanket of a squaw; and there, some tall warrior was grimacing delightedly as he grasped and sucked his long sticks of peppermint candy. Bright shawls, red squaw cloth, brilliant calicoes, and flashing ribbons passed over the same counter with knives and tobacco, brass nails and glass beads, and that endless catalogue of articles which belong to the legitimate border traffic. The room was redolent of cheese and herring, and "heap of smoke"; while the debris of munched crackers lying loose under foot furnished both nutriment and employment for little bits of Indians too big to ride on mamma's back, and too little to reach the good things on counter or shelves.

The *Wash ta-la!* ("very good") mingled with *Wan-nee-chee!* a very significant "no good," whether predicated of person or thing; and the whole scene was a lively episode, illustrating the habits of the noble red man in the mart of trade. Of course, all these Indians were thinking sharply, and many gave words to thought, so that an unsophisticated stranger might well doubt whether Bedlam or Babel were the better prototype of the tongues in use. The Cheyenne supplemented his words with active and expressive gestures, while the Sioux amply used his tongue as well as arms and fingers.

To all, however, whether white man, half-breed, or Indian, Mr. Bullock, a Virginia gentleman of the old school, to whose hospitality and delicate courtesy we were even more indebted in 1867, gave kind and patient attention, and his clerks seemed equally ready and capable, talking Sioux, Cheyenne, or English just as each case came to hand.

Outside everything was characteristic of the existing state of affairs, not to say prophetic of the future; and literal truth, in all its details, would furnish unrivaled scenes for stereoscopic views of Indian character and characteristics.

The council chamber was, of course, the first object of interest to us ladies after the shopping had been completed; and while the gentlemen were busy at quartermaster and commissary details, the ladies visited it. Pine boards had been arranged as benches in front of one set of quarters, and over these boards were once fresh evergreens. There was a unique and perfect simplicity in the arrangement, and such considerate abandon of all state and ceremony that no Indian need feel that he was kept at an awful distance, or must approach the agents of the Great Father with solemn awe or grave obeisance.

Under the eaves of all buildings, by doorsteps and porches, and generally everywhere, were twos, threes, or larger groups of hungry, masticating Indians of all sizes, sexes and conditions, covered with every conceivable degree of superficial clothing or adornment, with the special element of cleanliness just as critically wanting as is usual among the Indians of the Northwest.

During a long journey we had anticipated with more or less pleasure an attendance upon some of the deliberations, and it was understood that the Colonel had, without success, requested authority to remain at Laramie during the treaty, in order to become acquainted with the Indians and learn both their disposition and decision as to the new route we were to travel and occupy. But he hurried everybody up, kept his men to the camp, and our stay was cut down to the actual necessities of a marching command. Besides this, it seemed that during the little time we did stop some Indians had been sent for other Indians, and the Indians who actually held possession of the route in dispute were not on hand when they were wanted.

The Man Afraid of his Horses and Red Cloud made no secret of their opposition, and the latter, with all his fighting men, withdrew from all association with the treaty-makers, and in a very few days quite decidedly developed his hate and his schemes of mischief.[22]

There being nothing to see therefore but loafing Indians, and great work to be done in

---

[22] Red Cloud, who has been called "the red Napoleon of the Plains", was the ablest, and for some years the most persistent, opponent of the white advance into and across the Sioux country. In particular he headed the opposition to the opening of the Bozeman Trail by the Government, and in 1865 captured the first detachment of troops sent out to begin its construction. He refused to treat with the Peace Commissioners sent out that year, and he again defied the succeeding Peace Commissioners at Fort Laramie in 1866. Pointing a finger at Colonel Carrington he shouted: "You are the white eagle who has come to steal the road. The Great Father sends us presents and wants us to sell him the road, but the white chief comes with soldiers to steal it, before the Indian says yes or no. I will talk with you no more. I and my people will go now, and we will fight

preparation for winter and securing defensive positions before the rising war-cloud should break, we were all as eager to move on as the Colonel was persistent in hurrying us forward. Some of the chiefs, however, were seen by the officers, and when they knew that the command was going to the Powder River country in advance of any treaty agreement, they gave unequivocal demonstrations of their dislike. One pleasant intimation was given that in two moons the command would not have a hoof left. Another with great impressiveness thus explained his crude ideas: "Great Father sends us presents and wants new road, but white chief goes with soldiers

you. As long as I live I will fight for the last hunting grounds of my people." Saying which, he strode from the council with the threat to kill every white man who should venture to cross Crazy Woman's Fork of Powder River. See Hebard and Brininstool, *The Bozeman Trail*, II, 178. The warfare which followed, related in part by Mrs. Carrington, is still commonly known as "Red Cloud's War." For perhaps the only time in the long history of U.S.-Indian warfare, the Government was compelled to cry uncle and to yield abjectly to Red Cloud's demands for the withdrawal of the garrisons and the destruction of Forts Reno, Philip Kearney and C. F. Smith. His victory won, Red Cloud finally signed the Fort Laramie Treaty on November 6, 1868. Thereafter he remained at peace with the whites, taking no part in the warfare of 1870–1890. He died at Pine Ridge, South Dakota, December 10, 1909.

to steal road before Indian say yes or no!" Some of us called this good logic.

Just as the troops left, one of the commissioners came to our ambulance and advised that very little dependence should be placed upon the result of the deliberations so far as the new road was concerned, for a messenger sent out to the Indians had been whipped and sent back with contempt. This was the conviction of all of us; still the ladies kept up good heart, and as they could not well go back, concluded to go on, but agreed to limit their riding on horseback to the vicinity of the train.

On the 17th of June, though it was the Sabbath, we passed Laramie, and camped at the Nine Mile ranch, on the Platte. We bade farewell to Laramie with great composure and no regrets. Its North Platte and Laramie Rivers, its Laramie Peak, nearly sixty miles distant, and its adventitious charms as the locality of the Laramie Treaty sum up all its attractions. As at elegantly built Leavenworth, so at Laramie, water is hauled from the rivers, and a respectable fire would be ignorant of water in about a minute after it began.

This post was neglected, as were all frontier stations, during the war; being occupied by changing garrisons, whose jack-knives and bayonets, so useful in their proper sphere, had pretty much used up the pine and plaster wherever those appendages were ornamental or useful; while the parade ground was as barren and ignorant of sod as the great highway to Salt Lake City itself. General Dandy, the post quartermaster, with his good taste and skill, had, in 1866, originated a perfect plan to secure an exhaustless supply of water at reasonable cost, and should his successor carry his plans into effect much can be done to redeem the forlornness of the station.

Laramie has been a profitable place for traders, and not a few ranchmen and citizens have squaw wives, and a large Indian traffic; but with some exceptions, it was to us the most inhospitable and barren post on our trip. It was then a four-company post, but was reinforced during the autumn, thus giving rise to the report of General Sanborn, special Indian Commissioner, afterward published, that, "in 1866, at Fort Laramie, where all was peace, there were twelve companies of regular troops; while at Fort Philip Kearney, where all was war, only four companies were allowed."

Fortunately, this garrison proved ample for the defense of Fort Laramie, and the post was still safe on our return in 1867.

Chapter 9

LARAMIE TO RENO—CAMP PHISTERER CANON
—LARAMIE PEAK—WILD FLORA—PUMPKIN
BUTTES.

ON the 18th of June, at three o'clock
A.M., the bugle call started us from
Nine Mile ranch, and we were at last
directly en route for our new home, passing
the Dry Branch of Warm Spring, Bitter Cottonwood Creek, and, after a march of sixteen
miles, camped on Little Bitter Cottonwood,
where there was an ample supply of timber,
water, and grass.

June 19th. After eighteen miles of advance we came to the most remarkable defile
through which the Platte urges its way in its
passage from the Rocky Mountains. The
river, which along the line of the march from
Laramie had coursed through a prairie-like
bottom, here suddenly makes a short curve
of half a circle to the right, then, after passing for a few hundred feet between precipi-
tous cliffs, suddenly turns to the left by another short curve, nearly resuming the direction of its original northwestern course, and
again running through the prairie as before
it sought its peculiar hiding-place.

The eastern face of this gorge is perpendicular, and nearly four hundred feet in height. On either side of the entrance are conical summits, of even greater elevation, which stand like sturdy sentinels, but having many natural terraces, on which are placed long lines of cedars as true and uniform in method as if the subject of systematic arrangement. The one on the right is basaltic, and as truly significant of its volcanic origin as are the Palisades of the Hudson, or East and West Rocks near New Haven, Connecticut; and no part of the great wall which hems in the Niagara River, below the falls, has more stern and prison-like proportions. One or two of the ladies, with Adjutant Phisterer and Dr. Horton,[23] went around the first curve, quite within the gorge, to hunt for agates and try the effect of pistol shots, the echoes of which were startling and many times repeated. The deep, dark waters are closely pent in and shaded by these confines, so as

[23] Dr. Samuel M. Horton and his wife were members of the Fort Philip Kearney garrison, remaining there after the departure of the Carringtons in January, 1867, following the Fetterman Massacre. Sergeant Samuel S. Gibson, a survivor of the famous "Wagon Box" fight of August 2, 1867, supplies an attractive characterization of Dr. Horton, dwelling upon his kindness and consideration for "every man, woman, and child at the post." Hebard and Brininstool, *The Bozeman Trail*, II, 69.

never to enjoy the sunlight; but all of us enjoyed the sublimity and grandeur of this wonderful natural curiosity. Old Major Bridger, in his peculiarly quaint and sensible way, dropped the sentiment: "Better not go fur. There is Injuns enough lying under wolf

CAMP PHISTERER CANON,
North Platte River, D. T.

skins, or skulking on them cliffs, I warrant! They follow ye always. They've seen ye, every day, and when ye don't see any of 'em about, is just the time to look out for their devilment." The experience of the next morning confirmed his suspicions.

As this was the last camp before the final crossing of the Platte and entrance upon the territory of the Mountain District, it was named Camp Phisterer, in honor of Adjutant Phisterer, who selected the site, and was most conspicuous in all that contributed to the pleasure or progress of the march.

June 20th. Nine miles of travel brought us to Bridger's Ferry. Here we learned that Indians had, on the previous morning, made a descent upon the stock of Mr. Mills, the proprietor of the Ferry ranch, although his wife was a Sioux, and, besides his half-breed children, an Indian lived with him in his employ. This Indian had promptly pursued and recovered part of the stock, which they undoubtedly supposed belonged to emigrants. This Indian said that the marauders were "Bad Faces," of Red Cloud's band, and that we would certainly have trouble if men or animals were permitted to stray from the command. Major Bridger and Mr. Brannan were of the same opinion; and both claimed, as they had at Laramie, that we were advancing directly in the face of hostilities; and Major Bridger went so far as to affirm that the presents which were made to Indians at Laramie were given to positive enemies, or to those who had no influence at all over the warlike bands of the Big Horn and Powder River country.

Our next movement was to cross the North Platte. The beef herd was forced into the deep, swift current, and compelled to swim,

EAST VIEW OF NORTH PLATTE, 4 MILES EAST OF MOUTH OF SAGE CREEK

The road has crossed the ridge of sand hills, reaching point nearly opposite Fort Fetterman

and as a hundred men on the south bank kept them from returning, all were safely drifted across. The train and command crossed in the ferryboat, which ingeniously works its own way to and fro by such adjustment of cables and pulleys, and such adaptations to the current, that the round trip was made in about eleven minutes.

The march of June 22d was sixteen miles, finding wood, water, and grass in abundance.

The march of the 23d was fifteen miles, with ample supplies of all kinds at our camp on the North Platte, near the mouth of Sage Creek. In the morning we turned northward from the Platte, passing over the red buttes and lofty sand hills and rocky ridges which rise at least five hundred feet above the valley, and these proved in a few places to be very difficult for the more heavily loaded wagons. Occasionally the windings of the river are seen far beneath, and when the road has completed its circuit, and returning descends to the river, the panorama is exceedingly beautiful.

The river can be traced backward for miles in all its course, bordered on the north by the bluffs just crossed, and on the south by the nearly level plains, which, with slight modification, extend as far west as Platte Bridge, at Fort Caspar.[24] Near this point a new fort

[24] Near present-day Casper, Wyoming, Louis Ganard, a French-Canadian squaw-man, constructed a substantial bridge across the North Platte and charged toll to travelers on the Oregon Trail for the privilege of using it. The place was known as Platte Bridge, and

is being erected, with the certainty that Fort
Caspar will soon be abandoned or treated as
an immaterial position on the route.

Just before reaching the basin, where the
Fort Reno road turns northward, following
Sage Creek, and the northern Mormon road
passes westward toward Salt Lake City, we
found an extemporized shed of boards, where
Louis Gazzons (French Pete), with his Sioux

close by it a detachment of soldiers sent from Kansas
established Camp Dodge in the spring of 1865. Frequently taunted and bedeviled by the Sioux, who
swarmed around in vastly superior numbers, the garrison succeeded in escaping serious disaster until July 26,
1865 when a detachment led by Lieutenant Caspar
Collins, seeking to effect a junction with a small force
coming from Sweetwater Station, was wiped out, together with most of the approaching party of soldiers.
Lieutenant Collins was not yet twenty-one and his
boyish appearance had led to taunts that he was afraid
to fight Indians. The circumstances of his death led to
making him a popular hero. On November 21, 1865
General Pope issued an order renaming the post at
Platte Bridge for Caspar, "Who lost his life while
gallantly attacking a superior force of Indians at this
place." In 1905 a prize was offered for the best poem
about Collins who "rode to death nor cared to know
The fearful numbers of his foe, How great the odds,
how sure his fate; He rode to lead and not to wait."
The winning poem, from which these lines are quoted,
is printed in I. S. Barlett, *History of Wyoming* (Chicago,
1918), I, 151–53. For ample data concerning the history
and naming of Fort Caspar see Hebard and Brininstool,
The Bozeman Trail.

wife and half-breed children, were opening
their merchandise to catch travel over the
new route. Here the inevitable display of
canned fruits, liquors, tobacco, beads, cut-
lery, crackers, and cheese were modestly conspicuous, and the good-hearted trader decidedly congratulated himself that he had the
first stock of goods on the route to the land
of game and gold. Little did he anticipate
the doom that awaited him. Mrs. Dr. Horton was the recipient of a young antelope
from Louis, and for months after we were
well settled at Phil Kearney, this antelope, a
spotted fawn, and two colts of Captain Ten
Eyck, had each evening a spirited scamper
on the parade ground, until Indians stole the
ponies and the antelope poisoned himself by
the substitution of fresh paint for his usual
treat of sweet milk.

French Pete will be remembered as the first
citizen killed during that campaign, and especially as his long course of trade and intimacy
with the Indians seemed to promise, at least
for himself and family, some considerable
favor if not entire immunity at their hands.

June 24th. Marched fourteen miles;
camped at the head of Sage Creek; found
water, but used sage brush and buffalo chips
for fuel. Tufts of buffalo grass were scattered
between the sage brush and cactus, so that

the herds found forage without any considerable departure from the camp.

June 25th. Marched fifteen miles, and camped on the South Fork of the Cheyenne, where there is plenty of grass and timber; but the great body of the water, in extremely

LARAMIE PEAK—FROM THE NORTH,
5900 feet above sea level.

dry weather, passes under the sand and needs slight digging to start it to the surface and secure an abundant supply. At the middle of this day's march, just at the summit of the divide, there is the best view of Laramie Peak, showing its peculiar formation, where cone after cone rises gradually until a central shoot overtops them all.

June 26th. Was enlivened by a successful attempt to open a shorter route to Wind River, avoiding Humphrey's old camp; and after a march of twenty miles we found wood, grass, and water, besides realizing a gain of over five miles in the general line of travel.

June 27th. Marched twenty-one miles, to the Dry Branch of Powder River, finding wood, grass, and water, though the grass was largely intermingled with the inevitable sage brush and cactus. Early in the morning we obtained our first view of the Big Horn Mountains, at a distance of eighty miles, and it was indeed magnificent. The sun so shone as to fall with full blaze upon the southern and southeastern sides as they rose toward Cloud Peak, which is nine thousand feet above the level of the sea,[25] and the whole range so closely blended with the sky as to leave it in doubt whether all was not a mass of bright cloud; while many, even with the aid of a glass, insisted that they were immense gleaming sand hills, with no snow at all. In half an hour the air itself was invigorated by the currents from the snow banks; and even at that distance shawls became necessary, the ambulance side curtains were closed, and it seemed

[25] Over 13,000 feet. See *ante*, note 4.

as if a November day was to succeed the summer's morning. In front, and a little to the northeast, could be seen the four columns of Pumpkin Buttes, nearly twenty-three miles east of Fort Reno. These buttes are landmarks for the traveler from all directions, and nearly seven hundred feet high. East of them lie the Black Hills of Dakota, and the once talked of direct route from Sioux City to Reno and Virginia City, which has been referred to in connection with the pamphlet of Colonel Sawyer published by the government.

July 28th. Passed Buffalo Springs, and down the Dry Fork of Powder River, sixteen miles, and over one divide, to Fort Reno.

The road, from early morning, was in the very bed of the stream, which, but a few inches deep, was constantly crossed by the train, and being bordered by abrupt ledges of lignite, clay, and sand, is surely indicative of an abundance, if not a surfeit, of water during the thaws of spring; while, for nearly twelve miles, the traveler is hemmed in and confined to this narrow basin, subject to constant exposure and annoyance from Indian attacks. The grass is poor, but wood and water are abundant. Many cottonwood trees have been felled by travelers and Indians for the bark with which to feed both mules and horses; but this leaves a supply of dry wood equal to the increasing demand.

Our first view of Fort Reno was most unprepossessing; but, expecting it to be abandoned, its ugliness and barrenness did not so decidedly shock the sensibilities as if it had been gazed upon as a permanent home, or even a transient dwelling-place. We passed through more than a mile of river bottom, densely studded with large cottonwood trees, and after fording Powder River, encamped just south of the fort, glad to have accomplished more than five hundred miles of our journey with such substantial success.

Before long, some enterprising post commander will recommend the final demolition of the fort, or shrewd emigrants will avoid it, by carrying out the feasible project for a short cut-off under the Big Horn Mountains, which was partially inaugurated in 1866, and which affords abundant supplies of grass, as well as an equal amount of timber with the present location.

So we were finally at Powder River. We had known some such hot days as are never found in the Eastern or Middle States; had drunk water that had small virtue beyond its name and moisture; had used sage brush and buffalo chips for variety of fuel; but, so far, were all right and even fast seeing the country. The cactus, which annoys a horse as much as it does the pedestrian, had partly compensated for its thongs and sting by the beauty of its blossoms; and the prolific sage brush had imparted odor as well as fuel, and thus regaled the sense while it heated our coffee.

The wild tulip, larkspur, sweet pea, convolvulus, and a vine, closely resembling the Mexican plant, were among the flora that were abundant, and these, with others, were duly pressed for future care and admiration. The Indian potato and wild onion were gathered constantly by the men, and both are valuable when antiscorbutics are scarce and salt pork most abundant.

The march which brought us to Reno closed up all possibility of meeting any resident traders; and indeed, with the exception of the fort itself, there was then not a resident white man between Bridger's Ferry and Bozeman City, Montana. We were about to pass the last log cabin, and realize practically the experience of pioneers and test our own capacity for building, keeping house, and living in the land of Absaraka! Single trains of emigrants had passed through the country. Bozeman had made one trip and had succeeded admirably in the selection of his route, and our sterling friend Bridger had a head full of maps and trails and ideas, all of the utmost value to the objects of the expedition.[26] So we stopped at Reno, to prepare for the next, and final advance!

[26] John M. Bozeman was a native of Georgia who in 1861 left his wife and two small children to embark upon a gold-mining career in the Cripple Creek, Colorado area. The following spring he joined in the rush to the Montana mines, arriving at Virginia City in June, 1862. The Mullan Road from Walla Walla eastward to Fort Benton at the head of navigation on the upper Missouri afforded fortune seekers access to the Montana mines from the West. Those from the East, however, could find no direct route to them. Some went by boat up the Missouri to Fort Benton, whence they made their way overland as best they could. Others followed a round-about route by way of the Oregon Trail to Fort Hall, near present-day Pocatello, and thence northward to Virginia City. Bozeman, whose undoubted enterprise was matched by a corresponding lack of judgment, with one companion undertook in the winter of 1862–63 to open a more direct eastward route through the Indian country. Although attacked and plundered by the Indians he made repeated successive efforts to open a road through the Indian country until he was finally slain at the crossing of the Yellowstone, April 20, 1867. His pioneer efforts to open the Bozeman Road constitute his chief claim to fame. For a more adequate account of his career see Hebard and Brininstool, *The Bozeman Trail.*

Chapter 10

FORT Reno was first located in 1865, under the name of Fort Connor.

Absolute sterility excludes all elements of vegetable beauty or production. The single redeeming feature is the fact that the river bottom for miles in either direction is abundantly supplied with timber, so that emigrants will always find the material for fuel or building; but the same old sage brush and cactus persistently monopolize the soil for miles, and Powder River itself, flowing from the south side of the Big Horn Mountains, is muddy and so strongly alkaline as to be prejudicial to both man and beast.

In June, 1866, Fort Reno was an open post, except that the warehouses and stables had a rough stockade. Officers' and men's quarters, guard-house and magazine, were on the open plain. Being nearly one hundred and forty feet above the river, the water was brought up in wagons, and no effective effort had been made to seek for better water than that of the river, although after our second day in camp a spring of clear water was discovered, by the enterprise of the mounted command, immediately under the bluff. Subsequently it was decided to retain the post as part of the district command. New buildings were erected, the parade was inclosed, suitable bastions and block houses were built, and a substantial stone magazine was completed under the immediate direction of Captain Proctor.

At the date of our arrival the garrison consisted of two companies of the 5th United States Volunteers, who were simply waiting to be relieved before proceeding eastward to be mustered out of service. A company of Winnebago Indians had been at the fort, and we passed them near Laramie on the 17th of June. Many of them wished to go back with us, but there was no existing authority to employ them, and it was generally understood and distinctly affirmed by Major Bridger that some of the Sioux at Laramie expressly demanded, as a condition of their own consent to peace, that these Indians should leave the country. If this be true, it was sharp in the Sioux, for the service lost its best scouts, and no depredations had taken place about Reno while it was known that they were there. Upon the first alarm these Winnebagoes would spring to their ponies, with rifle and lariat, regardless of rations or clothing, and, with one good whoop, disappear in pursuit. Being deadly enemies of the Sioux, it is not to be wondered that the latter should wish them out of the country; but until peace could be absolutely realized, it would have been no prejudice to that line of operations, as events transpired, to have had a few soldiers who knew the Indian styles of warfare, and were up to their tricks.[27]

Nevertheless, the Winnebagoes departed, and their substitutes were not provided. So,

[27] The Winnebago are themselves a branch of the Siouan family although their separation from the remainder of the tribe antedates recorded white history. When the French penetrated the interior of the continent they found the Winnebago living in the vicinity of Green Bay, Wisconsin. They gradually spread southward until they occupied the Rock River Valley almost to its mouth, and all the country of Illinois and southern Wisconsin lying between the Rock River and the Mississippi. Pressed westward by the whites in successive removals, following the Sioux outbreak of 1862 they found an unwilling refuge on the Missouri River in South Dakota. About half the tribe has since found a seemingly permanent home in northeastern Nebraska. The remainder, nostalgically yearning for their ancient homeland, trekked back as individuals to Wisconsin,

as we began to live in Absaraka, we began to learn contemporaneous history.

Our camp at Fort Reno was adapted to the location. The mounted infantry were at the base of the hill, for ready access to water. Brevet Major Haymond's command was on the river's bank above, just over a slight rise, but out of sight from the fort. Headquarters tents were near the flag-staff, which had been located with a view to some future expansion of the post for the accommodation of twelve companies. After a night's rest, everybody seemed busy. Three emigrant trains were in the river bottom waiting for the Colonel's instructions as to their advance westward; and we were quite surprised to find that the lady travelers with those trains had no fear of Indians, and did not believe there were any bad Indians on the route. One train captain told us ladies we never would see an Indian unless he came to beg for sugar, flour, or tobacco. This was all very gratifying, as this captain had been many years on the Plains, and said

where the Government, as a matter of practical necessity, has allowed them to remain as permanent residents. Mrs. Juliette Kinzie's *Wau Bun*, the Lakeside Classics volume for 1932, affords much interesting information about Winnebago ways and personages, since the book is chiefly a narrative of the author's residence at Fort Winnebago (at present-day Portage, Wisconsin) from 1830 to 1833.

"he couldn't be scared worth a continental."[28]

About ten o'clock the ladies went to the sutler's store of Messrs. Smith and Leighton to do some shopping. Suddenly a breathless messenger rushed in with the cry of "Indians," and said, as intelligibly as he could, that the sutlers' horses and mules were all gone. Sure enough, upon going to the door, the horses and mules were galloping up the hills across the river, while a party of Indians were following, throwing out flankers to keep the stock in the desired direction, and evidently bending their course toward the Pumpkin Buttes. No doubt they had been eager observers of our progress, just as Major Bridger said, and no less watched the emigrants. Probably they supposed the small headquarters camp, with its large corral of wagons, was that of emigrants. At all events, they crossed the river through the timber, taking advantage of a deep ravine, and struck the herd suddenly without loss to themselves, yet passing two or three of our herds, which

[28] The expression "not worth a continental," denoting the utmost extreme of uselessness, derived from the valueless character of the paper currency issued by the Continental Congress during the American Revolution. It remained in common use at least in certain portions of the Middle West, until within the present Editor's memory.

were under guard, without venturing an attack.

At this unexpected message all became activity. The Colonel was entering the door as the messenger gave the alarm. The bugle brought the mounted men to the saddle and Brevet Major Haymond and Lieutenant Adair led eighty men in pursuit. It was excessively provoking to see the coolness of those Indians as they favored their ponies in bad places and seemed to calculate exactly how long they could take things easy and when they must hurry; but they had not long to tarry, and soon were pressing their plunder at the top of their speed.

Before the return of the party the next day, they had ridden nearly seventy miles, passing along the Pumpkin Buttes, but failed to recapture any of the stolen stock. But they brought in an Indian pony which the Indians abandoned when closely pressed; and this same pony was loaded with favors recently procured at Laramie. Among the variety were navy tobacco, brown sugar, a cavalry stable frock, calico dress-patterns, and other articles, which from their style and condition showed that they had not long since been taken from shelves or packages.

Indeed, the opinion expressed by everybody was afterward confirmed from Laramie, and it was thus early understood that the Indians who received presents at that post had immediately violated their obligations and commenced a new career of robbery and war.

Ten days were spent at Reno in arrangements to distribute the battalion, in reloading wagons, and relieving the companies of the 5th U. S. Volunteers. The mercury rose to 113° in the shade; wagon tires began to break or fall off, and there was no charcoal (so Mr. Brown said) for welding and putting them in order. The warehouse was full of old supplies, and these had to be invoiced and distributed, while the quantity was twice or three times a complement for all the wagons of the command.

Business was hurried, and it was decided to leave Captain Proctor and Lieutenant Kirtland with one company to guard the stores in depot until trains could be sent back for them and the fort could be dismantled.

Meanwhile the Fourth of July came in its proper annual course, and the usual salute was fired, under the charge of Major Henry Almstedt, paymaster, an old artillery officer, and a welcome visitor at all times, especially just then, when a few things more were to be bought before launching out in that wilderness, where, except from Messrs. Beal and

Hughes, our sutlers, there was nothing of civilization to be had.

At length, on the morning of July 9th, at 4 o'clock, the command started. Its organization was a matter of interest to us ladies, as there were but three wives of officers left after the parting at Lodge Pole Creek, and new partings were to be anticipated, to complete the constant series which began at Fort Sedgwick.

Brevet Major Haymond, with two companies, had been assigned to the post on the Upper Yellowstone; Brevet Lieutenant-Colonel Kinney, with two companies, had been assigned to the post on the Big Horn River; and Captain Ten Eyck had been given command of the post at district headquarters, new Fort Reno, to which the change of post was to be made. By a mail received before starting, we learned from the officers that the order for a battalion of the 13th U. S. Infantry, to operate from Fort Reno eastward, had been countermanded, and thus we had no rivals to compete for the honors of opening, protecting, and defending the new route and territory of Absaraka. The news gave us women a little scare, which the officers did not condescend to notice; but they, no doubt, were all laboring under the infatuation that the second battalion, with its fresh recruits, could do perfectly what under ordinary circumstances would have required two or three regiments to accomplish.

An order was posted at the sutler's store, telling emigrants how to corral their trains, how to deal with or not deal with Indians, and how to procure authority for proceeding beyond the post; and it is a singular fact that every reported disaster to emigrant or other train during 1866 would have been avoided, had the terms of that order been reasonably complied with.

We started westward July 9th, 1866.

The twenty-six miles to Crazy Woman's Fork, in the blazing sun, was a severe trial. It was fully night before camp was well established, and the next morning revealed the fact that half of our transportation was disabled, although inspected daily and repaired according to all the means at hand.

Crazy Woman's Fork has been described in general terms. The stream, just at the crossing, makes a sharp turn, giving two separate fords, but having quite a steep ledge or bank on the east side as the traveler enters its basin, but on the west gradually rising to the summit of the divide between its waters and those of Clear Creek.

Inspection was made, timber was cut, a charcoal pit was fashioned and fired, and every available blacksmith was put at work.

One means of repair was resorted to which was supposed to be as novel as it was effective. Gunny sacks were cut in strips and thoroughly soaked in water. These strips were tacked on so nicely that when secured with the heated tires they not only withstood the summer's use, but even in the winter of 1867 some of those wagons were doing excellent service without additional repair. Of course this would only answer where tires were unbroken; neither could it be afforded that all the corn should be emptied, except as the expenditure of the journey should permit, and thus allow an accumulation of those empty.

On the morning of the 12th, the companies that were to build New Fort Reno marched with headquarters to select and occupy its site. The four companies destined for the more distant posts were left to perfect repairs and follow as soon as possible. Our first camp was at Clear Fork, just at noon, and its perfect beauty and completeness of natural supplies have been anticipated in the general description of this portion of Absaraka. Little episodes, of course, occurred here, as they did elsewhere. With Mrs. Horton and Mrs. Bisbee the splendid sunset was watched with real pleasure. Our camp chairs were near the tents on the banks of the creek. A chance interruption of our meditations led to the agreeable information that we were sitting just over three voluble rattlesnakes, which an orderly was kind enough to find and mangle to death. We sat no more by the brink of Clear Fork, but dreamed of rattlesnakes until the bugle sounded the reveille the next day.

On Friday the 13th we had our next indication of Indians. A few were seen upon a high hill to the left; and after passing Rock Creek, close under a commanding ridge, our attention was called to two small pieces of cracker-box planted by the roadside, on which were notes in pencil, stating that two trains had been attacked on the previous Tuesday and Friday, and that some of the stock of each had been driven off.

These were trains that were in advance of our expected arrival, but gained greater distance than they expected, through our detention at Crazy Woman's Fork.

At 11 o'clock A.M., July 13th, we had passed Lake De Smet and were in camp on Big Piney Fork, just east of the crossing of the Virginia City road, and about four miles from the Big Horn Mountains. At last, we had the prospect of finding a home, and Cloud Peak seemed to look down upon us with a cheerful face as the sunlight made his features glow and glisten.

Chapter 11

RECONNAISSANCES — INDIAN MESSENGERS — WARNINGS — LOCATION OF FORT PHILIP KEARNEY—CONDUCT OF THE TROOPS, AND ITS CAUSE.

THE headquarters camp of the expedition of 1866 was organized on the 13th of July of that year with special care, and greatly to the annoyance of teamsters, as the Colonel had the corral formed three times until it was sufficiently compact and trim to suit him.

At 1 o'clock he was off with a small party to visit the surroundings as far back as the mountains, and seven miles westward, to determine the most eligible site for the post. A beautiful plateau had been passed just before the command halted, which seemed particularly inviting; but as Major Bridger and Mr. Brannan had both urged that the valleys of Goose Creek and Tongue River should be first visited, no decision was announced.

On the morning of July 14th, at 5 o'clock, Colonel Carrington, Adjutant Phisterer, Quartermaster Brown, Captain Ten Eyck, Guide Brannan, and Jack Stead, interpreter, with a mounted escort, left for a reconnaissance of the region of country which had such an exalted and widespread reputation as being the richest, loveliest, and grandest of all the lands of Absaraka, viz., Tongue River Valley.

Brevet Captain Adair was officer of the day, and all was unusually quiet in camp until nearly 9 o'clock, when it was found that some men had deserted to seek the gold mines of Montana. A detail started in pursuit. They returned before noon with the tidings that they had been stopped by a band of Indians, were refused permission to go on, and were instructed to return at once with a message to the white chief, that he must take his soldiers out of the country.

This party had met that same traveling ranch of Louis Gazzons about seven miles out, and a young man in his employ as teamster, who had been discharged by Lieutenant Brown at Fort Reno, had been impressed by the Indians to see that their message was correctly delivered and an answer returned.

This lad brought peremptory orders for the white men to decide for peace or war, and if they wanted peace, to return at once to Powder River. They promised not to trouble the old post, but declared that they would not let soldiers go over the road which had never been given to the whites, neither would they let them stay and build forts. These Indians were reported to be Oglala Sioux, under Red Cloud as their principal leader, and they had been negotiating for several days with certain bands of Cheyennes, with whom Louis Gazzons was trading, to induce them to join on the war-path and obstruct the road and all travel upon it. French Pete had already traded for a great many skins, and was preparing to visit the camp to sell as many as he could to the officers and men of the command.

The absence of the Colonel induced Mr. Adair to detain the messenger in the guard tent, and shortly after an Indian messenger approached, but quickly retreated when he found that he was not promptly joined by the white man sent in advance. A demand had also been made that the white chief, in company with Jack Stead, whom they knew at Laramie, and whose wife was a Cheyenne squaw, should go and visit their village and settle the question of peace or war.

Shortly after 6 o'clock in the afternoon, and after an absence of thirteen hours, the Colonel's party came in, having found two brush tepees, where there were signs of recent occupation by Indians; but as the detachment had crossed buttes and ridges nearer the mountains for the purpose of

119

testing Major Bridger's recommendation
that a new and shorter road should be opened to Tongue River Valley, they met neither
Cheyenne nor Sioux.

After due examination, the prisoner was
sent back, in company with Jack, to invite
the principal chief and some of his braves to
come into camp, when the sun was overhead,
after two sleeps (at noon of Monday the
17th), and promising that they should be
kindly entertained and allowed to depart in
safety.

Jack returned the following night and reported that the Indians, having been alarm-
ed by the protracted absence of their messenger, had moved off to Tongue River,
nearly thirty miles, under apprehensions of
an attack, but he followed their trail, delivered his message, and secured their pledge
to make the proposed visit.

The reconnaissance of the day had settled
the location of the fort, as Tongue River
Valley was not only more remote from pine
timber, too far from Powder River, and less
advantageous as a position, but its selection
would have left to the Indians the control of
the trails about Pineys and Peno, and thus
given them the very gate to Tongue River
Valley itself; while the abundance of grass,
pure water, choice timber, and wild grain in

the immediate vicinity of the site selected, left no necessity for those elements to be sought elsewhere.

Accordingly, early next morning, July 15th, although Sunday, the camp, which had been temporarily on the low ground where the underbrush of the creek and dense cottonwood might afford shelter to an enemy, was abandoned, and the plateau before referred to was occupied.

Very early in the morning, the Colonel and Captain Ten Eyck, with the pioneer party, had staked out the dimensions of the future post, according to plans and drawings matured at old Fort Kearney in the spring; while, to secure at the very outset a handsome and permanent parade-ground, the long train of wagons was repeatedly driven about the designated rectangle, four hundred feet square, and officers, teamsters, and soldiers, alike were forbidden to cross, except by designated avenues, while a mowing machine soon cut the grass and gave the start to the present beautiful lawn of the Fort Philip Kearney Plaza.

The tents were pitched along the streets appropriate to the respective building sites of officers' and soldiers' quarters, warehouses, sutler's store, band quarters, and guard-house; while the established general and picket guards, with the artillery parked on the parade, soon imparted form, comeliness, and system to the whole.

By 12 o'clock a stranger might have supposed the camp to have been a fixture for weeks.

We had one episode while moving: Black George ran in, in great haste, to tell missis that it was snowing, sure; while other reports were, that the grass of Peno Valley had been fired by the Indians, and the smoke was already sweeping down upon us. All proved to be a complimentary visit from grasshoppers as large as locusts, and for a time it seemed as if wagon-covers and tents were all to be eaten up in just about five minutes. In vain were turkeys and chickens let loose against the destroyers: the whole camp hummed with the rustle of their wings as they filed themselves on the blades of grass and became familiar generally. A kind wind from the mountains came along in the afternoon, and they left as suddenly as they had arrived.

The scout of Friday afternoon had determined available points for ready acquisition of building timber, and, while Engineer J. B. Gregory was soon at work trying to put in shape and operation a horse-power saw-mill until the steam mills should arrive, the whole garrison was broken into details for ditching, chopping, hauling, hewing, and such other varied duties as loomed up like a vast burden, to be overcome before winter should overtake us.

Neither was the undertaking a light one, as the district headquarters would at once become a partial depot, and supplies for a whole year had been estimated for, before the command left old Kearney.

Subsequent events confirmed the wisdom of this immediate and incessant labor; for when cold weather actually developed its power there were no surplus quarters, and the eventual, constant hostilities no less demonstrated the value of the defense and the whole arrangement of the post.

Thus, Monday morning was as busy in progress as Sunday had been necessarily occupied in location and occupation of the site.

It was deemed wise also to secure something like shape and a tenable position before the expected interview with the Indians, so as to give our visitors as good an impression as possible of our purposes and determination to remain.

As the diagram and map furnished illustrate the plan and surroundings of Fort Philip Kearney so far as completed on the 1st of January, 1867, no further comment need be made than to say that, with all the prophecies and liabilities that the soldiers would desert for gold leads or diggings, it was found that their almost universal impulse was cheerfully to take hold of every duty and put the work through.

The fact that gold color had been found in the creek the very first day, perhaps combined with doubt as to the safety of deserting only to run the gauntlet of hostile tribes, may have stimulated labor; but never did a command apply themselves more diligently to real hard work and exacting guard duty, nor did men ever exhibit more ready obedience and willing self-sacrifice, in order to carry out the plans requiring their co-operation in execution.

To be sure, there was little kicking and cuffing and cursing administered, after the theory of some, that this is the acme of all discipline, and that soldiers are like cattle, to be worked by the whip and the yell; and instances of such discipline were publicly reprimanded and corrected, but no work, however tedious, no exposure, however protracted, no order, however sudden or urgent, failed to find willing and spirited response. Obedience was unquestioning and immediate; justice was equal and certain, and it was well understood that the Colonel hated the popular theory of oaths and blows, while none the less positive in the enforcement of law. Fort Philip Kearney will be a monument of the spirit and skill of companies A, C, H, and E, 2d Battalion, 18th U. S. Infantry, now the 27th Regiment; and its own soldiers need not fear that any rivals will do more or better work, or do it under more adverse circumstances than was their mission in the summer and fall of the year of grace 1866.

Chapter 12

ARRIVAL OF INDIANS—THE CHEYENNES IN
COUNCIL—BLACK HORSE, THE RABBIT THAT
JUMPS, RED SLEEVE, DULL KNIFE, AND
OTHERS HAVE MUCH TALK AND "HEAP OF
SMOKE."

AT twelve o'clock, July 16th, a few
Indians appeared on the hills, and
after showing a white flag and receiving assurance of welcome, about forty,
including the squaws of chiefs and warriors,
approached the camp and bivouacked on
the level ground in front. Meanwhile, hospital tents had been arranged for this first
interview with the inhabitants of Absaraka.

A table covered with the national flag was
placed across one tent, chairs were placed behind and at the ends for officers of the garrison, while other seats were placed in front for
visitors.

Trunks were opened, epaulettes and dress
hats were overhauled, so that whatever a
full dress and a little ceremony could do by
way of reaching the peculiar taste of the
Indian for dignity and finery, was done. The
band of the 18th played without, as the
principal chiefs were brought across the

parade-ground to the tents and introduced to their seats by Mr. Adair. The Cheyennes came in full state, with their best varieties of costume, ornament, and arms; though there was occasionally a departure from even the Indian originality in apparel. One very tall warrior, with richly wrought moccasins and a fancy breech-cloth, had no other covering for his person than a large gay umbrella, which, as his pony galloped briskly up, had far more of the grotesque and ludicrous in its associations than it had of the warlike and fearful.

Some were bare to the waist, others had only the limbs bare. Some wore elaborate necklaces of grizzly bears' claws, shells, and continuous rings, bead-adorned moccasins, leggings, tobacco pouches, medicine bags, and knife scabbards, as well as armlets, ear-rings, and medals.

The larger silver medals included, one each, of the administrations and bore the medallion heads and names of Jefferson, Madison, and Jackson. These medals had evidently belonged to their fathers who had visited Washington, or had been the trophies of the field or trade.

Those who claimed pre-eminence among the band were Black Horse, Red Arm, Little Moon, Pretty Bear, The Rabbit that Jumps,

The Wolf that Lies Down, The Man that
Stands Alone on the Ground, and Dull Knife.

As these were the Indians who had sent
the message of the 14th, or were in their
company, the question of their inclination
and temper was one of no little interest to
all.

The formal assurance of the Laramie
Peace Commission before its adjournment,
that satisfactory peace had been made with
the Oglala and Brulè Sioux, and that the
Arapahoes and Cheyennes had only to come
in for their presents, inspired some hope that
possibly the reception this first band encountered, might result in substantial advantage
beyond the mere range of the band itself.

As the front of the canvas was open, the
ladies gathered in the headquarters tent
close by, parted its folds and enjoyed a dress-
circle view of the whole performance. As
pipes passed and the inevitable "how," the
rising up, and the shaking of hands were
interludes between all solemn declarations,
as well as the prelude to a new speech, or
the approval of something good that had
been said, the scene seemed just about as
intelligible as a rapidly-acted pantomime
would be to a perfect stranger to the stage.

The red-sandstone pipe had its frequent
replenishing before a single "how" indicated

that either visitor wished to make himself heard. The scene was peculiar.

In front of them all, and to the left of the table, sitting on a low seat, with elbows on his knees and chin buried in his hands, sat the noted James Bridger,[29] whose forty-four years upon the frontier had made him as keen and suspicious of Indians as any Indian himself could be of another. The old man, already somewhat bowed by age, after long residence among the Crows as a friend and favorite chief, and having incurred the bitter hatred of the Cheyennes and Sioux alike, knew full well that his scalp (Big Throat's)

---

[29] James Bridger shares honors with Kit Carson as a scout and "mountain man." He was born at Richmond, Virginia, in 1804 and died at his home near Kansas City in 1881. At the time of the Carrington expedition he was past sixty years of age and he retired from scouting and trapping activities a couple of years later. He had first gone to the mountains as a member of the William H. Ashley expedition of 1823, when he was a youth of nineteen. In 1843 he established Fort Bridger on the Oregon Trail in southwestern Wyoming. Driven from his station by the Mormons in 1853, he repaid the account by guiding General Johnston's army on its invasion of Utah in 1857–58. Many of the notable narratives of western travel in the period of his activity speak in highest terms of Bridger's character and ability. Almost the last of these testimonials is Mrs. Carrington's warmly appreciative comment. For a longer sketch see Hebard and Brininstool, *The Bozeman Trail*, II, 205–52.

would be the proudest trophy they could bear to their solemn feasts; and there he sat, or crouched, as watchful as though old times had come again, and he was once more to mingle in the fight, or renew the ordeal of his many hair-breadth escapes and spirited adventures. Many stories are told of his past history, and he is charged with many of his own manufacture. He is said to have seen a diamond in the Rocky Mountains, by the light of which he traveled thirty miles one stormy night, and to have informed some inquisitive travelers that Scott's Bluffs, nearly four hundred feet high, now stand where there was a deep valley when he first visited that country. When inquired of as to these statements, he quietly intimated that there was no harm in fooling people who pumped him for information and would not even say "thank ye." Once he was wealthy, and his silver operations in Colorado might have been very lucrative; but he was the victim of misplaced confidence, and was always restless when not on the Plains. To us, he was invariably straightforward, truthful, and reliable. His sagacity, knowledge of woodcraft, and knowledge of the Indian was wonderful, and his heart was warm and his feelings tender wherever he confided or made a friend. An instance of this will close the sketch of one who will soon pass away, the last of the first pioneers of the Rocky Mountains.

He cannot read, but enjoys reading. He was charmed by Shakspeare; but doubted the Bible story of Samson's tying foxes by the tails, and with firebrands burning the wheat of the Philistines. At last he sent for a good copy of Shakspeare's plays, and would hear them read until midnight with unfeigned pleasure. The murder of the two princes in the Tower startled him to indignation. He desired it to be read a second and a third time. Upon positive conviction that the text was properly read to him, he burned the whole set, convinced that "Shakspeare must have had a bad heart and been as devilish mean as a Sioux, to have written such scoundrelism as that." But to return to the council.

Near Major Bridger stood Jack Stead, the interpreter. Born in England, early a runaway sailor boy, afterward a seaman upon the *Peacock* when it was wrecked near the mouth of Columbia River;[30] then traversing

[30] The *Peacock* was one of the ships of Captain Charles Wilkes' notable exploring expedition of 1838–42. It was wrecked on the Columbia bar in July, 1841. Peacock Spit, near Cape Disappointment, preserves the memory of the vessel's fate.

the Rocky Mountains as one of the first
messengers to report the Mormon preparations to resist the United States, and the
renewal of Indian hostilities, the same year;
with hair and eyes black as an Indian's, and
a face nearly as tawny from hardship and
exposure; a good shot, and skilled in woodcraft; with a Cheyenne wife; fond of big
stories and much whisky; but a fair interpreter when mastered and held to duty; and
watchful as Bridger himself to take care of
his scalp, Jack Stead was the first to break
the silence and announce that Black Horse
wanted to talk.

Adjutant Phisterer, called by the Indians
Roman, or Crooked Nose, acted as recorder
of the council, keeping full notes of the conference; and few were the diaries or letters
home that did not embody the history of
our first visit from Indians, and repeat some
of their expressions of purpose or desire.

Neither did the Indian advocate appear to
disadvantage, as the exponent of his rights

Before joining the Carrington expedition Stead had
lived among the Pawnee of Nebraska for several years.
They were inveterate foes of the Sioux, for whom, accordingly, Stead was an object of hatred. One chronicler, who was a member of the Fort Philip Kearney
garrison, relates that Stead, on his part, entertained an
aggravated fear of the Sioux. See Hebard and Brininstool, *The Bozeman Trail*, II, 95–96.

and wants. Erect and earnest, he cast off the buffalo robe that had been gathered about his shoulders and in his folded arms, and while it now hung loosely from his girdle, stepped halfway toward the table and began.

With fire in his eye, and such spirit in his gesture as if he were striking a blow for his life or the life of his nation; with cadence changeful, now rising in tone, so as to sound far and wide over the garrison, and again sinking so as to seem as if he were communing with his own spirit rather than feeling for a response from the mind of another, the Cheyenne chief stood there to represent his people, to question the plans of the white chief, and solemnly advise him of the issue that was forced upon the red man. It was an occasion when all idea of the red man as the mere wild beast to be slaughtered, quickly vanished in a prompt sympathy with his condition, and no less inspired an earnest purpose, so far as possible, to harmonize the intrusion upon his grand hunting domain with his best possible well-being in the future.

Other chiefs followed Black Horse, in harangues of varied length and vigor; and all agreed that they preferred to accept protection and become the friends of the whites. They came to represent one hundred and seventy-six lodges, and had been hunting on Goose Creek and Tongue River, when they met Red Cloud; but said that one hundred and twenty-five of their young men were absent with Bob Tail, having gone to the Arkansas on the war-path and hunt. They had quarreled with another band of Cheyennes, who lived near the Black Hills east of Powder River; and said there was a third band south of the Republican hostile to the whites. Two of the chiefs had with them Comanche wives whom they had married in excursions to the south.

They gave the history of a portion of our march, and stated correctly, what Red Cloud had assured them, that half of the white soldiers were left back at Crazy Woman's Fork. They said that Red Cloud told them, the morning before the messenger was sent to the camp, that white soldiers from Laramie would be at Piney Fork before the sun was overhead in the heavens; that the white chief sent soldiers from Reno after Indians who stole horses and mules; but the white soldiers did not get them back.

They also stated that the Sioux were having a sun-dance, insisting that the Cheyennes must make common cause with them and drive the white man back to Powder River; that some of Red Cloud's men had already gone back to interrupt travel on the road; that they had left their squaws in the village with thirty of their old men, and were afraid the Sioux would rob them in their absence if they should stay too long in the white man's camp; but that if they could have provisions, they would make a strong peace, and let a hundred of their young men, whose return would be in two days, go with the white soldiers against the Sioux.

Before the council broke up, Brevet Major Haymond arrived with his four companies and went into camp northwest of the fort near the river crossing.

The Indians became very restless as the afternoon progressed, and at last bade good by; receiving papers indicative of their good behavior, and entering into an agreement to leave the line of road and go upon or south of the upper plateau of the Big Horn Mountains. They afterward visited Fort Caspar, behaving well, and no doubt observed their obligations as best they could.

The presents given consisted of some secondhand clothing of the officers, twenty pounds of tobacco, a dinner of army rations, and enough flour, bacon, sugar and coffee to give them a meal in their village and convince the absent of their kind treatment. They left with apparently cordial good feeling, and the understanding that they were not to approach emigrant trains even to beg; but might go to Laramie, or other military posts when hungry, as long as they remained the friends of the whites.

There is no evidence that any of these chiefs have violated their pledges.

Chapter 13

MASSACRE OF LOUIS GAZZONS' PARTY—IN-
DIAN RAID AND GREAT LOSS OF MULES—
THE CHEYENNES AGAIN—FORTY HOSTILE
DEMONSTRATIONS OF THE "PEACEABLE
TRIBES"—THE LARAMIE TREATY INCIDEN-
TALLY TESTED—MASSACRE OF LIEUTENANT
DANIELS—A FIGHTING PARSON.

AT five o'clock A.M., July 17th, the
herds of Brevet Major Haymond were
surprised, the Indians crawling within the picket, and with great sagacity starting Wagonmaster Hill's bell mare first, so as
to secure all in company. Major Haymond,
with one orderly, started in pursuit, as we
afterward learned, although no information
was given at the post until two hours after.
He left orders, we heard, for the mounted
men to saddle and follow. The party thus
pursuing in haste was ultimately surrounded
by several hundred Indians, and when a
messenger was sent in with report of the
condition of affairs, two companies of infantry and fifty mounted men, with ammunition, rations, wagons, and ambulances,
were at once started to the relief.

But very soon sad reports came from Peno valley, only a few miles over Lodge Trail Ridge. The casualties of the command had been two men killed and three wounded; and, more painful than all, was the report of the massacre on the road of Louis Gazzons and most of his party.

Brevet Major Haymond, finding the Indians so numerous and the ground impracticable for the use of his men, while the Indians were not only perfectly at home, but specially watchful of stragglers and fully versed in that style of warfare, fell back toward the post. On the retreat he came up with the wagons of French Pete, which had already started for camp. About the plundered wagons lay the mutilated remains of his party, with the exception that his wife, a Sioux woman, with her five children, had been able to hide in the brush until the arrival of the troops furnished an escort to headquarters.

Six men lay dead and mutilated upon the road. Such was the first lesson to the expedition of the kind of peace to be expected for the future. Henry Arrison, of St. Louis, partner of Gazzons, was among the number. The cattle, wagons, and goods that the Indians had not broken open, for want of time, were brought to the post and taken

charge of by Mr. John W. Hugus, adminis-
trator, on behalf of the widow, creditors,
and friends of the deceased.

The Sioux wife of Gazzons said that the
Cheyennes had traded largely and pleasantly with Pete, and that the chiefs who had
visited the post on the 16th were with them
until midnight, smoking and trading; that
during the evening some of the Sioux chiefs
came up from Tongue River Valley and
asked Black Horse what the white man said
to them, and whether the white chief was
going back to Powder River. To this Black
Horse answered that the white chief would
not go back, but his soldiers would go on.
They then asked what presents were given.
Black Horse told them that they had all they
wanted to eat, and the white chief wished
all the Arapahoes and Sioux, and all other
Indians of that country, to go to Laramie
and sign the treaty and get their presents.
At this the Sioux unstrung their bows, and
whipped Black Horse and the other Cheyennes over the back and face, crying *Coo!*
which by the Indians is deemed a matter of
prowess and a feat which secures them credit,
as they count their *Coos* in a fight almost
as proudly as they do the scalps of enemies.[31]

[31] "Coo," or Coup (meaning blow, or stroke) was the
French-Canadian term in use among the Plains tribes to

After the Sioux left, Black Horse told French Pete that he must go to his village and from there to the mountains, for the Sioux meant war, but advised him to send a messenger to the white chief quick, or the Sioux would kill him. French Pete neglected the advice; but was on his return in the morning, when the Sioux, who had stolen Major Haymond's mules, and had come in contact with his men, came across the train and destroyed all the men who were with it.

On the same day Major Haymond's four companies were ordered to change their position and encamp just below the fort.

On the 19th a train with military escort, under Captain Burrowes, was sent back to Fort Reno for provisions. The young men of the Cheyennes also returned from the Arkansas, and Bob Tail had an interview with the Colonel, leaving his own robe as a pledge of his friendship.

designate the formal signal of victory in battle. The practice of counting coups was considerably complex. Ordinarily a coup was attained by killing an enemy, taking his scalp, or being the first to strike or touch him, whether alive or dead. Coups might be counted also for being the first to strike a tepee in an attack upon a hostile camp. Red Cloud in 1891 claimed to have counted 80 coups. See Hodge, *Handbook of American Indians*; Ware, *The Indian War of 1864*, 568–70.

About one o'clock A.M., July 24th, a courier from Clear Fork brought a dispatch from Captain Burrowes that the Sioux were very numerous, and additional force was needed at once. Mr. Thomas Dillon also wrote that Mr. Kirkendall's train had been engaged all the afternoon, and he could not move without troops. A company of infantry, with a mountain howitzer, was soon started, and upon their approach in the morning, the Indians, numbering several hundred, fled. Torrence Callery, of Company G, had been killed; and one of the trains relieved, which had been taken back to Fort Reno temporarily, contained five officers of the regiment, with servants, baggage, Mrs. Lieutenant Wands and child, all of whom had been forwarded from Fort Laramie, under the prestige of the Laramie Treaty, with only ten men as escort to headquarters. When this train had reached Crazy Woman's Fork it was attacked by fifty Indians, and Lieutenant Daniels, of Indiana, who was a little in advance selecting camping ground, was killed, scalped, and mutilated, while one of the Indians put on his clothes and danced within view of the party.

Chaplain David White, Lieutenants Templeton, Bradley, and Wands, with Mrs. Wands and child, survived, and the Henry rifle of Mr. Wands was specially efficacious in warding off and punishing the assailants.

Chaplain White, like the preachers of Cromwell, only prayed internally, while putting his time physically into the best exercise of self-defense. He thinks he did his duty; and the officers say that he thought it was just about the right thing to kill as many of the varmints as possible.

Lieutenant Kirtland's rescuing party from Reno was also very prompt, and Lieutenant Daniels' remains were escorted to that post and suitably buried.

The Cheyennes of Black Horse met Kirkendall's train and gave warning of the approach of the Sioux, just as they had at the council given indications of this same movement. The warning was disregarded, but the Sioux did come.

Thus commenced our first two weeks in our new home. A few more incidents will illustrate the experience that followed.

July 22d. At Buffalo Springs, on the Dry Fork of Powder River, a citizen train was attacked, having one man killed and another wounded.

July 22d. Indians appeared at Fort Reno, driving off one public mule.

July 22d. Mr. Nye lost four animals near Fort Philip Kearney, and Mr. Axe and

Mr. Dixon each had two mules stolen by Indians.

July 23d. A citizen train was attacked at the Dry Fork of the Cheyenne, and two men were killed.

July 23d. Louis Cheney's train was attacked; one man was killed, and horses, cattle, and private property were sacrificed.

July 28th. Indians attempted to drive off the public stock at Fort Reno, and failed; but took the cattle of citizen John B. Sloss. Pursuit; recovered them.

July 29th. A citizen train was attacked at Brown Springs, four miles east of the East Fork of the Cheyenne, and eight men were killed, two were wounded, and one of these died of his wounds. Their grave is still memorial of the confidence with which they left Laramie, assured that all was peace. These men, though too few in numbers, were well armed, but were deceived by a show of friendship; and one Indian shot a white man in the back just after shaking hands and receiving a present.

Meanwhile, the necessity of maintaining Fort Reno as an intermediate post on the route had been established. Another company was sent to reinforce its garrison. The Upper Yellowstone post was abandoned for want of troops, and early in August, Brevet

Lieutenant-Colonel N. C. Kinney, with Captain Burrowes and their two companies, were sent to the Big Horn River, distant ninety-one miles, to establish that post, subsequently known as Fort C. F. Smith.

The narrative of all hostile demonstrations need not be traced. Enough will be given to correct false ideas as to the feelings and operations of Indians during the year; and the reader will not be astonished that ladies, as well as gentlemen, perused the President's message of December 8th, 1866, which congratulated the country that the Indians were at peace, with something like inquisitiveness as to whether the Colonel had reported the true condition to department headquarters, and whether department headquarters had read his report.

But to proceed. Glover, the artist, correspondent of *Frank Leslie*, was scalped one Sunday morning, while only a few minutes' walk from the post.[32]

[32] *Frank Leslie's Illustrated Newspaper* was America's most enterprising illustrated periodical in the Civil War period and for some years thereafter. The artist here noted, Ridgeway Glover was killed on or about September 15, 1866. Sergeant B. M. Fessenden, one of the finders of the slain artist, relates that despite warnings he was in the habit of taking long walks alone. Several arrows were in his body, and his long yellow hair had been removed in the process of scalping him. See He-

August 9th. In one of the frequent attacks upon the timber train, four mules were taken after the driver had cut them loose; but a party from the fort under Corporal Phillip recaptured the mules, killing one Indian and wounding a second.

August 12th. Indians drove off horses and cattle belonging to citizens encamped on the river bank near Reno. The cattle were recaptured.

August 14th. Joseph Postlewaite and Stockley Williams were killed within four miles of Fort Reno.

August 17th. Indians appeared in force near the same post, and drove off seven public horses and seventeen mules. Other similar depredations occurred in August.

September 8th, at 6 o'clock A.M. Twenty mules were driven from a citizen herd, during a severe storm, within a mile of Fort Philip Kearney; and two other demonstrations were made the same day. The Colonel

bard and Brininstool, *The Bozeman Trail*, II, 96–97. Colonel Carrington reported on September 17: "This morning Mr. Ridgeway Glover, citizen artist, who went out on a geological tour Saturday (Sept. 15) was found two miles from the fort naked, scalped, and his back cleft with a tomahawk." Glover was a Philadelphian and an artist of much contemporary note. In 1865 he had followed the route of the Lincoln funeral train, making numerous pictures of that historic tour.

with one party, and Lieutenant Adair with another, were out until after 9 o'clock at night in pursuit.

September 10th. Ten herders were attacked a mile south of the fort, losing thirty-three horses and seventy-eight mules. Pursuit was vigorous, but unsuccessful.

September 13th. At midnight a summons came from the hay contractors, Messrs. Crary and Carter, at Goose Creek, for help, as one man had been killed, hay had been heaped upon five mowing-machines and set on fire, and two hundred and nine cattle had been stolen by the Indians, who had driven a herd of buffalo into the valley, and thus taken buffalo and cattle together out of reach.

Lieutenant Adair went at once with reinforcements, but found the Indians in too large force for continuance of the work.

The same day at 9 o'clock, Indians stampeded a public herd, wounding two of the herders. Captain Ten Eyck and Lieutenant Wands pursued until late at night. Private Donovan came in also with an arrow in his hip; but, just as he was always in an Indian fight, brave as a lion, started out again as soon as it was withdrawn.

September 14th. Private Gilchrist was killed.

September 16th. Peter Johnson, riding a few rods in advance of his party, which was returning from a hay field near Lake De Smet, was suddenly cut off by Indians. Search was made that night by a party under Quartermaster Brown, but his remains were not recovered.

September 17th. A large force demonstrated from the east, and took forty-eight head of cattle; but all were recaptured on pursuit.

September 20th. Indians attacked a citizen outfit lying in the angle of the two Pineys; but were repulsed by aid from the fort, losing one red man killed and another wounded.

September 23d. Indians attacked and drove off twenty-four head of cattle. They were pursued by Quartermaster Brown, in company with twenty-three soldiers and citizens, and after a sharp fight at close quarters, the cattle were recaptured, and a loss was inflicted upon the Indians of thirteen killed and many wounded.

September 23d. Lieutenant Matson, with an escort, bringing wagons from the hay field, was surrounded and corraled for some time by a superior force. He found upon the road the body of Contractor Grull, who had been to Fort C. F. Smith with public stores, and was killed on his return with two of his drivers.

On the 17th, 21st, and 23d Indians had also been active near Fort Reno, driving off horses and cattle. Casper H. Walsh was killed; and at the Dry Fork of the Cheyenne, citizens W. R. Pettis and A. G. Overholt were wounded.

September 27th. Private Patrick Smith was scalped at the Pinery, but crawled a half mile to the block-house, and survived twenty-four hours.

Two of the working party in the woods were also cut off from their comrades by nearly one hundred Indians, and were scalped before their eyes. A party of fifteen dashed at the nearest picket but did no harm.

Captain Bailey's mining party lost two of their best men.

On one occasion a messenger came in hot haste from the Pinery, reporting that they were besieged; that the Indians had fired through the loop-holes of the block-house; that the men were constantly under arms, unwilling as well as unable to work, and asking for a force to clear the Indians out of the bottom lands underneath, where the woods were very dense. The Colonel went out with a small party and howitzer, shelled the woods, restored confidence, and the men resumed work. A person ignorant of the effect of a case shot, which scatters its eighty iron bullets quite dangerously, might think it very foolish to explode one where no enemy was in sight: but we saw those experiments repeated, where otherwise quite a skirmishing party would have been required, and as the Indians invariably ran away, and sometimes got hurt, the little howitzers were soon favorites and no objects of ridicule or contempt.

The foregoing are instances out of many Indian visits, but do not give all, even of the first two months of our residence in that country. Alarms were constant; attacks upon the trains were frequent, and this kind of visitation continued during the whole season. The ladies all came to the conclusion, no less than the officers affirmed it, that the Laramie treaty was *Wau-nee-chee*, NO GOOD!

Chapter 14

IT was quite early after the establishment of Fort Philip Kearney that measures were taken to hold communication with the Crow Indians, to consult with the authorities of Montana, and determine the condition of the entire route to Virginia City. Major Bridger was selected for the mission, accompanied by Henry Williams, assistant guide, who proved himself valuable in almost every work he undertook. They made the through trip with comparative expedition, made complete notes of the journey, and besides their official reports, were very courteous in contributing their information to those who were desirous to keep a full record of all that transpired during our sojourn on the frontier.

They had first an interview with nearly six hundred warriors, not far from Clark's Fork. On that occasion White Mouth, Black Foot, and Rotten Tail declared their uniform and unanimous voice for peace; but said that in some instances the young men desired to join the Sioux, and thus come to some accommodation as to their title to the lands of which they had been robbed by both Sioux and Cheyennes.

Red Cloud had made them a visit and they had returned the visit, but would not join him against the whites. The Man Afraid of his Horses told them that his young men were going on the war-path, and that the Sissetons, Bad Faces, Oglalas from the Missouri, the Mineconjous from the Black Hills, the Unkpapas, some Cheyennes and Arapahoes, as well as the Gros Ventres of the Prairie, were united to drive away the whites, and would have big fights at the two new forts in the fall.

They also represented that Iron Shell, with some of the young men of the Mineconjous and Brulès, would go with Red Cloud, notwithstanding the Laramie Treaty; that the Nez Percés and Flatheads were friendly, but the Piegans and Bloods were hostile, while the Blackfeet, Assiniboines, and Crees were friendly with both parties and would join no league against the whites.

Besides the visits of Bridger to other bands of Crows along the route from Big Horn to the Upper Yellowstone, James Beckwourth, the famous mulatto of the plains, who had also lived among the Crows as an adopted chief, and had several Crow wives, was em-

ployed as an assistant guide, and was sent
to their villages, where he subsequently sick-
ened and died.[33]

From these sources it was learned that in
the fight of September 23d the Sioux lost
thirteen killed and had a great many
wounded.

Other parties of Crows came to Fort C. F.
Smith to hunt and trade in that vicinity,
and not only showed uniform friendliness
toward the whites and the new road, but
offered two hundred and fifty young warriors to engage in operations against the
Sioux. Major Bridger had great confidence
in this proposition; but the officers had, it
would seem, no authority to employ so
many, as well as no means of arming and
equipping them when employed.

All the statements of the Crows were substantially confirmed by Cheyennes at a subsequent visit. They represented Red Cloud
and The Man Afraid of his Horses to be in
Tongue River Valley, and Buffalo Tongue,
to be on Powder River; that the Big Bellies,

[33] Like Bridger, James P. Beckwourth joined the William H. Ashley expedition from St. Louis to the Rocky
Mountains in 1823. Almost all of the succeeding four
decades were spent as a trapper and squaw man, and
the details of his activities are necessarily considerably
obscure. He married a succession of Indian wives and
for several years lived with the Crow tribe. His post-

the Bad Arrows, Those that Wear a Bone in the Nose, and Those that Put Meat in the Pot were near the Big Horn River, and though friendly to the Crows were opposed to the road; that Bob North, a white man with but one thumb, with twenty-five lodges and the Big Medicine Man of the Arapahoes, had also joined the aggressive party.

Still later in the season there was renewed and cumulative evidence that the Crows were truly friendly, but were unwilling to venture very far eastward for any purpose until the Sioux were out of the way or the white soldiers were sufficiently numerous to guarantee their safety without sacrifice of life or property.

White Mouth and Rotten Tail told Mr. Bridger that they were half a day in riding through the hostile villages in Tongue River Valley, and that fifteen hundred lodges of war parties were preparing to attack the white man at Fort Philip Kearney and Fort C. F. Smith.

humous fame is largely due to his chance encounter in 1856 with T. D. Bonner, a writer, who recognized Beckwourth as the source of a good story. The resultant book has given Beckwourth a reputation for imaginative artistry in narrating his life story. Yet such authorities as William E. Connelley, veteran secretary of the Kansas State Historical Society, and others have been disposed to credit much of it.

All these statements were believed, and it is known that they had important influence in that vigorous prosecution of necessary work which followed, and rendered impossible any system of aggressive war on the part of the troops of the garrison.

Chapter 15

THE last days of August brought Brevet Brigadier-General Hazen on a tour of inspection, and his visit was greatly enjoyed by us all. He also brought the welcome news that two companies of regular cavalry had been ordered up immediately from Laramie, and that although he had waited a week for them at Fort Reno, they would certainly be but a few days behind him. The next day it was understood that official orders had been received to the same effect—that one regiment of infantry had left St. Louis by way of reinforcements westward, and that General Cooke had acquired the other two battalions of the 18th, with control of all operations on the Platte. This inspired everybody with good cheer, and the time was eagerly anticipated, by ladies no less than gentlemen, when adequate means would allow some opportunity to punish Indians more thoroughly and thus insure the integrity and security of the route.

On the last day of August General Hazen, accompanied by Lieutenant Bradley and twenty-six picked men of the mounted infantry, with Mr. Brannan as guide, started overland for Fort Benton and other posts on the Upper Missouri. The loss of one-third of the mounted force seemed less annoying, as the two companies of cavalry were supposed to be not far behind, and yet, in fact, they did not come that fall. Half armed portions of one company straggled along in November, having old Enfield rifles or old-fashioned carbines, and the first installment of this company was but sixteen strong, under a sergeant, with orders to escort a train to Fort C. F. Smith. All this no one could know in advance; and the constant looking for somebody to help watch, work, and fight was kept up until, as in respect of almost everything else relating to the post which was of importance to be known to the people at large, or at least the authorities at the head of affairs, it was left for the massacre of December 21st to arouse the impression that there were really some untamed red men roaming loose on the plains.

The mounted infantry were the sole dependence for carrying the mails, as these had been ordered to be carried weekly, at the rate of at least fifty miles per day; and the horses, which by the 10th of October had been reduced to less than forty, were poorly adapted for a swift express of over two hundred and thirty-five miles without a relay, and especially when they were almost daily required for active picket and outpost duty at the fort.

This mail was our sole reliance, as it made the trip both ways, and no cavalry or other mail parties came from Laramie to exchange with it, and so divide the labor between the two posts until subsequently, when mails were left at the ferry. Fort Philip Kearney, therefore, did not receive its mails from the east, but sent east when it wanted some news, and thus occupied a very prominent and independent position in Absaraka and the region adjacent thereto. Sometimes these trips were as long as three weeks, because night travel had to be relied upon through a portion of the route, and neither wagon-teams nor pack mules maintained their ambition as to speed and exactness, when they found that their natural inability to perform the feat was not regarded as excuse for failure.

The Indian habit of calling as early as daylight for loose stock required also that

the horses, when in garrison, should be early
saddled, so that, at any moment, the girths
could be tightened, the bridles be bitted,
and a dash be made after such persistent
trespassers. It was a source of congratulation, alike to men and to horses, that this
habit never cost the garrison a life or a
horse, while in many cases it defeated the
plans of the Indians and secured the recapture of stolen stock. Mounted infantry,
however, are a peculiar institution in that
country. The long rifle, however well cared
for, is forever in the way, and the soldier is
spoiled for a footman and is almost useless
in the saddle. It became a settled opinion,
which the ladies shared with others, that
the Sioux and Cheyenne light cavalry were
much better adapted to the hills and valleys, the gorges and mountain passes, especially in a long race, or steeple-chase, than
even the mounted men of the 18th. Of
course, it was difficult for men, unused to
horseback-riding, to take to it kindly, at
first; and the manual of arms was less convenient when yelping Indians were shaking
buffalo robes and speeding the flight of arrows and bullets. We had, of course, to keep
a mounted picket and prompt communication with working parties; and there was
also some responsibility for helping Fort

C. F. Smith to some communication with the outer world.

Such men as Brannan, with his daring, who was scalped through his imprudence on his return from the trip with General Hazen; as Van Valzpah, with his experience and quiet coolness, who, after a life in Oregon and Washington Territories, and many successful trips to Laramie, was butchered at last, with his whole party;[34] as miner Phillips, with his sound sense and solid honesty, who carried dispatches on the night of December 21st; and Captain Bailey, of the miners, who, after seventeen years in frontier explorations, retained the manners and habits of a pleasant gentleman, full of intrinsic worth and steady courage, could do anything with Indians or horses on a mail trip, that anybody could do; but in that bracing climate horses would need their forage when trips were frequent, and even the men were found to be limited to something like the ordinary finite range of physical ability and

[34] Van Valzpah was the mail carrier between Fort Laramie and Fort Philip Kearney. A member of the garrison relates that Van Valzpah's companions were carrying two pack loads of onions to Fort Philip Kearney to relieve the sufferers from scurvy at that post. The same authority places the date of the killing in the spring of 1868. See Hebard and Brininstool, *The Bozeman Trail*, II, 108.

endurance. And yet, nearly every ten days, and sometimes each week, brought us a mail, omitting such newspapers as were borrowed somewhere east, or were diverted to Salt Lake City, where there were more readers, as well as the leisure of security from the red men of the Plains. New York papers were often ten weeks old, and nearly half the letters, for a portion of the time, bore the postal mark of Salt Lake City, additional to several others.

When horses diminished in numbers, and mounted escorts could not accompany the trains to the Pinery, a new plan was adopted for the more prompt formation of the corral. Trains went out in two parallel lines with an intervening space of fifty or one hundred yards, so that, when an alarm was given, the front wagons turned in to meet each other; those on the flanks were trotted up with the mules inside, covered by the next wagon in advance; while the rear wagons of each line obliqued in to fill the fourth, or rear side of the square. It was a singular commentary on the recklessness of travelers, their ignorance of the feelings of Indians, their want of correct advice at Laramie, and the wisdom of the Indians themselves, that, of all the outrages committed on trains in 1866, there was never a single persistent attack upon a good corral, neither was there loss of life when proper rules were regarded. The apparent exception near Fort Philip Kearney, when Lieutenant Guinness was killed, in June, 1867, grew out of the great disparity of numbers, in part, and partly to the assurance of the Indians, derived from the massacre of December 21st, 1866. Brevet Major Powell, who resisted the attack of June, 1867, also resisted the tantalizing challenge of Indians, December 19th, 1866, and literally obeyed his orders, thereby saving himself and command from that utter destruction which befell others two days later.

For many months nearly all public references to attacks about that post, only made mention of attacks on wood trains; and the world at large seemed to regard it as if a detail had each time been sent for daily supply of fuel, instead of being employed on systematic labor in building a large post and fort.

The Pinery which is most accessible is just seven miles from the fort, as indicated on the map of Fort Philip Kearney and surroundings. At the base of the upper mountain, as well as on the island below, blockhouses had been built, and the men for a long time remained over night for early morning work. A train of over ninety wagons was employed at one period, and the timber would be cut, loaded, and hauled the same day. All sizes were accessible, from timber that would work out thirty-inch clear boards and plank down to the slender pine of the thickets from two to three inches thick, which made a close framework or skeleton for support of a clay covering. Innumerable straight trees of from four to fifteen inches in diameter were found, which cut from thirty to forty feet in length, without a knot or branch; and these lay so closely in a wall as to need no chinking before the plaster was applied.

These timber parties always had their armed teamsters, their armed choppers, and armed guard. Chopping details varied from sixteen to thirty, with a special guard of about the same number, making, with teamsters, a resisting force of from seventy to one hundred men, and sometimes, early in the season, the force of teamsters and wagonmasters alone was nearly that number.

Timber was procured much nearer, but with more difficulty, in July and August; and the place last adopted proved ample for all purposes.

This work blended all kinds of labor appropriate for tools that chop, saw, hew, or finish wood. Shingles were rived from bolts

sawed by the men, and many a shingle bee
was held, at night, to expedite work and
convince the skeptical that shingles, or anything else, could be made or done, when it
had to be, and that civilization was still
westward bound.

Chapter 16

BUT for the presence of hostile Indians, the country about Fort Philip Kearney would be a charming field for hunting and picnic purposes. Soon after our arrival, the ladies ventured twice to the mountains, and the second time descended to Pine Island, where choice elk steaks, furnished by the timber choppers, and suitable accessories, supplied a delightful meal, and no Indian disturbed the pleasure. Judge J. T. Kinney, formerly Chief Justice of Utah,[35] representing the business interests of Mr. Botsford, the sutler, was chief manager and steward, and under his skillful catering a dinner was provided that would not have dishonored a city restaurant.

[35] Judge Kinney was a native of Oswego County, New York. He studied law, migrated to Iowa, and from 1847 to January, 1854 served as a member of the Supreme Court of that state. From the latter date until March, 1863 he was Chief Justice of Utah Territory, save for a three-year interval, 1857–60, when he practiced law in Nebraska. President Lincoln removed him

The bill of fare was not printed; but canned lobster, cove oysters, and salmon were a very fair first course; and, associated with the game, were jellies, pineapples, tomatoes, sweet corn, peas, pickles, and such creature comforts, while puddings, pies, and domestic cake, from doughnuts and gingerbread up to plum cake and jelly cake, with coffee, and Madame Cliquot for those who wished it, and pipes and cigars for the gentlemen, enabled everybody to satisfy desire.

A trip to Lake De Smet, which is but a little more than two miles distant, is another locality which could be made a pleasant summer resort, to say nothing of skates in winter. The western end of the lake is accessible by a gentle slope after crossing Starting Creek; and a few hours' work and the use of pine timber would make a convenient landing for sail boats and dock boats. The north shore is rugged and the hills are covered with fragments of coal, red lava, and melted boulders, which seem as if they

from office on charges of pro-Mormonism and he was promptly elected Territorial Delegate in Congress. After serving one term (1863–65) he resumed the practice of Law in Nebraska. In February, 1867 he was appointed by President Johnson to investigate the causes of the Fort Philip Kearney massacre. From 1884 to 1889 he was Indian Agent to the Yankton Sioux in Dakota. He died at Salt Lake City, August 16, 1902.

had been thrown out of some great furnace. The south shore is hilly but less rocky. The water is deep and intensely alkaline, and there is neither inlet nor outlet as the little creek which is crossed before reaching the lake passes by the west end at a few hundred yards distance, and turns westward to the Piney Forks, emptying its stream below their junction.[36]

A third ride, which requires the saddle, is to climb the mountains by an Indian trail just below the point where the Little Piney makes its exit, and visit Fort Ridge, more than seven hundred feet above the fort. This ridge received its name from an Indian

[36] Lake De Smet, in northern Johnson County, Wyoming, is named for Father Pierre Jean De Smet, who is reputed to have been its white discoverer. However this may be, he was a notable character in the development of the Rocky Mountain and Pacific Northwest areas. A native of Belgium, he came to America in 1821 and entered the Jesuit order. In 1823 he was sent to the novitiate at Florissant near St. Louis which subsequently became the University of St. Louis. He was ordained in 1827, and in 1838 began the career as missionary to the western Indians for which he is chiefly remembered. He possessed remarkable physical strength and a remarkable capacity for winning the confidence of white men and red men alike. In carrying out his missionary labors he is said to have traveled 180,000 miles, crossing the Atlantic sixteen times. He mediated successfully between warring Indian tribes, and between the latter and the whites. Notable among the latter

fort near the summit. It is about thirty feet square, of loose stones of considerable size, and when visited, the inclosure was raised still higher by temporary abatis of pine logs. There were indications that a band had recently camped near it, having squaws with the party, and doubtless this place furnished one of the camp fires which had repeatedly been observed both by night and day. The view from the next higher range is fine beyond description.

Below the observer, the fort, the Pineys, Lake De Smet, and the branches of Peno Creek are drawn so near that it is difficult to realize that they are from seven to twelve

undertakings was his attendance at the Fort Laramie Council of 1851 and his intercession with the Sioux hostiles in 1868. According to his biographer, his "kindly tolerance extended to all except religionists of non-Catholic persuasion."

Mrs. Carrington's observation concerning the resort possibilities of Lake De Smet has long since been verified. The Wyoming State *Guide* of 1941 succinctly headlines it in the words "exceptional fishing and skating." Over it hovers the type of romantic legend concerning the tragic love of a red brave for a beautiful maiden (appropriately named Star Dust) which is widespread throughout the American West. According to this particular version the temporarily faithless lover was bound to a rock overlooking the lake by his inamorata's father and there left to die. When the wind moans over the Lake the warrior is supposed to be calling for his lost love.

miles distant. Beyond, and northward, the successive round-topped red buttes follow each other like an exaggerated style of the waves of some old cornfield which has been uncultivated for years; and thus they stretch on for nearly eighty miles before they are blended with the uneven horizon. In the northwest is the beautiful valley of Tongue River and its tributaries, with the Panther Mountains beyond. Westward, the Big Horn Mountain range continues its cragged front, past Piney Summit and Rocky Face Ridge, until lost to view. Eastward, the Black Hills, beyond Reno, and Pumpkin Buttes, loom up at a distance of a hundred miles, and Rock Creek and Clear Fork are traced until they disappear in the buttes of the north. Southward, Cloud Peak rises sublimely, with its hoary head piercing the clouds and furnishing an exhaustless reservoir for the hungry streams below.

The ascent is slow and requires frequent rests. Animals as well as men pant under the strain; the breath becomes short and labored, giving no little pain with a sense of suffocation, and the perspiration drops from mules and horses as if they had just been lifted bodily from a complete immersion. But, when the topmost summit is attained, after threading the intricacies of a pine or-

chard half choked by young balsam and
hemlock, the cup of coffee, with a sirloin of
mountain sheep cooked upon heated stones
or spitted before the coals, acquires peculiar
virtue and relish; and the mind never tires
in study of the magnificent panorama disclosed.

The Big Piney itself is possessed of a variety of natural charms. The gorge through
which the water rushes is nearly four hundred and fifty feet in height, and while the
river soon buries itself in the pines below, so
that the sighs of the winds through their
branches are blended in solemn murmurs
with the mad dash of cascades and the swift
rush of the rapids, it often breaks out to the
sunlight, and retains all its wildness and
tumult of sounds until it passes the fort and,
joined by its lesser sister, bears off for the
Missouri through the intervening channels.

These are all rides for the saddle, although
the ambulance can reach all but the mountain summit; and until two narrow escapes,
one on Big Piney and another beyond Pilot
Hill, had taught the ladies the risk of exposure, it was no rare thing to see Mrs. Wands
and others on a gallop for recreation and
change.

The road from the fort to the Pinery is
itself over the gentle southern slope of Sulli-

vant Hills, and at the highest point before entering the woods there is a fine view of Tongue River, the red buttes, and the lake, only surpassed by that of Fort Ridge itself.

Pilot Hill, only a few hundred yards from the fort, has its own fine views, and the traveler from Powder River can see at the distance of eleven miles its picket on the summit, watching for his arrival or keeping close scrutiny of the enemies of his peace.

The old road was abandoned the same week the site of the fort was selected; and though Colonel Sawyer soon after came over the old road as in 1865, all trains subsequently took the short cut-off from the lake to the fort.

Opposite the fort a gradual slope, slashed by occasional ravines, ends in a narrow tableland with another fine view of the fort, Peno Valley, the mountains and the lake. In every direction are natural beauties which minister to the refined taste, and furnish, even at that distance from civilized life, such choice intercourse with nature that separation from friends is softened and the hours of peace are like the moments of a pleasant dream.

The fort proper is six hundred feet by eight hundred, situated upon a natural plateau, so that there is a gradual slope from

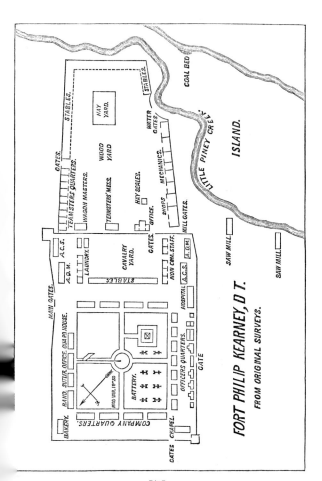

FORT PHILIP KEARNEY, D.T.

FROM ORIGINAL SURVEYS.

the front and rear, falling off nearly sixty feet in a few rods, thus affording a natural glacis and giving to the position a positive strength, independent of other defenses. A rectangle, two hundred by six hundred feet, is occupied by warehouses, cavalry stables, laundress quarters, and the non-commissioned staff.

About the parade-ground, already referred to, are officers' and men's quarters, offices, guardhouse, sutler's and band building.

The stockade is made of heavy pine trunks eleven feet long, hewn to a touching surface of four inches so as to join closely, being pointed and loop-holed, and firmly imbedded in the ground for three feet. Block-houses are at two diagonal corners, and massive gates of plank with small wickets, all having substantial locks, are on three fronts, and on the fourth or southern front, back of the officers' quarters, is a small gate for sallies, or for officers' use.

Three framed warehouses, the hospital, and four company quarters, built in 1866, are eighty-four feet long and twenty-four feet wide, with ceilings of ten feet. The windows to soldiers' quarters, as well as those designed for officers, have three sashes each, giving ample light and cheerfulness to the whole garrison. Regulation bunks, with arm

racks, shelves for knapsacks, boots, etc.,
are conveniently arranged, so that a company can form for roll-call between the
two lines.

A flag-staff, surrounded by an octagonal
band platform, stand, and seats, occupies,
the center of the parade, and diverging
walks, twelve feet wide, pass to each street,
the magazine being in the center of one of
the squares.

East of, and opening from the fort, extending with nearly an equal area to the
Little Piney is the corral, or quartermaster's
yard. This is surrounded by a rough cottonwood stockade and contains stabling for
mules, hay and wood yards, hay scales,
quarters for teamsters and mechanics, the
blacksmith, wagonmakers, carpenters, saddlers, and armorers' shops, and the general
apparatus and conveniences of such a place.

From this corral, one gate opens toward
the saw-mills, one toward the road from
Powder River, and one to the clear waters
of the Little Piney, which here makes a convenient bend perfectly protected by the reentering angle of the stockade just at that
point.

Two steam saw-mills just above the mill
gate and but a few rods distant furnish constant supplies of posts, plank, studding, raft-

ers, lath and boards, and all lumber for every use.

The stockade of two thousand eight hundred feet circuit was completed in October, notwithstanding all other work and constant skirmishing went on, and, with the exception of most of the Sabbaths, there was no cessation of labor, whatever the weather, until the holidays of October 29th and 30th. On the first of November the same diligence was renewed, and each day's close was a new testimony to what a few men could accomplish under systematized labor and the will to work.

Chapter 17

THE last day of October being the stated day of muster-for-pay, it was declared a holiday, as the previous day had been one of preparation. The completed flag staff was at last to receive its chief glory in flying the first garrison flag that ever rose over Absaraka.

The day was bright and lovely.

The whole command was in full dress, and after the inspection and review of the morning upon the plain before the fort, and the proper muster, the troops formed three sides of a square about the flag-staff, the fourth side having a platform for officers, ladies, and visitors, and the band taking station in the center.

Probably the program would not conform closely to all conventionalisms of army usage, or find precise antecedents in army regulations, but it appeared to be designed more particularly to bring hard-working day-laborers back to something like military dress forms of parade, and supply a little recreation to those whose only interval of rest was the occasional hours of sleep. Shut out from civilized life, the only drawback was the refusal of the Colonel to let everybody give some old-fashioned cheering when the work was done. But all went off about as well as it would elsewhere, and as it suited those whom it was designed to gratify, it made no difference to mankind at large.

Judge Kinney read an appropriate poem of Miss Carmichael's chaste and spirited collection, Chaplain White offered the prayer, and principal musician Barnes, who, with William Daily, fashioned the flag-staff, presented to be read an original poem of his own, which at least did justice to his patriotic spirit.

The following was the address, and is such a brief resumé of the preceding work, and the results attained by the expedition of 1866 in a little more than three months of labor, that no apology is made for its repetition, although already known to many:

"OFFICERS AND MEN:—Three and one-half months ago stakes were driven to define the now perfected outlines of Fort Philip Kearney. Aggressive Indians threatened to exterminate the command. Our advent cost us blood. Private Livensberger of Company F was the first victim, July 17th, 1866; Lieutenant Daniels, Private Callery, of G Company; Gilchrist and Johnson, of E Company; Fitzpatrick and Hacket, of D Company; Patrick Smith, of H Company; and Oberly and Wasser have also, in the order named, given their lives to vindicate our pledge to never yield one foot of advance, but to guarantee a safe passage for all who seek a home in the lands beyond.

"Fifteen weeks have passed, varied by many skirmishes and both night and day alarms, but that pledge holds good. In every work done your arms have been at hand. In the pine tracts or hay fields, on picket or general guard duty, no one has failed to find a constant exposure to some hostile shaft, and to feel that a cunning adversary was watching every chance to harass and kill.

"And yet that pledge holds good. Stockade and block-house, embrasure and loophole, shell and bullet, have warded off danger, so that women and children now notice the savage as he appears only to look for fresh occasion for you to punish him, and with righteous anger to avenge the dead.

"The Indian dead outnumbers your own fourfold, while your acquired experience and better cause afford you constant success in every encounter. This is not all. Substantial warehouses, containing a year's supply, spacious and enduring quarters, and a well-adapted magazine are other proofs of your diligence and spirit.

"The steam whistle and the rattle of the mower have followed your steps in this westward march of empire. You have built a central post that will bear comparison with any for security, completeness, and adaptation to the ends in view, wherever the other may be located, or however long in erection.*

"Surrounded by temptations to hunt the choicest game, and allured by tales of golden treasure just beyond you, you have spared your powder for your foes, and have given the labor of your hands to your proper work. Passing from guard-watching to fatigue-work, and, after one night in bed, often disturbed, returning to your post as sentry; attempting with success all trades and callings, and handling the broad-axe and hammer, the saw and the chisel, with the same

*Brevet Brigadier General W. B. Hazen, upon his tour of inspection, pronounced this stockade to be the best he had ever seen, excepting only one in British America, built by the Hudson's Bay Company, with great labor and expense. The previous description of Fort Philip Kearney is in substance derived from the *Army and Navy Journal* and the New York *Times*.

success as that with which you have sped the bullet, your work has proven how well deserved was the confidence I reposed in all of you; and that same old pledge still holds good.

"Coincident with your march to this point was the occupation of Fort Reno; first by Company B, afterward reinforced by Company F of this battalion, and the advance of Companies D and G to Fort C. F. Smith, nearly one hundred miles farther west. All these, like yourselves, having a share in the labor, the exposure, and the conflicts that throughout the whole length of the line attended its occupation, have sustained the past good record of the 18th Infantry, and thus also have vindicated your pledge.

"And now, this day, laying aside the worn and tattered garments, which have done their part during weeks of toil and struggle, the veteran battalion of the 18th Infantry, from which perhaps I shall soon be parted in the changes of army life and organization, puts on its fresh full-dress attire for muster and review.

"The crowning office, without which you would regard your work as scarcely begun, is now to be performed, and to its fulfillment I assign soldiers; neither discharging the duty myself, nor delegating it to some brother officer; but some veteran soldiers of good desert shall share with a sergeant from each of their companies, and the worthy man whose work rises high above us, the honor of raising our new and beautiful garrison flag to the top of the handsomest flag-staff in America.

"It is the first full garrison flag that has floated between the Platte and Montana; and this beautiful pole, perfect in detail as if wrought and finished in the navy yards of New York, Philadelphia, or Boston, will be to Sergeant Barnes, whose appropriate and well-intended verses will be read to you, a long remembered trophy of his patriotism and skill; a new impulse to your own future exertions; a new cause for pride as its stripes and stars are daily unfolded; a new source of courage to each traveler westward advancing; and a new terror to foes who dare to assail you.

"With music and the roar of cannon we will greet its unfoldings.

"This day shall be a holiday, and a fresh starting-point for future endeavor.

"And yet, all is not said that I wish to say! While we exalt the national standard, and rejoice in its glory and its power, let us not forget the true source of that glory and power.

"For our unexampled health and continued success; for that land of the free and home of the brave; for our institutions and their fruits, we owe all to the Great Ruler who made and has preserved us.

"Let me, then, ask all, with uncovered heads and grateful hearts, to pause in our act of consecration while the chaplain shall invoke God's own blessing upon that act; so that while this banner rises heavenward, and so shall rise with each recurring sun, all hearts shall rise to the throne of the Infinite, and for this day, its duties and its pleasures, we shall become better men and better soldiers of the great Republic."

At the close of the prayer, the flag slowly rose to masthead, while national airs, the booming of cannon, and the sharp ring of presented arms paid it such tokens of respect as the occasion enjoined.

The afternoon was pleasant, and such recreation was indulged in as the men found agreeable. About three o'clock, Indians came out of the creek and around the bend of Sullivant Hills so quickly as to almost pass the west gate before they were discovered. They evidently hoped by the suddenness of their movement to cut off a few private horses that were grazing just south of the fort, but were disappointed. Others appeared upon the hills, and flashing mirrors were constantly passing signals for nearly an hour. It would seem as if the salute had attracted their attention, and they had supposed that other Indians were near the fort, or the white men had some other exhibition for their gratification and surprise. They had at least the pleasure of seeing the Stars and Stripes, and thus getting new hints as to the proposed length of our visit.

In the evening all the officers, in full dress, and the ladies of the garrison, attended the muster evening levee at the Colonel's, where music, social dancing, and such an entertainment as was practicable, closed the day, and brought everybody up very closely to the grade of similar reunions in the States.

Chapter 18

A DAY OF INCIDENTS—HOSTILE SIOUX AND
FRIENDLY CHEYENNES—NARROW ESCAPE
OF THE LATTER—OUR PICKET MIMICKED—
MORE MASSACRES—CROQUET INTRODUCED
INTO ABSARAKA.

ONE September morning was peculiarly bright and clear. A full moon had fairly invited the Indian deities to their best endeavor, but as a slight fall of snow half covered the earth all expectations of seeing red men gradually vanished from our minds. The timber train went as usual to the Pinery. A water party was at the larger creek before the fort. Details were at work on the ditch. Others were hewing, pointing, cutting loop-holes, or placing the completed trunks in the trenches. The saw-mills were busy, and men who had just come off guard cheerfully lent their energies to work upon their company barracks. The touch of snow seemed to hurry everybody. The band was just marching from the guard parade when an alarm was given.

We could all see, and, after the children were looked up or accounted for, did our share of watching.

A party of seven Indians dashed out of the thick cottonwood at the confluence of the two Pineys and made boldly for the picket on Pilot Hill. It seemed that almost instantly the relief of the mounted picket, always saddled and ready, were out of the east gate upon a run, and yet it was plain that no riders or horses would be in time. The despised howitzers were brought into requisition, and a case shot was sent as a swifter messenger, with its relief of eighty bullets, and, as it hurtled through the air, the savages slackened speed a little to watch its advent. They found "the gun that shoots twice" too much for their dodging, and as its shell exploded over their heads, scattering its compliments and the earth in all directions, they turned their course and made for the brush as quickly as they had appeared. A second similar messenger dropped one Indian from the saddle, and all took to cover.

Directly opposite the fort, and only about seven hundred yards from the front gate, across the Piney, where Captain Bailey had encamped his party of miners, nearly fifty Indians made a dash for his horses; but the miners were as quick as their foe, and were after them with revolvers and rifles; while again, "the gun that shoots twice" achieved a success. One Indian pony was shot by a miner, but, to our great disgust, his rider coolly leaped up behind another Indian and galloped off beyond the reach of harm.

A case shot and shell turned aside another party demonstrating from the west; but, simultaneously with the operations of these parties, a still larger force was spread out on the summit and slopes of Lodge Trail Ridge, just as if they had in view an attack upon the timber train while the other parties should skirmish and draw the attention of the garrison. A detachment was at once sent toward the woods, but the flashing looking-glasses all along the hills passed the quick signal that their plans had been foiled, and very soon all Indians had disappeared.

A messenger brought in word that Patrick Smith, belonging to the permanent block-house party in the woods, had dragged himself nearly half a mile to his camp, badly wounded with arrows, and scalped. He had managed to break off the shafts, so as not to be impeded in crawling through the thickets. Dr. Reid, Acting Assistant Surgeon, at once went to his relief; but he died within twenty-four hours.

While the working party were felling trees, a party of Indians broke through the woods and killed two of the detail who were a little separated from their comrades.

About two o'clock in the afternoon the sudden, repeated shriek of the steam-whistle at the farther mill, and the equally hasty signal of the pickets, gave the alarm that Indians were again close by. We could all see fifteen Indians between the fort and the mountain, galloping from the west directly for Pilot Hill, with the plain purpose of capturing and scalping the picket under the very eyes of the garrison. Before they had half ascended the hill, Captain Brown and Lieutenant Adair, with a party, were in hot pursuit. Private Rover (who is of a good Chicago family, and enlisted under the false name of Rover) was in charge of the picket. He had been signally brave in several tight places before. On this occasion he dismounted his three men, turned the horses loose toward the fort with a good urging, and slowly fell off the northern slope, with arms at a "ready," to join the supporting party. The horses came down the steep grade toward the fort on a run, passing through the Indians, who dare not stop them and could only give them a few arrows as they passed. The chief warrior reached the summit, and for an instant turned his pony, to imitate the usual signal of riding in a circle until flags were used; but the pressure of Captain Brown's party soon put the Indians and their ponies to their mettle.

It was nearly night when the party returned, with wearied horses, to tell the tale of their adventures.

They brought with them a band of eight Cheyenne Indians and one squaw, whose broken-down ponies and miserable outfit showed that they were neither on the warpath nor very prosperous. It seems that Captain Brown, while pursuing the Sioux, saw them suddenly stop and have a short parley with a party coming from the east.

As the two separated, the latter came forward holding up a paper and showing themselves to be Little Moon, The Rabbit that Jumps, and The Wolf that Lies Down, with a few others, on their way to the fort for provisions, and permission to go to Tongue River Valley to hunt.

These chiefs were at the council in July, and said that Black Horse (who then was ill) was sick and in their camp at Rock Creek, and that old White Head, the oldest living Cheyenne chief, was with them also: that they had been in the mountains as directed, and had crossed as far as Fort Caspar, where Brevet Major Morris had treated them well, and given them a letter to the Colonel.

These Indians were permitted to camp on an island in Little Piney, under the notice of the saw-mill guard, and by dusk were cooking their bacon and coffee, which had been presented by Colonel Carrington.

Men of the timber train came in, and told the soldiers that some of this very party were with those who had killed Oberly and Wasser. This rumor spread through the garrison. Added to the fact that many officers and citizens had doubts whether some of the band of Black Horse were not among our active enemies, this developed a spirit of vengeance that soon made itself demonstrative.

It seemed too bad, when no man could go out of the stockade unarmed, and any negligence insured the most horrible death and torture, that any red man should be sheltered and fed by the garrison, its commander, or Colonel Carrington, the district commander.

About 9 o'clock Chaplain White called and said that the men talked about killing the Cheyennes; and soon after a soldier opened the door and said that the men were killing the Indians. The Colonel started at once, with revolver in hand, and three reports, soon after heard, showed that some issue had been made. As a matter of fact, nearly ninety men had quietly armed, and in the darkness of the night formed themselves opposite the Indians, cocked their

pieces, all ready to fire, when a guard arrived
and they were ordered back to post. Anxious
not to be recognized when the guard arrived
and they were ordered back, they disobeyed
Captain Ten Eyck and rushed for the east
gate; but the Colonel's shots, after hesitation to obey his order to halt, stopped the
party.

So far as the light could determine, they
were found to be some of the best men of the
garrison. They quickly realized the dis-
grace that would have fallen upon the post
and regiment had they perpetrated the massacre, and for many reasons were restored
to their barracks with only admonition and
caution as to future conduct.

In fact, the next day these same Indians
had a conference, and in the judgment of
everybody vindicated their good faith by
such information of their own movements
and those of the Sioux, as fully comported
with advices from other sources.

Old White Head also came, with a few
braves, and had a talk with some of the officers; but the band, after the risk of the night
before, and having been instructed to keep
off the road (as soldiers could no longer dis-
criminate when they met Indians on the
road, or about the working parties), left us
and returned no more.

Other days were as full of changing adventures as this. Few were without their share of less painful incidents. A game of croquet was planned, and while the ladies could neither ride nor walk beyond the gates, some amusement was attempted between Indian alarms; the evening found its recreation in the authors' game, a quiet quadrille, good music, conversation, and other varieties, besides the needle and cook-book.

It may be added, before this last reference to the Cheyennes, that when they were passed by the Sioux whom Captain Brown chased from Pilot Hill, the Sioux contemptuously struck them and cried *Coo!* as they did in July, when unable to induce the same party to engage in war against the whites and the occupation of the road.

Chapter 19

THE nights in Absaraka were peculiarly beautiful when cloudless. The rarity of the atmosphere gave full play to the star-beams, and it seemed as if there were twice as many as in any firmament elsewhere.

Their first appearance was often mistaken for Indian signal fires, as they rose above the horizon, like the sun or moon, having orbs as marked and light as brilliant as when they attained the zenith. In the glory of the full moon the snow-clad mountains shone as silver; while the deep roar of the cascades of Big Piney Fork was hardly less grateful to the wakeful soul than its lullaby was soothing to the weary.

From sunset until morning this melody increased in power, as if making most of its time when man was not too busy to notice or enjoy, or as if seeking to comfort and quiet him after his day of toil. Each midday's thaw upon the mountains in summer would reach the great gates of exit just at that grateful hour when the undisturbed slumber is sweetest and soundest, and all natural harmonies intensify the blessing of morning sleep.

Now and then the aurora borealis put forth its pyrotechnic energies in a profuse variety of merry dances, vaulting streamers, and gorgeous coronas; and then, again, the lunar rainbow, with its strangely unreal tints and novelties, would banish sleep and bring us all to a patient attention to its claims, and thorough admiration of its wonderful characteristics.

August and November contributed their aerolites and proper share of meteors, and the blazing sky-path of these eccentric visitors shone fresh and clear after the celestial traveler had exploded itself, or had been otherwise disposed of under the laws of its being or the program of the meteorologist and astronomer. Other nights were such as Æneas knew when the gods were angry, or Odin permitted when the storm-king was riding in state or in vengeance. Then, every mountain gorge had its own blast, and every gulch, ravine, and valley had its fitful and unruly current. Tent-flies took the proportions and direction of inflated balloons, and the snapping and flapping was suggestive of sky for the roofing and all out-doors for the inclosure of the habitation we dwelt in.

Such winds do justice to the theory and mission of winds. They blow as winds can only blow when in real earnest: and it is inflexibly certain that the classical Æolus of early times who used to cave and lock up the winds he was familiar with, never gained jurisdiction over the winds of Absaraka; or the whole history of his career and successes is simply a myth, or poetic fiction of by-gone days. In early school hours, when Madame M————s thought Latin was a special accomplishment as a basis of good English, we received the history and adventures of Æolus with as much faith as anybody did, and if compelled, at last, to question any alleged circumstances connected with his career, it is a matter of reluctant conviction, and not of captious skepticism as to the history of the past.

Other night scenes than those portrayed by Nature were frequently contributed by the native inhabitants of the land.

While the garrison were in tents few ladies slept soundly; and officers and men alike threw themselves down for repose as if expecting each moment a summons to duty. Beyond the general guard lines the pickets were thrown out in several directions to

watch for the approach of Indians; and as
each relief went out it changed its station, so
that enemies who knew the former position
of the detail could not know its place two
hours afterward. Scarcely had the post been
located, when these night visitations became
frequent.

On one occasion brisk firing was heard on
all sides, and the entire garrison was under
arms, while Lieutenant Adair's whole company was sent out to support the pickets and
ward off attack. Numerous fancies often
blended with the real facts, and false alarms
alternated with the genuine. Thus, wonderful reports would come in of the flight of
arrows that innocently whizzed past the men
on duty; and yet the closest scrutiny by lan-
tern or morning light would fail to discover
the projectiles themselves. Sometimes a
mule, straying from corral or parting his
halter, became the victim of that constant
vigilance which was the price of our lives
and liberty; or sneaking wolves would be
mistaken for sneaking Indians, whose habit
of borrowing wolf-skins and wolf-cries to de-
ceive us compelled instant attention to whatever had show of life. At other times crawling Indians would actually draw near enough
to attempt a shot at the tents or sentries;
and at all times dawn of day was the only

sure indication that an enemy was not close at hand. One sign, however, became a fair one. When wolves were loudest and nearest, the Indians seldom were near; and the old trappers claimed to distinguish between the genuine wolf-howl and the Indian imitation by the fact that the former produced no echo. Either the natural or the imitated was ugly enough, and sufficiently abundant for that style of music.

With completion of the stockade the guard was reduced, and some sense of security prevailed. Until then, it is certain that any considerable body of Indians, with a proper leader, could have dashed through the camp and performed substantial mischief. But while the stockade kept Indians out, it did not keep them away. Still they ventured their shots at the sentries, fired arrows into the beef cattle close outside, and tried all possible measures to decoy and capture any who were imprudent and careless.

About nine o'clock one evening a volley near the front gate aroused the garrison. Close to the stockade, and just at the foot of the natural slope which surrounds it, a small corral of wagons belonging to the sutler inclosed a group of teamsters engaged at cards. The first indication of the presence of Indians was a volley fired under the wagon beds, which wounded three, and one of them fatally. A detail from the guard was soon on the spot, and the low ground was scouted as far as the creek; but the night being dark, no Indians were found.

Another evening, just after taps, an alarm was given by the sutler that his stock, which had been left on herd half a mile south of the fort, on the Little Piney, was attacked; and besides his own men, Captain Brown, with forty infantry, moved out as skirmishers from that face of the fort toward the creek. Almost immediately a bright fire sprang up on the spur of Sullivant Hills, nearest the post on the west, around which the figures of Indians could be distinctly seen moving. The picket at the hay-ricks east of the fort, on Little Piney, fired two shots at horsemen on the creek, and there were other indications that several hostile parties were preying about us. The night was very dark, and objects could be seen but a short distance.

The bright fire, made up of pine flambeaus or torches, alone furnished any show of a fair target, and received complimentary attention.

A careful range was given to the field howitzer, loaded with a twelve-pound spherical case shot, and three twelve-pound mountain howitzers were also loaded and trained in three other directions, where there was any probability of stirring up the skulkers. All were discharged at one word, and the first shell exploded directly over the fire, scattering its bullets and the Indians as well, while the fire was instantly extinguished and the night passed without further interruption. The stock were brought in safely, with the report that the Indians abandoned their game as soon as the party on the hills was scattered. It evidently was a novel surprise that at night and at the distance of several hundred yards the white soldiers could reach them with such plentiful volleys as a case shot distributes.

The duties of the officer of the day at night were always exacting and full of incident; and indeed, while every day brought its probabilities of some Indian adventures near the fort or at the Pinery, every night had its special dangers, which, unanticipated, might involve great loss, if not the sacrifice of the post, its garrison, and stores.

Repeated attempts were made to approach the large hay-ricks for the purpose of setting them on fire; and while as a general rule large parties only appeared at the full of the moon, the forays of stealing and scalping bands were constantly harassing and probable.

Such demonstrations were seldom early in the evening. Just at daybreak, when sleep is soundest, and the faintest glimmer of light discloses unprotected stock or exposed positions, was the favorite hour with the sharp red man.

Two days after Captain Fetterman arrived, impressed with the opinion, to which he had often given language, that "a company of regulars could whip a thousand, and a regiment could whip the whole array of hostile tribes," he was permitted to make the experiment of lying in the cottonwood thickets of Big Piney from two o'clock until ten o'clock in the morning, using hobbled mules for live bait to decoy the aborigines.

A beautiful Sunday morning dawned, and no Indians were seen; and so close was the covert that the glass did not reveal the secreted party. About nine o'clock Mrs. Wheatley rode in front of the fort with Mr. Reid, passing it nearly a half mile, where her husband's cattle were feeding, and at least a mile from the expected skirmish. The team soon came back upon the run, some Indians having dashed forth, driven off the cattle, and not capturing the wagon and passengers because of a presented rifle, or the assurance that the stock was theirs at all events, while a moment's delay would expose them to quick pursuit from the fort. The Indians may or may not have known the plan for their surprise; but their sagacity and suspicion, their keen sight and knowledge of woodcraft are seldom at loss; and while they were often foiled and disappointed, or repulsed with loss, they were always innocent of being surprised, and shrewdly made their own advances so covered that they were near the desired object before their presence was known.

So it was that nights in Absaraka, so cool and suggestive of sweetest sleep, were associated with wakefulness and danger; and at least one officer, whose responsibilities were as large as any, slept for weeks in succession without removal of garments, and nightly made his rounds to secure personal knowledge of the deportment of the guard and the condition of the post.

Habit, however, soon accustomed those who were not immediately on duty to trust the vigilance of the guard, and to sleep by snatches that grateful sleep which elsewhere never could be beat.

Chapter 20

WOMAN had a choice field in Absaraka for the exercise of many industrial pursuits, and fortunate were those who in earlier days had been advised that other rooms than the parlor have their uses, and other fingering than that of the piano must be employed in roasting and boiling, in frying and broiling, in baking and stewing. It was found that yeast was to be made before the bread could be extra, that the hands were to be servants when no other servants could be had; and it was discovered by some that the dish-cloth and wash-cloth, the broom and the duster were susceptible of as graceful manipulation as prinking irons, or the strings of lute and guitar. In fact, every morning brought its round of antebreakfast labor, with that restoring process by which dishes once used are brought back to proper condition for future uses. Female servants were scarce, independent, and disputant. The few taken with families had learned that their market value for washing was above everything reasonable in a household, and that a fortune was soon to be realized by selling villainous pies to soldiers at half a dollar or more for a pie.

Ladies found themselves obliged to turn milliners and dressmakers; and we know experimentally that our experience in fabricating boys' clothes alone was worth a good apprenticeship, if it should ever become necessary to rush to a trade for support.

Frank Leslie's and Madame Demorest's magazines became each a desideratum, and linsey-woolsey, delaines, and calico nowhere else underwent such endowment with fashionable shapes as in Absaraka. Darning and stitching, hemming and hemstitching, cutting and basting were as inevitable as the need of clothes to wear. The triplet of "I never could, I never would, and I never will," became almost obsolete; and in their place were these other impulses, "I wouldn't, but I must and I will," or "I could, I can, and I do!" Unhappy were any who despised to begin, and, in the penalty of charcoal beefsteak, hot water soups, and dyspeptic biscuit, were driven to despair or disgust.

But any life on the Plains is a good school, and its practical suggestions take all the starch and false pride as to work completely out of the unfortunate human creature who expects the spoon to be carried to the mouth

by attendants, and a metropolitan table to
be spread by the hands of a striker.

Primitive ways are to be learned; but the
tent becomes neat and genteel, and the taste
of its arrangement and adornment gives
capital hints to the mind of the beauty of patience, and especially confirms the sacred
maxim, that content with godliness is great
gain.

The snapping of a tent-pole at midnight
under three feet of snow; the blaze of the
canvas, as the ambitious fire commissions
the red-hot pipe to unroof your earthly tab-
ernacle, at no small risk to bedding and
trunks; the pretty little drifts that gracefully
slip through the closely drawn entrance and
sprinkle your bed, your furniture, and your
wardrobe, all afford change and excitement,
and not unseldom bring occasion to begin
housekeeping anew. The frozen-up kettles,
pots, and buckets demand recognition; while
the milk, the cream, and the butter are in-
centives to new branches of industry and skill.

So when houses are used, one house will
differ from another house in glory. The
adobe, with its unplastered surface, and the
dropping of dirt from the earth-covered roof,
is one variety; and the log-cabin is another
variety; either of which involves much ingenuity, not to say genius, as the mind strug-

gles to give them neatness and comfort. Yet either of these soon becomes home; and its protection from summer's heat and winter's cold is often more grateful and complete than more pretentious edifices of wood or brick. It is, indeed, not always easy to adapt a carpet to dirt floors, or the changing sizes of army habitations; nor is it pleasant to break up and begin housekeeping several times a year. Always there is something you cannot carry with you, something which must be sold or given away. Always some favorite chair is broken and crockery mysteriously disappears, requiring new outlay at prices beyond reason, and trying the patience and temper by sound and certain tests. Custom familiarizes the different styles, shapes, and colors of plates and dishes, as they are replenished at different times and places; but while the tin-cup and plate are splendid on the march, they do not come up to the ideal of comeliness and elegance in preparation for a reception or dinner-party given to strangers.

When, after a successful trip of six hundred miles, our two cows were driven away one Sunday afternoon by some very mean Indians, there ensued another of those episodes which distract the mind and mar all plans as to butter and cream for cake and for coffee. The wolves took our nice turkey hen just as she was ready to give us a brood of little turkeys; while half of our young chickens in that bracing climate gaped themselves to death. Yet, with all these sacrifices and losses from repeated change, there were real cosy times in tents, houses, or in cabins. The good nature and good sense of Uncle Samuel had furnished canned provisions, greatly to our personal comfort and pecuniary convenience; but fresh vegetables were most precious and rare. A few potatoes from Bozeman City, sent with the regards of Brevet Lieutenant-Colonel Kinney, were a great treat; and Major Almstedt, paymaster, was good enough to spare a half cabbage and eleven onions, through one of his trips, to astonish the palate and minister to a craving for something novel from the United States. Ingenuity was tasked to invent new cookery for cove oysters and other savory preserved edibles; and wild plums, gooseberries, currants, grapes, and cherries furnished a preserve basis quite palatable and natural.

Wild meats would have been abundant; but the stringent Indian game laws of that country treated all hunting by the white man as poaching, and the preserves were skillfully guarded, to cut off so far as possible every impulse to trespass.

Evenings had their readings, their games, and quiet quadrilles. Music was a never-failing relief for body and mind; and the interchange of patterns, books, and recipes kept up material for new industry and new themes for deliberation or chit-chat. Sickness, though rare, brought its sympathies, and its little interchange of good things and delicacies; and with the occasional pressure of unsatisfied longings there was developed a peculiarly apt illustration of the idea that people really don't want much of anything, and the Scripture was confirmed that "a man's life consisteth not in the abundance of what a man possesseth."

Change and frequent parting brought those peculiar separations that nowhere else are so tender as in army life on the frontier. Captain Haymond, Lieutenants Phisterer and D'Isay left us for recruiting service only two weeks after we reached our destination; and subsequently, Lieutenant Adair and Lieutenant Bisbee, wife and child. Others came, and quite a coterie shared in the round of evening sociables, which relieved the tension of continual excitement, and brought into being some features similar in kind to those of by-gone times at home.

Nor was the Sabbath neglected. Each new building, that was available in turn, became our sanctuary, as there was not time to build exclusively for chapel purposes. The sutler's store, the commissary building, company headquarters, and the band pavilion of evergreens successively shared the honor. The string band accompanied the voices, and, far away from the church-going bell and the heaven-directing spires, the praise of God was sung and Divine help implored. Few are the sanctuaries in civilized states where the *Magnificat*, *Gloria in Excelsis*, *There is a light in the window*, *Old Hundred*, and *Coronation* were supported by a better orchestra or sung with more spirit.

The garrison itself had its own occasional social gatherings; and such was the general sobriety, the patient obedience and thorough absorption of the men in the plans of their commander that drunkenness was rare and profanity less than usual. The stringent orders against verbal or personal abuse, the public reprimand administered on one occasion, and the governing principle that while obedience must be cheerful and immediate, the rights of the soldier as a man must be regarded, inspired the men with confidence and new ambition to fulfill their full measure of duty.

Chapter 21

WHEN even a woman shares the contingencies of entering a new country with troops, she must learn something besides the lessons of housewifery, endurance, and patience.

When days, weeks, and months pass with constantly recurring opportunities of seeing Indians in small and in large parties dashing at pickets, driving in wood parties, harassing water details, and, with dancing and yelling, challenging the garrison to pursuit; when, now and then, one, two, or more casualties mark the issues of a day, and these culminate, until at last five wagonloads of bodies give evidence of the cunning barbarity and numbers of the foe; when night alarms are common, and three men are shot within thirty yards of the gates; when the stockade becomes a prison-wall, and over its trunks are seen only the signs of precaution or active warfare; when the men are never idle, but all are daily engrossed in essential labor, with no signs of reinforcement or aid; when the usual thankless task of opening a new country with its uncertainties and enmities, with resources absurdly deficient, meets only obloquy and abuse for the principal actors, she acquires somehow, whether by instinct or observation, it matters not which, an idea that Indians will fight, and sometimes do become quite wicked and dangerous. Surely, their ways are not as our ways, and their ponies are not like our horses. Their commissariat and their forage are not in trains or on pack mules; their campaigns are not extensively advertised in advance, nor do they move by regular stages or established routes.

Yes, even a woman, after several hundred miles of journey alternately in the ambulance or side saddle, sometimes in corral expecting its aid for safety, and again in the winding defile, where the very place excites the keenest scrutiny and is suggestive of noble red men with the nobility ignored, will see some peculiarities of Indian warfare when Indians are really venomous, and will draw conclusions for friends to consider, even if they only elicit a smile at her timidity, simplicity, or weakness.

James, the novelist, never compelled his solitary horseman to fight a Sioux, and, had the Knight of the Leopard, at the Diamond of the Desert, met more than one quiver of the darts of the Saracen, his adventures might have ended while his career was scarcely begun. Not unlike the Arab is the Indian of the Northwest. Isolated, yet in communication through the little mirrors which flash the sunlight and pass his signals for miles; separated, yet by the lance, pennon, and flags combined when opportunity is inviting; dashing directly forward at a run, with the person crouched on the pony's neck, and wheeling only to throw himself out of sight and pass his arrows and bullets under the animal's neck before he returns for a fresh venture; fleeing everywhere, apparently at random, so that his pursuer must take choice of object of quest only to find his hot pursuit fruitless, with gathered numbers in his line of retreat; shooting up and down red buttes, where the horse of the white man breaks down at once; running on foot, with the trotting pony just behind him seeking a rest from the burden of his master; imitating the cry of the wolf and the hoot of the owl, when it will hide his night visit, these Indians are everywhere, where you suppose they are not; and are certain to be nowhere, where you suppose them to be, sure.

In ambush and decoy, splendid; in horsemanship, perfect; in strategy, cunning; in battle, wary and careful of life; in victory, jubilant; and in vengeance, fiendish and terrible.

Too few to waste life fruitlessly; too superstitious to leave their dead to the enemy; too cunning or niggardly of resources to offer fair fight; too fond of their choice huntinggrounds to yield willing possession to the stranger, they wait and watch, and watch and wait, to gather the scalps of the unwary and ignorant, and bear off their trophies to new feasts, new orgies, and new endeavor.

So reluctant are they to attack a foe under cover that during the year 1866—once before stated—not a train was lost or seriously embarrassed when in corral; nor was any considerable party assailed when it sought judicious and substantial defense. Yet, daring and watchful, none better estimate the foe they contend with. When white men have delivered their fire and the gleam of the ramrod has shown that the single-shooting arm was in use, then follows the wild dash, with revolvers and arrows, so quick and so spirited that their loss is as nothing, and swift ponies take them safely away for renewal of attack. Circling and intermingling to confuse all aim, affecting retreat seemingly to break up their array, and by some ravine, gulch, cañon, or thicket to appear on fresh and better vantage-ground, they approximate ubiquity, and fill the terse description of the veteran Bridger, "Where there ain't no Injuns, you'll find 'em thickest."

Good judges of numbers, and quick to estimate the strength and designs of an enemy; keen to maintain their scouts and secure due notice of reinforcements; rarely, though sometimes, fighting in masses, but then with such involved and concerted disorder as to insure their purpose, when the plan is to overwhelm alive and capture for the torture, this same Indian must find in his final master a better-armed and well-disciplined foe, who has studied his country and his nature, and this before his peace-offerings will be abiding and honest or his hunting-grounds shall become the peaceful path of the traveler.

With all this, these same Indians have read the book of fate, and in the establishment of mutually supporting and well-garrisoned strongholds they will be foiled as to protracted interruption of emigration and travel. When this end is reached, and the great route through Absaraka is occupied and guarded, the game will flee the range of the white man's rifle, and the desperate Indian must abandon his home, fight himself to death, or yield to the white man's mercy.

Fired by the progress of the settler and the soldier; seeing as never before the last retreat of the buffalo, the elk, and the deer invaded by a permanent intruder; looking at his rights as violated, and the promises of many agents as unfulfilled; taught by nature, if not by the white man, that he is the lawful tenant of the waste he roams over until he has bartered his right away, he has some reason to exclaim, as Red Cloud assured Black Horse, when the latter, in July, 1866, said: "Let us take the white man's hand and what he gives us, rather than fight him longer and lose all," the answer was "White man lies and steals. My lodges were many, but now they are few. The white man wants all. The white man must fight, and the Indian will die where his fathers died."

Growing conscious of the white man's power, knowing how vain is an open field struggle, they avoid such determining issues, and waylay in detail, gradually enlarging their sphere of action, and thereby gathering in the young men and disaffected of other bands, until common cause may be had of all whose wrongs or temper inspire them to keep the war-path longer.

The frequent change of dwelling-place in a great area of hunting-ground gives them peculiar aptitude for this warfare and peculiar immunity from punishment. A single pony will bear and drag the lodge poles of a tepee, and the squaws will not only relieve the warriors of all menial details, but with the old men and boys are no despicable protectors of a village when the fighting men are in pursuit of game or scalps.

Thus Indian fighting is no parade of ceremony specifically described in regulations, nor an issue between fair and generous opponents. It is at all times destruction for the white man to fail, and his exposures, his perils, and even his successes, so much less heralded and estimated than in more artificial war with those of his own race, only bring him the personal consciousness of duty done to balance wasting years, loss of social life, and a bare support. With all this, and the sometimes recurring feeling of bitterness prompting the desire to exterminate his foe and thereby visit upon him some of the horrid scenes he has passed through, there comes the inevitable sentiment of pity, and even of sympathy with the bold warrior in his great struggle; and in a dash over the plains, or breathing the pure air of the mountains, the sense of freedom and independence brings such contrast with the machinery and formalities of much that is called civilized life, that it seems but natural that the red man in his pride and strength should bear aloft the spear-point, and with new resolve fight the way through to his final home in the spirit land.

Chapter 22

POPULAR opinion has regarded the Indian bow and arrow as something primitive and well enough for the pursuit of game, but quite useless in a contest with the white man. This idea would be excellent if the Indian warriors would calmly march up in line of battle and risk their masses so armed against others armed with the rifle. But the Indian comes as the hornet comes, in clouds or singly, yet never trying to sting until his ascendency is assured and his own exposure is slight.

At fifty yards a well-shapen, iron-pointed arrow is dangerous and very sure. A handful drawn from the quiver and discharged successively will make a more rapid fire than that of the revolver, and at very short range will farther penetrate a piece of plank or timber than the ball of an ordinary Colt's navy pistol.[37]

[37] Although the Plains warrior lacked the white man's power of organization and the latter's persistence in waging war, until the introduction of the revolver and the breech loading rifle the bow and arrow warrior was

The arrow-head varies in length and shape, and the shaft itself slightly changes, according to the tastes of different bands or tribes; and yet so constantly are arrows exchanged in gambling or barter that the character of the arrow used does not invariably determine the tribe engaged. Such were many of the arrows taken from the bodies of Captains Fetterman, Brown, Lieutenant Grummond, and others after the massacre of December, 1866. All the peculiarities there

at least a fair match for his musket-equipped white antagonist. Even after the revolver became commonplace, veteran observers testify that the Indian armed with bow and lance was still a formidable antagonist. On this point Captain Ware writes: "The Indians were all well armed, and in one sense better armed than our soldiers. They had firearms and quivers full of arrows. A bow and arrow is a much more effective weapon than a revolver in the hands of an Indian. While a revolver could shoot six times quickly, as then made, it could not be reloaded on horseback on a run with somebody pursuing. But the Indian could shoot six arrows that were as good as six shots from a revolver at close range and then he could shoot twenty-four more in rapid succession. And so, when a soldier had shot out all his cartridges he was a prey to the Indian with a bow and arrow who followed him. In addition to this, the Indians carried lances, which they used to good purpose. Our boys [cavalry] had sabers. An Indian could not hit a soldier with a lance if the soldier had a saber, nor could a soldier saber an Indian if the Indian had a lance." *The Indian War of 1864,* 452.

found have been seen in the quivers of the
Kittekehas, Chowees, Petropowetaws, and
other Pawnees, all of whom are friendly, and
some of whom are now, as in the winter of
1865–66, in the employ of the United States.
The head is often barbed, but not generally,
and is from two to three and a half inches in
length, made of iron, and ground to a double
edge. The shaft, which is about twenty-five
inches in length, is winged by three feathers
of the eagle, sage-hen, or wild-goose, and
from the sinew wrapping of the head to that
which binds the feathers is deeply marked
by three grooves or blood-seams, so that
when the flesh of man or beast closes about
the shaft, these seams act as conduits and
gradually bleed the victim to death. These
grooves are with some Indians straight, and
with others are zigzag or winding from midway down to the feathers.

The bows of Oglala and Brulè Sioux, Arapahoes, Cheyennes, and most of the Indians
east of the Rocky Mountains, are from
thirty-two to forty inches long, of great
elasticity and tension, so that they easily
drive an arrow through a two-inch plank,
and even through a man or buffalo.

The hatchet is generally that which is furnished by Indian agents or traders, often
having the head and handle hollow and con-

nected for use as a pipe; and, when possible, the handle itself is profusely studded with brass nails such as once distinguished parlor sofas and chairs.

Rifles, both English and American, abound. The Hawkins is a favorite, carrying what is called the trade ball, and requiring a patch; but many of the old guides, trappers, and half-breeds still cling to their use as in the days of Pathfinder and other heroes of Cooper.

The quiver and bow-case are made of deerskin, bearskin, otter and other hides, or furs; and the armament of Hawkeye, which now hangs before the writer, is elaborate with tassels and pendants from well-dressed beaver.

The shield is worn by many of the leading braves, and is formed of several thicknesses of hide fastened through and through about the edge with sinew, and studded with brass nails, or ornamented with silver and other bright metal.

The spear varies from five and a half to seven feet in length, having a head nearly eighteen inches long, with a small pennon; and the heel of the shaft is balanced with eagle feathers, while others are caught along the shaft, giving steadiness to the flight, and suiting the diversified tastes of the owner.

The right and left hair of the warrior or brave is brought before the ear, braided or twisted, and wrapped with strings or ribbons, and falling upon the breast; while a third braid, falling behind and below the scalp-lock or tuft, often is covered with a succession of silver medallions hammered from coin, gradually diminishing in size from four inches to one inch as the series approaches the ground.

Earrings, necklaces, bracelets, and armlets are of brass, beads, bears' claws, or silver, but more generally of beautiful combinations of shells from the Pacific, seventy-five of which have been the price of a pony, and show the close relations of trade maintained between the tribes of the opposite slopes of the Rocky Mountains.

Moccasins, leggings, breech-cloth, and a buffalo robe belted about the waist, leaving the breast bare, is the sole dress of the majority. Others have jackets more or less fancifully decorated with small bullet buttons, and every article of dress that an American soldier uses is at once assumed when its possession is acquired. Trousers are, however, cut off at the hip, as their own style of protection is habitually preferred. Gifts of clothing are quickly put on; and a present of gentlemen's underclothes once given to a Pawnee was so quickly substituted for his original garments as barely to allow escape from the room during the process.

The women vary little in costume except in a wrapping something like a petticoat or skirt, but wear less paint. The hair-parting is, however, invariably painted vermilion when visiting or in full dress, and cheeks, chin, and arms have their share of brilliant tints. Warriors, squaws, and children alike use the bow and arrow, but the women are peculiarly apt with knife and hatchet. The youngsters have a javelin exercise which is admirably fitted to prepare them for their future life. A small hoop is held by the thumb and forefinger of the right hand, while within the hand is the spear. The hoop is thrown forward on the ground, and the javelin is sent after and through the ring with great dexterity and success. This, with the cast of the hatchet and play of the knife, takes the place of the white boy's baseball or marbles; and the blunt-headed arrow brings down birds and small game that would be spoiled by the keener shaft.

The revolver is becoming quite common, and is used with more dexterity and skill than is the rifle. The following instance will illustrate a remarkable failure in rifle firing. Soon after Captain Fetterman arrived, he rode to the Pinery with Lieutenant Bisbee, Captain Ten Eyck, and one or two other officers who had just arrived, to see the locality. They descended to Pine Island just after the last timber-wagon had come out on the road, and in advance of their escort. They were received by a volley of from fifteen to twenty rifle shots, which were fired from a rest upon a fallen tree, at a distance of only fifty paces, as actually measured, without injury to anybody. A second volley equally failed to touch a man. A little bugle-boy brought word to the garrison that all were killed, for he saw the Indians as they fired and the officers as they disappeared. They were compelled to skirmish down the island before they could extricate themselves from the dilemma. A supporting party went out, but met them returning, and thus relieved the anxiety of the garrison.

The Indians not only use mirrors and flags for signal purposes, but many carry with them good field and spy-glasses, some of English styles, procured from Canada, and others are supplied by traders on the frontier.

The domestic life of the Indian, with the barbarity of the sun-dance and the filth of his home, have often been described; but the plenitude of furs in the land of Absaraka have furnished peculiar facilities for adornment and somewhat better wardrobes than are usual nearer the Lower Missouri and Mississippi waters. Their tepee is the model from which the Sibley tent was derived, and will accommodate several families; but nothing else on the face of the earth will furnish a more curious medley of contents than does a tepee where two or three families, of all ages and sizes, with all their worldly goods and hopes are huddled, piled, and crammed about its fire, and where the fitful wind and lazy squaws are combined in the effort to smoke buffalo tongues, strips of meat, and *Injun* all together. The picture is complete, by way of contrast, if a kettle of boiling water over the fire has received a fat dog just after his throat felt the knife, and a white officer, on a pile of furs, is doing his best to show how gracefully he can endure the honors and dinner specially designed for his presence. All this, too, while other officers and ladies are cheerfully waiting outside in the glad consciousness of escape from the hospitality of a chief.

Bells, triangles, and common horns have found their way among these Indians, and they eagerly adopt from the white man whatever makes noise or show.

Chapter 23

FORT PHILIP KEARNEY, December 6th, 1866. I hardly know how to take up my sadly interrupted journal. This day, with its bright morning, brought its sweet promise of rest from Indian alarms, and throughout the garrison all work was pushed with vigor; but the evening adds another sad chapter to the history of our frontier life.

The garrison waited anxiously until nearly nine o'clock before the distant bugle-note indicated the return of parties which, since nine in the morning, have been in pursuit of Indians. It seems hardly possible that poor Bingham, the gentle, manly, and soldierly young officer, who has already won the esteem of everybody, has already, so soon after his arrival, fallen a victim to his ardor and the craft of our foes. It seems that such a disaster has been necessary to check the natural impulse of every one who comes here to chase Indians, regardless of number or rules. Mr. Grummond and Mr. Wands have given me the whole history, and it is of God's mercy that any one escaped. Captain Fetterman has been in, and says he has learned a lesson, and that this Indian war has become a hand-to-hand fight, requiring the utmost caution, and he wants no more such risks.

When the Indians attacked the wood train in the morning, Captain Fetterman was sent with mounted infantry and a part of Lieutenant Bingham's cavalry to drive the Indians over Lodge Trail Ridge, while the Colonel, with Lieutenant Grummond and about twenty-five or thirty mounted men, crossed Big Piney to intercept the party chased by Captain Fetterman. Nearly two hundred Indians were in front of Captain Fetterman, hotly engaging his party, when fifteen of the cavalry, with Lieutenant Bingham, left him, for some reason unknown to everybody. The Colonel's party pushed for the scene of action, and met the cavalry dismounted on one of the forks of Peno, but without Mr. Bingham. It seems that he had dashed westward after he saw the Colonel's party galloping down the hills, and Mr. Grummond, by some sudden impulse, was led to leave his own party and join Mr. Bingham, both disappearing suddenly and nearly alone.

The Colonel's party followed down the valley, according to original plan, until the opening below showed a large force of Indians beyond, and fast gathering on the flanks. Only seven men and a bugle-boy turned the point with him, and Indians were constantly circling around to draw their fire. Private McGuire's horse went down with him, as he gratefully tells his story, and an Indian was crawling along to scalp him, when the party stopped for him and he was lifted up. The recall was sounded, and Corporal Baker hearing it rode over a hill from the north, reporting that Lieutenant Bingham had certainly gone beyond the second hill, though just then there were at least eighty Indians in sight before that hill. Soon after Captain Fetterman came up, having crossed over to the other party after the defection of the cavalry, and a movement was made at once for the rescue of Lieutenant Bingham. Lieutenant Wands, who had superseded Captain Brown as regimental quartermaster, was to have started with the Colonel, but being delayed to exchange his horse, by mistake joined the other party. He had been grazed by a ball, and probably his coolness and his Henry rifle saved that detachment after Lieutenant Bingham left it, as the others fired revolvers, even at several hundred yards, and Lieutenant Bingham threw his away.

The party rode but a few rods on the hill when suddenly a shout was heard: "For God's sake, come down quick," and through a gulch where the road was visible seven Indians were seen with their spear-heads close upon the backs of four of our men, one of whom was Lieutenant Grummond.

Mr. Wands thinks, from the formation of the ground, that had they passed that ravine a moment sooner or later, they would have seen nothing of Mr. Grummond's party until they should have found their bodies on return.

A few moments later the body of Lieutenant Bingham was found and that of Sergeant Bowers, who was still living, though his skull was cleft through with a hatchet. He had killed three Indians with his revolver before he was overpowered. Private Donovan, always so brave, was with the party. They had been surrounded by thirty Indians while Lieutenants Grummond and Bingham were pursuing a dismounted Indian and cutting at him with sabers.

An ambulance was sent for, and Captain Arnold went out with forty men to reinforce the party. The remains of Lieutenant Bingham are in hospital, to be cared for and prepared for burial.

December 9th, 1866. Lieutenant Bingham and Sergeant Bowers were buried today.

Lieutenant Grummond conducted the Masonic services, assisted by Mr. Weston, Mr. Saunders, Mr. Beckwourth and others, while Chaplain White conducted the religious portion.

Thus our cemetery fills up with only the victims of violence! Everything in nature is so beautiful, and the climate is so restoring and healthful, that one could look upon such frontier life with something like complacency were it not for these savages, or even if the long and anxiously expected reinforcements could be seen or heard from. Sometimes it seems as if nobody cared if we had help or not.

Sergeant Bowers was such a favorite with Captain Brown that he placed his own corps-badge upon the breast of the remains; and the men feel especially vindictive and anxious for revenge, as Bowers had so often led the hay parties and successfully skirmished in defense of their work.

The officers feel more than ever the necessity of completing all necessary work and preparing for winter, and many believe that we may shortly expect, as the Crows indicated, the return of Indians in still larger force, to try and cut off work and supplies, if they do not dare to come near the fort and attempt its capture by surprise.

After the funeral, Lieutenant Grummond came in to speak of the services at the grave, which were very impressive, and again expressed his gratitude for his preservation. The lesson will not be lost, and shows what madness it is to follow these Indians very far with insufficient force, and what great peril may come to the post and whole line of road by rash impulses and disregard of the special work that presses so hard.

We think now that we shall not soon hear from Fort C. F. Smith, as Lieutenant Bingham had just returned from that post, having an escort of twenty-five men; and Brevet Lieutenant-Colonel Kinney, who has just made us a week's visit, thinks it unsafe to undertake the trip with less than an escort of fifty good men.

Our mail is overdue, and no doubt the courier and mail party are detained as guides to troops. The sentries understand they are not to fire at messengers coming from the east, and we shall soon have letters and papers after a long intermission. Perhaps the news of our difficulties has by this time been received, and nearly six months of trial may be succeeded by six months of triumph. We learn, as did Crusoe, how much can be done during comparative isolation from a civilized world.

Chapter 24

DECEMBER, 21st, 1866, was to us the saddest day of the year. Though snow covered the mountains, and there was every indication of the return of severe weather, the morning was quite pleasant. Men only wore blouses at their work, and the train, although much later than usual, went to the Pinery with a strong guard, so that the teamsters, choppers, and escort, all armed, numbered not far from ninety men.

The children ran in about 11 o'clock, shouting "Indians!" and the pickets on Pilot Hill could be distinctly seen giving the signal of "many Indians," on the line of the wood road; and news was also furnished that the train was in corral only a short distance from the garrison.

The officers and all the ladies were soon watching for other usual demonstrations, while a detail was being organized to relieve the train.

Brevet Lieutenant-Colonel Fetterman, then walking back and forth before his quarters, near where the Colonel was giving his instructions, asked and obtained permission to go with the detachment.

Lieutenant Grummond, also at his own request, took a part of Company C, 2d United States Cavalry, making the whole force just seventy-eight officers and men. Captain Brown, unknown to the officers of the garrison, as well as citizens Wheatley and Fisher, both experienced frontiersmen and good shots, also joined the party.

It was just at the time when a few more trains of saw-logs would furnish ample lumber material to complete the office building and a fifth company quarters, already well under progress.

The orders were given in front of Lieutenant Grummond's house, next the Colonel's, and those who were present heard them repeated with distinctness and special urgency. Lieutenant Wands was also instructed to repeat them. As if peculiarly impressed with some anticipations of rashness in the movement, the Colonel, just after the command left, went across the parade-ground to a sentry platform, halted the mounted party, and gave additional orders, understood in the garrison, and by those who heard them, to be the substantial repetition of the former.

The health of Mrs. Grummond was such that Lieutenant Wands and other friends urged him, for his family's sake, to be prudent, and avoid all rash movements and any pursuit that would draw them over Lodge Trail Ridge, and to report to Brevet Lieutenant-Colonel Fetterman the orders he had received. These orders were, in so many words, "to relieve the train, and under no circumstances to cross the ridge." Everybody knew why special emphasis was given to these orders.

Only two days before, Brevet Major Powell had been sent out to relieve a train, and obeyed his orders literally, although, as he afterward said, he was sorely tempted to pursue, but became afterward convinced that certain destruction would have been the result. Major Powell was in fact assigned to command the relieving party on the 21st; but when Brevet Lieutenant-Colonel Fetterman stepped forward and claimed it by seniority of rank, he was permitted to go and received his instructions.

The day before, and succeeding that on which Major Powell had reported several hundred Indians present, the Colonel himself took charge of trains to the Pinery, spending the day in building a bridge over the creek and superintending the chopping parties and guard detail. All the indications were that the numerous Indian villages on

Tongue River would lose no chance to do mischief, and the garrison was insufficiently supplied with arms, even of old styles, for the men actually at the post. Before Captain Fetterman left, a few Indian pickets were seen on Lodge Trail Ridge, and a few were below the fort at the road crossing. Two or three case shot, dropped near them, dismounted one and brought nearly thirty out of the brush. These at once disappeared. After the detachment had been gone a short time, finding that Captain Fetterman had left without a surgeon, the Colonel sent Dr. Hines, with one of his own orderlies, to join the train and report to Captain Fetterman; Doctor Hines started, but soon returned with the news that the train had safely pursued its route to the woods; that Captain Fetterman was on the ridge to the north, out of view, and that there were so many Indians in sight that he could not join the party. It was about noon, and a man rushed in to say that firing was renewed. Every shot could be heard, and there was little doubt that a desperate fight was going on in the valley of Peno Creek beyond the ridge. The presence of Lieutenant Grummond with the party gave us new anxiety, and many heartfelt prayers were offered that he might return in safety. The Colonel was on the "lookout," on headquarters building, and gave his orders before coming down.

It seemed long, but was hardly twelve minutes before Captain Ten Eyck, Lieutenant Matson, Dr. Hines, and Dr. Ould, with a relieving party, were moving, on the run, for the scene of action. We had all watched Captain Fetterman until the curve of Sullivant Hills shut him off, and then he was on the southern slope of the ridge, apparently intending to cut off the retreat of the Indians from the train. Wagons and ambulances were hurried up; the whole garrison was on the alert; extra ammunition for both parties was started, and even the prisoners were put on duty to give the guard and all available men their perfect freedom for whatever might transpire Couriers were sent to the woods to bring back the train and its guard, to secure its support, as well as from the fear that the diversion of Captain Fetterman from his orders might still involve its destruction; and shortly Captain Arnold came to report that the whole force of armed men left at the post, including guard and everything, was but one hundred and nineteen men.

Until the wagons galloped out of the gate, we could see a solitary Indian on the highest part of Lodge Trail Ridge; but he soon dis-

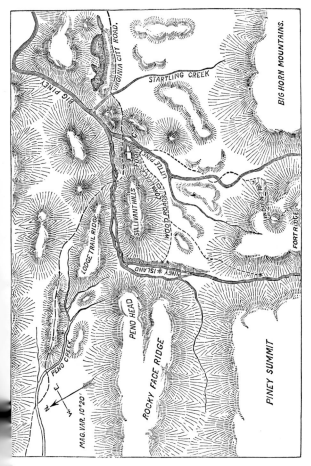

FORT PHILIP KEARNEY AND SURROUNDINGS, FROM ORIGINAL SURVEYS.

*Indicates block-houses in woods for working parties.
......Dotted line, roads to Pine Island and Mountain.
— — Broken line, road to Virginia City, crossing narrow divide
where bodies of Fetterman's command were found.
C, cemetery at foot of Pilot Hill.
☐Corral, on road to woods, where train was attacked December 21st 1866.

appeared. All this time firing was increasing in intensity, and in little more than thirty minutes,—after one or two quick volleys, the rattle of file-firing, and a few scattering shots, —a perfect silence ensued. There were then many anxious hearts, and waiting was perfectly terrible! The movements of Captain Ten Eyck were watched with intensest interest. The pickets could give no information, and a messenger sent upon Sullivant Hills could see neither Indians nor troops. It was just before Captain Ten Eyck's party reached the top of the hill across the Piney, north of the Virginia City road, that all firing ceased. Soon orderly Sample was seen to break away from the command and make for the fort, with his force, on the run. He brought the message that the valleys were full of Indians, and that several hundred were on the road below, yelling and challenging them to come down; but nothing could be seen of Fetterman. As was afterward learned, this party was on the very field of carnage, and doubtless they were completing their robbery and butchery. It was after dark when Captain Ten Eyck returned with forty-nine of the bodies and made the terrible announcement that all were killed.

To a woman whose house and heart received the widow as a sister, and whose office it was to advise her of the facts, the recital of the scenes of that day, even at this late period, is full of pain; but at the time, the Christian fortitude and holy calmness with which Mrs. Grummond looked upward to her Heavenly Father for wisdom and strength, inspired all with something of her same patience to know the worst and meet its issues.

The body of Lieutenant Grummond had not been rescued, and there was some faint hope that stragglers might yet come in and break the absolute gloom of the tragedy by some explanatory and redeeming feature.

At last the wood train came in, having seen nothing of Fetterman, nor even having heard the firing, or suspected any additional danger after repulsing their own immediate assailants. Imagination only can suggest how wide-sweeping would have been the massacre had any considerable portion of the hostile bands renewed the attack upon the train after the successful decoy of the others to inevitable destruction.

With the next morning came a meeting of officers, with universal disinclination, generally expressed, to venture a search for the remaining dead. The safety of any small party seemed doubtful, and the post itself might be imperiled by a large draft upon the garrison. But the Colonel had made up his mind, and freely expressed his purpose "not to let the Indians have the conviction that the dead could not be rescued;" and besides this, the very men who had passed through the war without blanching began to form ideas of the numbers and barbarity of the Indians which threatened to take away one-half their real strength. So the Colonel informed Mrs. Grummond that he should go in person, and would bring home her husband. Captain Ten Eyck, Lieutenant Matson, and Dr. Ould went with the party. Long after they left, and they left with the cheerful Godspeed of every woman and soldier of the garrison, on a holy mission, the pickets, which were distributed on the line of march, indicated their progress, and showed that neither the fort nor the detachment could be threatened without such connection of signals as would advise both and secure co-operation whatever might ensue.

Long after dark the wagons and command returned with the remaining dead, slowly passing to the hospital and other buildings made ready for their reception.

Lieutenant Grummond's body was found and eventually accompanied us on our midwinter's march back over the plains.

A careful roll-call of the garrison was had, and the body of every missing man was found. Wheatley and Fisher were discovered near a pile of rocks, surrounded by expended cartridges, proving that their Henry rifles had done good service. All the bodies lay along or near a narrow divide over which the road ran, and to which no doubt the assailed party had retreated when overwhelming numbers bore down upon them. Captains Fetterman and Brown were at the point nearest the fort, each with a revolver shot in the left temple, and so scorched with powder as to leave no doubt that they shot each other when hope had fled. So ended lives that were full of pride and confidence in the morning. Captain Brown's repeated dashes, and especially his success on the 23d of September, had inspired him with perfectly reckless daring in pursuit of Indians; and only the night before the massacre he made a call, with spurs fastened in the button-holes of his coat, leggings wrapped, and two revolvers accessible, declaring, by way of explanation, that he was ready by day and night, and must have one scalp before leaving for Laramie, to which place he had been ordered. He had inspired Captain Fetterman, who had been but a short time in the country, and already had great contempt for our adversaries, with the same mad determination to chase whenever they could, regardless of numbers; and together they planned an expedition of a week's trip to Tongue River Valley, with a mixed party of ninety citizens and soldiers, to destroy the Indian villages and clear out all enemies. Disapproval of the plan did not change their belief in its feasibility and wisdom; but here were eighty-one officers and men, and among them the veterans of a long war, utterly destroyed in their hands, only six or seven miles on the route to that same Tongue River Valley.

This massacre proved the value and integrity of Major Bridger and his statements, and no less showed the wisdom of a settled policy not to precipitate or undertake a general war while there was but a handful of men at the post; and the army had not yet received such increase as could promise any considerable support.

A kind Providence spared many, and the line of road opened in the summer of 1866 was maintained. Other regiments have strengthened the garrisons, and a year of changes finds the Indians still numerous and unpunished, but with the line still maintained; while the fruits of the labor of 1866 are yet to be valued when that country shall be occupied and sufficiently understood. If the line be abandoned by its garrisons, as is probable, to give better security for the Union Pacific Railroad, and if its choice hunting-grounds be given to the Indians, who seem to have a right to them at present, it cannot be doubted that the work done will have its value, and eastern Montana will ultimately perfect its communications with the Missouri through the field of so much struggle and duty.

Chapter 25

THE bodies of the dead were first deposited in the spare ward of the hospital, two hospital tents, and a double cabin. Details from each company assisted in their care and recognition. Many gave their best uniforms, decently to clothe their comrades, and the noblest traits of the soldier were touchingly developed as they carefully handled the mutilated fragments, drew out or cut off the arrows, and decently composed all for the burial.

A long line of pine cases, duly numbered, was arranged by companies along the officers' street, near the hospital, and as each body was placed in its plain receptacle, the number and name was taken, for the future reference of friends.

The detail to dig a grave for this great entombment was well armed, and accompanied by a guard; but so intense was the cold that constant relays were required, and the interment was not achieved until Wednesday after the fight.

Over the great pit, fifty feet long and seven feet deep, a mound was raised, and the dead were buried with a sad and solemn stillness that will long leave its memory with those who had souls to estimate the circumstances and lessons of that dire calamity.

As if Nature herself were shocked by the enormity of the Indian torture there inflicted, and would still the passions of all, or forbid their immediate indulgence, it so happened that from the very night of December 21st the winter became unmitigated in its severity, requiring guards to be changed at least half hourly, preventing out-of-door inspections of the guard, and driving officers, ladies, and men to beaver, buffalo, or wolf skins for protection from the cold.

The relief, as they hastened to their regular distribution, presented no bad idea of Lapland or Siberian life. The tastes, workmanship, and capital of the wearers were variously illustrated in their personal wardrobes. A uniform cap being useless and hardly endurable, even with coat-cape fastened, hood-like, over the head, the soldiers had permission to suit themselves in respect of substantial comfort. Mittens that ended at the shoulder; buffalo boots and leggings nearly to the thigh; hats as tall as a Poland-er's, with bushy wolf tails pendant; and tippets, comforts, coats, and vests of skins made an odd style of uniform under the existing Regulations for the better Government of the Army of the United States. There were, indeed, times when the smallest possible number of men were allowed to be exposed, and only while the corporal could return to the guard-house and fresh relief might promptly follow up the same routine of constant change. Some were frosted in crossing the parade, some on their sentry platforms; and guard duty with keeping warm were the principal work of all who had no part in hauling water, cutting wood, the care of stock, or the issue of supplies.

The holidays were sad as they were cold. Lights were burned in all quarters, and one non-commissioned officer was always on duty in each building, so that in case of alarm there could not be an instant's delay in the use of the whole command. Each company knew its place and the distribution of the loop-holes; the gunners slept in tents near their guns, and all things were ripe for the destruction of assailants should any venture to attack.

The constant and drifting snow-storms soon so lifted their crests by the west flank of the stockade that officers walked over its trunks, and when a trench ten feet wide was cleared, the next snow or wind would fill it, as only snow can snow and winds can blow in that suburb of Cloud Peak, the home of perpetual snow.

The men themselves, who, at the October muster, looked forward to the holidays and December muster with glad anticipations, forbore all demonstrations usual to such a period, and sensibly felt the weight of the great loss incurred.

Of the sergeants who had distinguished themselves in the previous war, or had actively operated in the labors of 1866, nearly all of the most prominent had fallen: Lange, a martinet, trim, upright, and soldierly; Bissell, calm, mature, and carrying into his profession the sturdy habits of business which had marked his life in Chicago before a hasty indiscretion impelled him to the army; Smith, the pride of the mounted infantry; Morgan, and many others, deserve an enduring monument over their last resting-place no less than heroes of more exalted stations from more memorable battle-fields.

The whole garrison shared the gloom. Charades, tableaus, Shakspearian readings, the usual muster evening levee at the Colonel's, and all the social reunions which had been anticipated as bringing something pleasant, and in the similitude of civilized life, were dropped as unseasonable and almost unholy. Present and exacting duty admitted no dalliance with pleasures that were at other times rational and refreshing; and a calm, sedate, but genial sympathy brought most to a closer fraternity, almost confirming the sacred proverb, "That it is better to go to the house of mourning than to the house of feasting."

But no calm review, no wealth of language can bring before the minds of strangers to those scenes any conception of the realities experienced; neither would a literal catalogue of mutilations and outrages upon the persons of the fallen bring within the range of any imagination the capacity to present them as they were to the understanding of others. The aggregate of wrongs to single individuals would sum up the shocking features of many battle-fields; and the sum of all inflicted upon the entire party can have no precedent by which to estimate their horrors.

Nor was the abandonment of the proper recreation of the holidays the sole result.

Plans had been made looking to a short winter expedition, under the advice of General Cooke, that "three hundred infantry, with much suffering, could perhaps do more in winter than three thousand cavalry in summer." The exact method of doing this had not been settled upon, it is believed, though much talked of in social circles, where the ladies had the privilege of listening; and it was known that the Colonel was determined, as soon as reinforced, to make such reconnoissances and outside movements as would test its practicability without risk to the post; but the destruction of Fetterman's command within a few miles of the post engendered doubts, which were freely expressed by the officers, whether the force that could be made available, even after a successful march and surprise, could entirely or signally destroy the villages of Red Cloud, with his warriors, his kniving squaws, and shooting papooses. Underlying these facts was the general congratulation that a successful maintenance of the post until spring should reopen the road to travel, would be a practical assurance to the Indian of the ultimate extinction of his hunting-grounds and the end of his supremacy in Absaraka. Others suggested that perhaps Red Cloud had concluded to keep himself vigorously awake, and try the surprise party himself, or so occupy himself as to consolidate all hostile bands into some comprehensive system of hostility to the post and the white man generally.

Besides this, it was a matter of notoriety and fact that, while the officers were anxious for repeating arms or breech-loaders, only old styles of rifles were on the way, and also that ammunition, not more than four or five months previously started from Leavenworth, was resting itself at some place not disclosed to the white warriors of Absaraka.[38] Then the reinforcements had not come; and as the affair of the 21st, with the details of the same, had actually engrossed the time

---

[38] Although the Spencer repeating rifle had been adopted by the army at the beginning of the Civil War, that conflict had been chiefly fought without its aid. Down to the summer of 1866 hardly more than 100,000 Spencers in all had been purchased by the army. Colonel Carrington had managed to equip the regimental band with Spencers before leaving Fort Kearney, but his subsequent appeals for the weapon had been ignored or overruled. After his removal from the command, a supply of Spencers arrived at the fort, to be used with deadly effect upon Red Cloud's warriors in the Wagon Box fight of August 2, 1867. The stupid refusal to supply Colonel Carrington with them may well have determined the issue of Fetterman's fight. As for ammunition, the garrison of Fort C. F. Smith was at one time reduced to 10 rounds per man, and at Fort Philip Kearney there were but 45 rounds; this in a state of active war in the heart of the hostile country, when General Cooke was ordering an expedition against the enemy in their strongholds.

and energies of the whole garrison, the entire plan of destroying the Indians of the Northwest while the mercury was motionless and the snow was all in motion was temporarily dropped.

True it was that the spirit which drove Fetterman to hasty disobedience and certain destruction, viz., a desire to settle accounts for some of the outrages perpetrated during our six months' sojourn, had somewhat decidedly inspired all the ladies, as well as the officers and men, with a longing to do something explosive and brilliant; but the ladies had so often been told not to discuss military matters, and the tide of events having unfavorably settled the prospect of our husbands' gaining glory by miraculous adventures with Red Cloud, there was a quiet acquiescence in the condition of self-defense.

A stranger might have almost thought we were besieged. The commanders of Forts C. F. Smith and Reno so construed their condition; and the constant watchfulness, strict discipline, and ever-present preparation for all contingencies savored not a little of the same essence, as we passed the holidays of 1866–67 at Fort Philip Kearney, Absaraka.

Chapter 26

HAS any military event in history, whether sacred or profane, immediately after its occurrence called forth more elaborate and general explanation, and involved more contradictory and absurd criticism, all "founded upon fact," yet ignorant of that valuable article, than the massacre near Fort Philip Kearney, December 21st, 1866?

Of course the public could not be expected to know, nor the press to announce, that the only means of communication between that post and Fort Laramie, the nearest mail and telegraph station, was through two hundred and thirty-five miles of hostile country and through couriers sent by the post commander himself.

Neither could the great American people wait for information; but they must know exactly and fully all the particulars for perusal while coffee was cooling at the next morning's breakfast table.

It was, of course, to be expected that the illustrated papers should act promptly and perspicuously, with all the embellishment and accuracy which wood engraving affords, and do this so truly to life that it would be at once recognized by all actors in its scenes; and it was equally certain and necessary that a "special artist," some "actual observer," or a "special correspondent," should furnish the editor's sanctum with the right material for his use in advance of the mails. There was certainly no difficulty as to historical precedents or illustrations of Indian warfare from which to combine a proper sketch, and accordingly the work was begun, even before the couriers had reached Laramie with details of the transaction itself.

As there was no one to contradict, and no one who knew the truth, a large margin was left for the play of the fancy, and the imagination was drawn upon with great freedom and success. The people were of course greatly shocked by the tragedy, and were certain that somebody was terribly to blame. The Indians were supposed to be so quiet and peaceful that nobody asked whether the massacre was one of a series; but statesmen as well as editors, those who claimed to know all about Indian affairs and those who never saw a live Indian outside of a city show, de-vised theory upon theory, to the great delight of their own complacent souls and with all the wonderful wisdom of absolute ignorance.

It could not be expected, in the urgent demand for particulars, that truth and justice would be the essential features of the whole; and the sensation had to be used just at the time, or somebody's paper or somebody's friend would suppose that somebody else, who was regularly compensated to cater to the popular passion for the startling and novel, was ignorant of that of which he knew nothing. So it happened that numberless journals obtained, at last, the true version of that sad affair.

Not to name those papers and thus arouse invidious distinctions where so many showed brilliant powers of imagination, a few choice selections will do honor to them all and injustice to none.

Albany, a city set on a hill, Argus-eyed and sagacious, had a corresponding pre-eminence in the way of invention and preciseness of detail. It portrayed, as "from reliable information," the fearful climax, "when the last band of survivors were driven to the gates of the fort, knocking and screaming in vain for admission; when the last cartridge from revolver, carbine, and rifle was expended;

when the sabers and butts of muskets were broken; and when, leaning against the gates, weary and bleeding and all resistance fruit-less, all fell in one heap of mangled human-ity, unsupported and uncared for." This sketch closed its recital with the startling announcement that the commanding officer, whom it doomed to future obloquy, with two full companies, was looking on, afraid either to fire or open the gates lest the garrison within should be massacred by the infuriated savages and the post should be sacked!

Block-houses, of course, reserved their fire! Loop-holes shone with the glaring eyes of frightened soldiery, but not with the gleaming rifle! Four howitzers, which could have swept the slope and bottom land, were silent and innocent of harm to anybody!

And yet, as a matter of fact, the fight was not within sight of the fort; and its capacity for defense or the support of any party near by was superior to the whole force of Indians in Tongue River Valley.

One illustrated paper had a report "from the only eye-witness of the massacre." This person was said "to have been cut off from his party by Indians, and from a thicket only two hundred and fifty yards distant from the fight he saw the repeated charges of the cavalry, the dashing adventures of officers and men, and the last shot discharged by the last survivor through his own brain."

And yet, as a matter of fact, the very person accredited with this narrow escape and these providential aids to a close observation, did not see a shot fired by the party, or any part of the conflict; but went out with Captain Ten Eyck's relieving party, after failing to find Fetterman's party when firing was heard, and saw what Captain Ten Eyck saw of the fight, and that was—nothing.

A second illustrated paper had an engraving of the fight, and indicated in advance what should be done with the post commander. Others were hardly outdone by this. All had a convenient scapegoat for the whole affair. The gallantry and prowess of some were praised, while dereliction and cowardice were branded upon others.

Even the metropolitan papers of New York and Washington could not possibly wait, but discharged their shafts, regardless of character or truth. Thus pamphlets, letters, editorials, and pictures expressed their theories or positive statements; so that beyond the opinion of Lieutenant-General Sherman accompanying a soldier's letter, published at Washington in a pamphlet, with other documents sent to Congress upon the massacre, and a critique of the Cincinnati *Gazette* upon the pamphlet itself (author unknown to us), no correct account of the tragedy has ever gained access to the people at large.

To those who were present under the shadow of such a calamity, it seemed harsh and brutal that, more than two thousand miles away, there should be such quick and morbid ambition to criticise and abuse; and the ladies were not a whit behind the officers and men in thoroughly wishing that delegations from the eastern cities could spend some days in that country to try a few dashes after Indians, and take a turn at guard or picket duty, and live a time where newspapers are sometimes two months in coming, where bacon takes the place of seafood, and desiccated materials put on the name and function of vegetables.

We had become perfectly accustomed and hardened to correspondents from the Plains, whose warped or false representations discredited every good thing. Thus, for instance, three papers among those of the largest circulation in the country declared that the commanding officer was constantly giving powder to his enemies, and that ladies threw packages of sugar and coffee over the stockade to the squaws. A tender-hearted sympathetic, but temporary attaché of the Indian Bureau knew just how the massacre occurred—viz., that the poor, hungry, starv-

ing women of the Sioux had come to beg, and
their husbands had come to ask a little powder for hunting and to have an order re-
voked as to gifts of arms to Indians, and,
being fired upon, they became desperate and
took immediate vengeance. This critic,
whose narration had its place on the tables
of members of Congress, said a wood train
could not have more than six men with it,
and could not possibly have been attacked
by three hundred Indians. He did not know
how slowly six men would have built a post;
nor that the timber trains sometimes numbered ninety or more wagons, each drawn by
six mules; that each team required a driver;
that the work required choppers and loaders
and a guard to protect them; and that six
men could not do this.

Some supposed that the whole was caused
by ignorance of the Indian tricks and habits,
and of the surrounding country, notwithstanding the fact that some of the officers
not involved in the skirmish had spent the
summer and fall in just such warfare and in
reconnoissance of the country for miles in all
directions.

Every conceivable hypothesis but the correct one was adopted, and everybody,
without seeming to think that possibly
the authorities of the fort itself knew

something of the affair, and were old enough to make some official report of the matter.

One said that the soldiers abused the squaws and the women of the country, although, except at the July meeting with the Cheyennes and the short stay of French Pete's rescued wife, there was never a squaw at the fort.

At least three disappointed aspirants for civil berths became newspaper correspondents and traducers; but the sting of their falsehoods was innocuous, as their inducement was understood.

One and all gloried in abuse; and no wonder is it that the hard labor of 1866, its skirmishes and exposures, its chases and its losses, were never told, lest credit should inure to the pioneer expedition to Absaraka.

The information supplied, and that manufactured, alike furnished some amusement to the garrison; but, for the sake of many friends who were anxious to learn the truth, it would have been grateful to the feelings had the truth been made known, to accompany the false as its antidote. At last the United States Senate called for the report of the commanding officer, at the April session, 1866, and again at the July session; and when it appears, some additional light may be furnished by which to confirm or disprove this comedy of errors.

Chapter 27

NEW YEAR'S DAY, 1867, was without its anticipated festivities. All honor to the 27th Infantry, until then the 2d Battalion of the 18th Infantry, and which on the last day of December severed its relations with the old regiment, that during the holiday week they accepted their sad lesson, and with manly self-denial refrained from those indulgences which are so common at Christmas and the advent of a New Year.

On New Year's Day the Military Reservation was finally announced, in orders, giving to the burial-place of the victims of that great disaster a memorial character, honorable to the courage of the fallen.

A few days after, Brevet Brigadier-General H. W. Wessels, Lieutenant-Colonel of the 18th, a soldier with laurels and a gentleman without blemish, arrived with two companies of cavalry and four companies of infantry, of which one company was to be left at Fort Reno, his former post.

Orders came to remove headquarters to Fort Caspar, and all preparation was duly made. General Dandy, Chief Quartermaster, with discernment and courtesy, fitted up army wagons for the women and children, and deserves due thanks for our earthly salvation, as that preparation alone secured us a safe deliverance during the trip that ensued.

"After night cometh the morning," and at Crazy Woman's Fork, January 25th, 1867, the order of nature was regularly preserved. We left Fort Philip Kearney at half-past one P.M. of the 23d, just at the hour fixed. Packing had been done, wagons were loaded, houses had been evacuated for new-comers, and although the snow again began its fantastic drifting and plentiful resupply, the march had to be made, and the extinct road could hardly become more distinct, but possibly even worse.

By ten o'clock at night, by dint of shoveling and picking at proper intervals, nearly six miles had been attained, and the train corraled on a commanding summit to wait for the coming moon.

Lieutenant Bowman had been detailed to command the escort of twenty cavalry and forty infantry as far as Fort Reno, and discharged his trust with unwavering diligence and acceptance.

At one o'clock A.M. the bugle sounded, and just at three o'clock our invaluable guide and scout, Captain Bailey, reported that himself and moon were ready. The sky had cleared, the stars were brilliant, and the aurora borealis faintly endeavored to show itself and cheer our onward way.

It is picturesque so to travel. Napoleon, it is reported, traveled over snow, but left his family; and the novelty of the movement of officers, their wives and children, and the usual families of band musicians, with their liberal allowance of future trumpeters, flutists, and drummers, gave this march a distinguishing feature not usually credited to that masterly winter trip of Napoleon to Italy by the way of the Alps. The wheels creaked, the mules made their usual vocal sounds at the early disturbance of their feed, and everybody shrunk into clothing as closely as possible to evade the increasing cold.

The thermometer hanging in our wagon allowed the mercury to do its share of shrinkage, and lingered about thirteen degrees below zero, with great apparent hesitation, if not positive reluctance, at being kept out of the bulb. Stalking in front, leading his pony, stamping through drifts and feeling his way, guide Bailey led off with inordinate self-possession, not to say coolness, and soon after daylight we were once more in camp at Clear Fork. Breakfast was soon over, the mules were fed, and the march proceeded. It was the remark of Captain Arnold that it was "stunning cold," and before twenty-four hours more were passed it became clearly evident that he had the right idea, and that expression will hereafter be to us not a provincialism of doubtful origin, but a simon pure exponent of that style of cold.

Of course for awhile there was a keen watch for Indians, since as they see everything and know everything, it was just possible that they might envy us our horses, mules, and scalps; but the country was covered with buffalo, who did not even pay us the compliment of being scared, and in fact for twenty-five miles they were never out of view. Their quiet labor in the snow, wallowing and trampling for grass, was also a positive assurance, so said Bailey, that they had no red men in company.

So we plowed, dug, and plodded on. Before night we were at Crazy Woman's Fork. That any one of the party left it alive, and made the next march, now seems a wonder. The corral was formed in the grove at the bend of the stream, and wood was abundant after digging it out of the snow, but there a wood fire actually lost one-half its virtue.

As fast as snow melted and rolled from the billets, which were heaped on as high as a man could reach, the same melted snow turned to ice, and each fire was soon girt about by constantly thickening ice. To stand fronted to the flame, then reversed, and to do this constantly that fearfully long night, was the resort of almost everybody. Cooking was out of the question. Hatchets broke our bread, and water was sufficiently warmed to thaw the chunks. Slices were not attempted. Thanks to our little stoves, the ladies essayed the luxury of steeped, not to say hot coffee, and with partial success. None of the special artists who portrayed the massacre accompanied us, but the picture of an entertainment given to Lieutenant Bowman, escort commander, and Captain Arnold, is still before us.

The general train formed a complete circle, with headquarters wagons in the center. By every fire were groups bending forward with outstretched hands to gather a little vital warmth. Hopeless of supper, most of the women and children closed themselves up in their wagons, and from each little stove-pipe the white smoke told all night how hopefully they were struggling to worry it through. Children were crying of cold, and men were multiplying expletives. Drivers left their teams, and began to avow that they never would drive another rod until it was warmer. All at once the Colonel and a party of officers approached our wagon and knocked. The door partly opened, and we know how it must have looked as a tin cup suddenly gleaming by the camp-fire was quickly delivered, and its recipient hastened to a blaze to imbibe its contents while yet unfrozen. Then another and another went out in the same careful way, and the door slammed again. Next, with the same caution, were passed forth bread, with pieces of the last turkey of Fort Philip Kearney, which, having been chopped with the hatchet, had also been softened over the fire, after the coffee had been concocted. As the door opened, we suppose the view must have been about as follows: In the foreground, a lady sitting upon a pile of wood, with feet to the stove, though these were covered with high buffalo boots, her head enveloped in a beaver hood, her form wrapped in linsey-woolsey and buffalo skins, and her hands stirring something like turkey knobs and bread chunks over the stove. In the background, in a perfect nest of wolf skins and beaver, two boys with caps, boots, and coats trimmed with the same material, and pushing themselves as close to that little sheet-iron arrangement as safety and culinary duties would permit; on the right and left a saber, shotgun, rifle, and revolver, with pendant pails and cooking utensils; at the extreme end, a thermometer, worn out and desolate.

The iron itself seemed jealous of doing any radiation whatever, and some dry pine wood which had been brought with us burned out so quickly, and lost so much courage and efficiency by constant replenishing, that it really was not the fault of the stove, for it could not possibly be heated through between times. It never was red hot, and its very top would neither thaw nor toast bread, unless when a kettle let down within had contact with the flame that struggled to do its best.

Lieutenant Wands, with indomitable tact and energy, was everywhere, between the necessary warnings, encouraging drivers, cheering up soldiers, keeping himself alive, and doing good generally. Everybody had some adventure. Mules got mad and broke loose, dashing just where they pleased, as if bound to keep up circulation by constant exercise.

Sometimes a party would be seen coming with a great log, struggling through snow nearly waist deep, and now and then some desperate character would throw himself down, determined to have a sleep if he froze to death. This was of course stopped, and with chattering teeth and aching limbs and benumbed feet, general stamping was resorted to, to keep circulation busy after the manner of the mules.

Mrs. Wands and Mrs. Grummond had the same school of practice in keeping up fires, and little Bobby Wands had the same ambition to burn his buffalo boots as other little boys we know of.

The convenient window in the wagon door, when the frost was scraped off, was a capital place for study of human nature under adverse circumstances; and it is morally certain that any one of those wagons, in the exact condition as then seen, would have been worth to P. T. Barnum the restorative equivalent of his loss in the great fire.[39]

At last the sentry called "one o'clock," and all through camp was repeated, "Good! it's one o'clock!" Some were for having reveille sounded at once; but guide Bailey, who

[39] P. T. Barnum conducted the American Museum in New York City for thirty years before embarking upon his career with the circus in 1871. The Museum was several times burned down, the last time on March 3, 1868. Although unaided by the possession of one of the winter expedition's army wagons, the great showman managed, by clever publicity, to extract profit even from his fires.

had tried the ascent out of the bottom to the summit, eastward, found that no exit could be had until daylight. It was no doubt a lovely place for Indians, if they had been on that bluff, but they were not; and but for the shelter of the hill no living creature could have withstood the exposure.

From one o'clock to three, each hour was called, and at three the thermometer gave out entirely. The mercury settled in the bulb, froze itself stiff, and treated that sheet-iron stove with outrageous contempt.

FORTY BELOW ZERO! and the night dragged its hours so slowly! By four o'clock patience gave out also. Do or die was the impulse of all, and the slow work of getting frozen hands to put on frozen harness began, or rather such a thing was ordered to be done. Whether the teamsters thought the bugle summons was the thawing out of an old call, as once happened in the experience of the celebrated traveler Baron Munchausen, or they were too nearly frozen to appreciate their import, is not certain; but call after call failed to get them from their fires, until a verbal order, concise and to the point, promised all to be left behind, without wagon or rations, that were not ready to start punctually at six.

With the dawn came the report of the sad work of the night. Assistant Surgeon Hines had the fingers of both hands frozen, and they were already quite black; while many teamsters and nearly half of the escort were more or less frozen, some of them requiring amputations as soon as we reached Fort Reno.

With great difficulty, by the assistance of those comparatively uninjured, and the exercise of the positive authority of the officers, the train was at last ready.[40] From the bottom land there was a sharp rise of nearly sixty feet to the bluff, and the first teams that tried it, even after the drifts had been shoveled away, repeatedly fell for want of foothold, and back came loaded wagons, dragging the kicking, tangled mules with them. Details of men took charge of the wheels, whips on either side and ropes ahead gave additional impulse; and in three hours the entire train had successfully passed the first sixteenth of a mile out of twenty-six to be made to Reno.

[40] Colonel Carrington stated that blacksnakes were applied to those who ignored all other appeals. The blacksnake—familiar to the present Editor's boyhood—was an extremely flexible, tapering rawhide whip, ten or twelve feet long, attached to a very short wooden handle and terminating in a cracker. Wielded by an expert drover, it could inflict deadly execution upon the hide of a stubborn bull or other animal, while the cracker could be made to snap like the discharge of a pistol.

Just as the last wagons were buried in a
deep cut, half a mile from the river, the
alarm of "Indians" was given. A messenger
came and reported that the rear was attacked. Teams were put to the gallop, the train
was closed up, half frozen men in the wagons
took their arms, and Lieutenant Wands,
with a mounted party, dashed back to bring
up the rear, and ascertain the facts. All
proved a false alarm; but an hour was lost.

Fortunately the day was still and clear.
The glare of the sun was at times blinding;
but the goggles, which on the Plains are used
both against snow-blindness and dust, enabled all to get along tolerably well. Buffa-
los kept us company until within a few
miles of Reno. Messengers were sent on in
advance, and at dusk we safely passed its
gates and received at the hands of Captain
Proctor, Adjutant Kirtland, and other officers not only quarters, but all creature comforts for the whole party. Such was the
first sixty-five miles march returning from
Absaraka. Such were three days of our
second winter on the plains. If we claim no
special credit for endurance, and have never
questioned the necessity of such a march at
such a season, certainly, like good wives, we
followed wherever led, and we do not envy
any officer's wife, of however long expe-

rience, her claim to have had a harder trip
after such a summer. Perhaps some have.
Ours was ample for us.

It is now like a dream, when it comes to
mind, that nearly one-half of more than fifty
demonstrations of hostile Indians in the
Mountain District were under the very eyes
of the ladies of the garrison and their children. The lesson is not forgotten, as we no
less recall the Mercy that spared us. Nor
does a single sentiment of complaint or re-
flection upon the Indians, the weather, or
anybody else, have its place in our recollec-
tions of the past. It was our impulse and
duty to go, and we went. No regrets are
entertained; but sometimes it seems that we
should have had more enjoyment and quiet
had there been more men along, and that
the Indians would have treated larger numbers with greater respect; and sometimes it
seems very strange that that trip to Fort
Caspar, just then, was such a matter of life
or death to the nation as to make it a question of life or death to us.

Chapter 28

NEARLY three days were spent at Reno changing the infantry escort and providing for those who suffered. Lieutenant Jacobs, son of Dr. Jacobs, an old friend at our birthplace, Danville, Kentucky, was its commander.

Our days' marches were forced, as far as snow would permit, and were—1st, Dry Fork of the Cheyenne; 2d, Wind River; 3d, Brown Springs, four miles east of the South Fork of the Cheyenne; 4th, the North Platte; near mouth of Sage Creek; 5th, Deer Creek Station, burned by Indians in 1865; and 6th, to Caspar. Indians had kept out of sight, and the headquarters of the 18th were again approaching a home. Lieutenant Wands, guide Bailey, and others rode forward to give notice of our speedy arrival; when, all at once, we found our ambulance closed in by others, and upon looking out discovered the whole train on a trot, in column of six wagons front, and thus moving all in mass. The quick passing of an orderly was all that had been noticed, and without the sound of a bugle or other warning we found ourselves preparing for Indians, only six miles from Caspar. A party of red men had passed between the train and those who with Lieutenant Wands had gone in advance, and galloping close up to the telegraph office, had run off the stock of horses just after the officers had dismounted at the fort.

The Colonel, who was riding along a ridge somewhat in advance, recognized a mounted party crossing the Platte to be Indians, closed up the train and moved on; but pursuit was hopeless, as the Indians had seen the escort turn the hill in full view, and were nearly across the Platte three miles distant when discovered.

Soon we were met by Brevet Major Norris, a friend of old times, with his company of the 2d Cavalry, and returned with him to the post, where he had already anticipated our wants. Here also Brevet Major Morris, Captain Freeman and wife, and Lieutenant Carpenter, all old officers of the 18th, competed in their welcomes, with other officers previously unknown, to us all. Here also, to our great delight, we met Mrs. Potter and her husband, the new adjutant of the regiment, who, after long service as acting assistant adjutant-general during the war, and as commandant of the District of Utah, while colonel of the 6th U. S. Volunteers, had been appointed to the 18th Infantry and at once placed on the staff. Mrs. Potter and little Carroll had just arrived from Laramie upon advices of change of headquarters.

The first thing done was to disencumber ourselves of blankets and furs. The next, was to open our eyes as Lieutenant Wands inquired where most would we prefer to go rather than remain at Caspar, the most barren and insignificant post on the plains. The apparent joke as to preference was earnest of a welcome fact; for sure enough, General Augur, upon assuming command at Omaha, had changed the headquarters station to McPherson, and thus we at once began to prepare ourselves to double our track to Sage Creek and extend our winter's march over the path of 1866, and within ninety-seven miles of old Kearney. Orders had miscarried, or the trip to Caspar would have been spared us.

The next day Captain Kellogg of the 18th, with his most estimable and lovely wife, arrived, and the associations of olden times were agreeably renewed.

Good-bys quickly followed, and with Brevet Major Morris of the 18th in charge of the new escort we were again on the way. The second day we reached the North Platte again, where Lieutenant Jacobs, who had now to return to Reno, bade his farewell, leaving pleasant memories of his courtesies as a gentleman and efficiency in charge of the escort.

Before stopping, on the sixth day of February, the Colonel had the misfortune to be accidentally shot while riding rapidly to close up the train, by the discharge of his revolver, which had been badly repaired at Caspar, the ball entering the scarpal space, grazing both femoral artery and sciatic nerve, following the bone around to the outside of the limb, where it lodged. Instead of returning to Caspar, he ordered the train crowded forward to Laramie, and at noon of Saturday, the ninth of February, the corral was formed in the Laramie River bottom near the post.

The whole-hearted Mr. Bullock threw open his house, and, with Surgeon Snell, heaped upon the party that remained for twelve days with the Colonel every comfort and attention that home itself could have furnished. The second day heavy snow fell, and the last of headquarters did not reach Fort McPherson until March 2d, although

Adjutant Potter and Quartermaster Wands, with their families and part of the baggage, were sent a few days in advance. The trip from Laramie was without escort, none being attainable, although there had been an outrage perpetrated but a few days before between the post and Fort Mitchell; still, no danger was apprehended. The ride of fifty-three miles to the latter post was made in one day; and two or three days of rest passed delightfully, as Captain Hughes of the 18th, and Assistant Surgeon Cunningham, nephew of Lieutenant-General Cunningham of the British army, were our excellent and willing entertainers. They had given the same cordial greeting to the advance train, and thus Reno, Caspar, and Mitchell had alike kept up that old army hospitality which was once its pride and is the essential and redeeming feature of its isolated social life.

Scott's Bluffs, Fortification Rocks, Chimney Rock, and Court House Rock, had a different language as they rose before us, cold and snow-clad; but even winter could impart no more gloom to their barren features; and the same cedars peeped through the snow that had dotted the sterile sides and cañons in the heat of summer.

Captain Neill, Dr. Latham, Mr. Adams and wife, and young Janney, of Columbus,

Ohio, were still at Sedgwick, but otherwise few old friends were met. Brevet Lieutenant-Colonel Dodge of the 30th Infantry, which was in camp across the river, and Lieutenant Bennett also called. The sight of a full regiment reminded us how constantly General Wessels and the upper garrisons were watching daily for their arrival, and how long we had lived in the same expectancy.

The Platte was crossed on the ice; but it would hardly have been the fair thing to have passed it without recognition, so our ambulance broke through a few times, and three or four little scares were undergone for old acquaintance sake.

From Fort Sedgwick to Fort McPherson the drifting sands of summer had been overshadowed by the deep and drifting snows of winter; but with Valentine and Baker and Morrow to yield their best for our physical necessities, the journey soon came to an end.

We had been to Absaraka and back again! All phases of life, all eccentricities of climate and temperature, all grades of exposure and danger, and intercourse with all styles of human nature had been experienced or encountered.

Fort McPherson became home for a time. Here were some reminders of old times, as the spring of 1867 brought Indian depredations to the very vicinity. Here, too, were Indian councils, Indian visits, and Indian promises. Here, too, the Special Indian Commission spent a month in seeking interviews with the Oglala and Brulè Sioux of the Republican, and taking the testimony of Colonel Carrington as to the facts concerning the Fetterman Massacre.

Here, too, a court of inquiry met to take testimony, and we had the pleasure of again meeting Captains Haymond and Phisterer, who left Fort Philip Kearney, August 1st, 1866, and had been summoned from Pittsburg and New York as witnesses respecting the affair of December 21st following their departure.

Here, also, were visits from Generals Sherman, Augur, and Custer; and here, also, Spotted Tail, Standing Elk, Swift Bear, Two Strike, Pawnee Killer, The Whistler, Long Bull, The Man that Walks Under the Ground, Joe Smith, Sharp Nose, and The White Antelope had talks, and gave pledges of friendship.

Here, also, the courtesy of Brevet Lieutenant-Colonel Mizner, of the 2d Cavalry, and his wife, and the officers of his command, and the sisterly welcome of Mrs. Potter made our arrival pleasant and our stay delightful, crowning with something like the amenities of old-fashioned times in the States, our return from Absaraka, Home of the Crows.

But changes still occurred! Mr. Wands had been transferred to the 36th Infantry, and with his family soon returned westward again. Lieutenant Brent succeeded him as regimental quartermaster. Colonel Mizner took his turn to visit the Indian country farther west, and his accomplished wife anticipated our own trip eastward a few weeks. As at the outset so at the close of our trip across the Plains and back again, the same kind Providence guided and guarded our footsteps, and more than ever brought home to the soul the sweet assurance of His presence

> Wherever we wander,
> Wherever we roam.

Chapter 29

THE dead of 1866, in the occupation of Absaraka, were those who were worthy. Officers and men alike had done duty well, and the majority had an honorable record before they engaged a new enemy in a new country.

Brevet Lieutenant-Colonel William J. Fetterman, son of Captain George Fetterman, deceased, an old army officer, was born in garrison, and was instinct with the ambition of a soldier.

He was appointed a lieutenant in the 18th United States Infantry in May, 1861, and joined the regimental headquarters almost immediately. In the School of Instruction for officers, organized by the Colonel of the regiment in July, 1861, he was ambitious and proficient, and in his duties as recruiting officer in Ohio realized substantial success, while, no less, commanding esteem by his refinement, gentlemanly manners, and adaptation to social life.

After he accompanied the regiment to the field, and when the changes incident to the war had placed the field officers of the regiment on detached duty, as generals of volunteers, Captain Fetterman commanded the detachment, and earned the reputation of being a brave soldier.

His return to the regiment in November, 1866, had been sought, and no less looked for with glad anticipation, as officers were so few, and his social and professional character alike made him a favorite.

As the senior officer serving with the 2d Battalion, just taking the new style of the 27th Infantry, it was naturally expected that he would take command of it whenever the Colonel should join the 1st Battalion, which was to retain the old number, but had its companies on the lower route.

That he was impatient because Indians were not summarily punished, and permitted this feeling and contempt of the enemy to drive him to hopeless ruin, where a simple deference to the orders and known policy of his commander, and still higher authority would have brought no loss of life whatever, is matter of history; yet, such was the esteem entertained for him by his Colonel and many friends, that as the grave received his remains, and the battle-field evinced the vigor of his desperate defense, no bitter reflections mingle with the necessity of rendering equal justice to the living.

In the prime of manhood and the pride of a noble spirit he reached forth for laurels that were beyond his reach; and with all the support that human energy and quick haste could furnish, the error could not be retrieved, and his brief Indian campaign and life closed together, when he had just reached his new field of labor, inexperienced in its methods and contingencies, and incurring the saddest penalty for neglect of the experience of others.

In life he was a gentleman. In death he was mourned and honored.

Captain Frederick H. Brown enlisted in the 18th Infantry at Columbus, Ohio, was at once appointed a sergeant at regimental headquarters, and then quartermaster sergeant. Among the first appointments from the ranks, under the then existing law requiring the Colonel to fill the vacancies of second lieutenant, Mr. Brown was second. He was almost immediately appointed regimental quartermaster and commissary, as his antecedent experience in the commission business at Toledo had peculiarly fitted him for such duty. This office, in the field and out of it, he filled until promoted captain, late in 1866, when he received orders to join his company at Fort Laramie.

He had become so attached to the country about Fort Philip Kearney, and so enthused by his purpose to take the scalp of Red Cloud, that Indian skirmishing fastened itself upon his nature with the hold of some constitutional disease.

With it all he felt a deep sense of neglect that the flood of brevets which rolled over the regiment omitted his name; and when one officer was brevetted for services in the Atlanta campaign, although, during the whole period, that officer was at the North, and others had honors for similar erroneously designated services, he became impatient, eager, and reckless.

His intimacy in the family of the writer brought forth frequent sketches of his history and disappointments; and while he could cheerfully accept and reason upon the circumstances of the command, and intellectually recognize the impossibility of doing more than was being done to punish the savages, his restless spirit would hardly let him fill up the measure of his necessary duty, so set was his purpose to do some service that would command the recognition of his six years of connection with the 18th Infantry.

On the night before his death, already adverted to, when he called, equipped for im-

mediate duty, and at a time of the evening
when there was no show for service, he was
peculiarly earnest in his regret that he must
leave without Red Cloud's scalp. He asked
for the Colonel, and said he wished they
would hurry up reinforcements. He was
going to have one more fight if he had to
work night and day to finish his papers. He
adverted to the Colonel's refusal to permit
himself and Captain Fetterman to go to
Tongue River Valley on a trip with the
mounted men, and said he knew it was impossible, but he just felt that he could kill
a dozen himself.

Those who knew Captain Brown, or, as
all the officers styled him, "Fred," know how
he overflowed with genial humor, and interested himself in whatever imparted social
life to the march, or garrison life. His relation of an Indian skirmish on the 23d of
September was frequent; and just before his
death he made up its history, which he said
showed one good fight he had with the
rascals.

That his impulses led Brevet Lieutenant-
Colonel Fetterman to disobey orders on the
21st of December, at the sacrifice of the
whole detachment, is not questioned; and
yet we have no heart for blame when the
strength of his friendship, his pride in his

regiment, his disappointment as to honorable mention, and his brave but false estimate of the spirit of the Indian, challenge so much of our regard as memory brings him back to us, as when we parted but a few hours before he left earth's scenes forever. He said he would always keep a shot for himself; and doubtless thereby saved himself from torture.

Lieutenant George W. Grummond, who fell in the same memorable slaughter, had achieved success in the war of the rebellion as captain and field officer of Michigan volunteers, and was understood to have been brevetted brigadier-general of volunteers before he ceased his connection with the Army of the Cumberland. Our narrative has shown how narrow was his escape on the 6th of December; and the sketch of the Fetterman Massacre shows how closely he obeyed his orders to remain with Captain Fetterman. His ambition prompted him to volunteer to accompany that party, and the fact that his remains were found with those of Sergeant Lang and a few others more than a quarter of a mile in advance of the other dead, indicates that he either was covering the retreat or was disabled and killed in a gallant defense. He had a soldier's spirit, and in social relations was genial and already esteemed by all. He alone, of the fallen, left a widow to mourn his loss, and his remains returned with her to Tennessee, where they received their final burial.[41]

[41] Grummond was a resident of Detroit and listed in the Detroit directories as a sailor from 1857 to 1861. Although the definite connection has not been established he was probably a younger brother of Stephen B. Grummond who was born at Marine City in 1834. His father had migrated from New York State to the St. Clair River prior to the War of 1812 and there married Mary Harrow, whose father had served as a captain of British naval vessels on the Upper Lakes during and after the American Revolution. The St. Clair River was, and still remains, a nursery of sailors and seamanship, and Stephen Grummond while still in his teens became a sailor and at twenty-one obtained control of a tiny vessel which became the basis of his subsequent fortune. In 1855 he removed to Detroit, where in time he became the owner of a steamship line and operator of one of the largest lines of tugs on the Great Lakes. He held various local public offices, including that of Mayor of Detroit in the eighties.

George Washington Grummond, who we infer was a younger brother of Stephen, appears in Detroit directories from 1857 on as a sailor. Evidently he joined the Light Guard Company, Detroit's most notable military organization, for when the news of Fort Sumter aroused the nation in April, 1861 he was serving as first sergeant of the company. It offered itself as a body to become Company A of the First Michigan Regiment of three months' troops on April 16, 1861, and as first sergeant, Grummond, then aged 21, was the fourth man to sign the roll. By reason of the character of the membership and their familiarity with military discipline the Company provided an astonishing number of commissioned officers to regiments subsequently organized. One of them was Grummond, who in September, 1861, was commissioned captain in the First Michigan Regiment of three-year troops. Subsequently he served as major and as lieutenant colonel of the Fourteenth Michigan Infantry, from which he was honorably mustered out in July 1865. In May, 1866 he was commissioned a second lieutenant in the Eighteenth U.S. Infantry, Colonel Carrington's Regiment. His further story is sufficiently related by Mrs. Carrington.

Chapter 30

THE foregoing narrative has given the distances for the best day-by-day marches, and such facts as to wood, grass, and water as are of practical value along the route from the Union Pacific Railroad to Fort Philip Kearney.

The westward-bound traveler will find at Omaha such extensive supplies of merchandise and outfit, at the establishments of W. R. King & Co., Jewett & Ely, John M. McCormick & Co., Hurfords, Lehmen & Co., Stephens and Wilcox, C. F. Catlin, S. & A. B. Saunders, and fifty other grocery, hardware, dry goods, and stationery houses, that he will find himself not a whit at loss if he has reached that city without much antecedent outlay; while the Union Pacific Railroad regularly transports its burdens beyond the first spur of the Rocky Mountains, passing en route the wagon departure at Horse Shoe Creek, and again at Cheyenne, affording a comparatively easy route to Laramie and points beyond.

To those who travel with their own wagons and substance, this narrative gives many hints; but the whole line from Leavenworth, or Nebraska City, on the south side of the Platte, has been temporarily impaired by the Indian encroachments, the westward tide of travel, and the natural laws of that advance. With no affectation of scientific research more than to collect such botanical, floral, and geological specimens as the circumstances of the march would permit and a natural taste for such study would prompt, our information from competent sources, in company, sets forth southern and middle Nebraska as full of promise. The beautiful farming lands back of Omaha will find their contesting claimants; while salt, building material, and indications of coal show that the State is capable of expansion and self-support with little extrinsic aid.

Beyond Nebraska, and apart from the accommodations of the Union Pacific Railroad, the ox and mule teams still hold supremacy, and for their benefit some further information is given.

The trip of Major James Bridger and guide Henry Williams in 1866, who were sent forward by Colonel Carrington to visit the authorities of Montana and survey the route, or shorten it and open a new route, furnishes many facts additional to those contained in the report of Colonel Sawyer,[42] and their notes, somewhat abridged, are by permission freely used for our present purpose, with the confidence that this will always be an avenue for travel, though interrupted in the settlement of Indian questions for a time.

The following statement closely approximates the odometer measurement of General Hazen in 1866, and while this is twenty miles less than Colonel Sawyer's route, the course of travel adopted by Major Bridger confirms his opinion that nearly thirty miles more can be saved as soon as the government or emigration can safely operate and improve the road:

Fort Philip Kearney to Fort C. F. Smith..........................	91 miles.
Fort C. F. Smith to Clark's Fork...	63 "
Clark's Fork to Yellowstone Ferry ..	90 "
Yellowstone Ferry to Bozeman City.	51 "
Bozeman City to Virginia City.....	70 "
Total..........................	365 miles.

The first distance is divisible as follows:

Fort Philip Kearney to Peno Creek Branch........................	5 miles.

[42] James A. Sawyer's report of his survey of a wagon road from Niobrara to Virginia City in the summer of 1866 was published as Sen. Exec. Doc. 58, U.S. Serial 1277; also as House Exec. Doc. 59, U.S. Serial 1256.

To North Bank of Peno Creek, with timber, grass, and water.........	7 miles.
To Second Crossing of Peno Creek, with same supplies.............	6 "
To Crossing of Goose Creek, with same supplies..................	4 "
To Brown's Fork of Tongue River, with same supplies.............	13 "
To East Fork of Little Horn River, with same supplies.............	17 "
To Grass Lodge Creek, with same supplies.......................	15 "
To Rotten Grass Creek, with same supplies.......................	16 "
To Fort C. F. Smith, Bridger's Cut-off...........................	8 "
Total........................	91 miles.

Between Tongue River and Little Horn River eight forks are crossed, the largest of which, Colonel Kinney's Fork, is quite a stream of clear water, with nearly two feet of depth in the autumn.

Between Little Horn and Big Horn Rivers are nine small streams of constant water.

The Big Horn River is nearly three hundred and thirty yards wide, with from three to six feet of water, and is crossed by a substantial ferry. In 1866 Kirkendall's train lost a wagonmaster by attempting to ford it; but it can be forded, with some little risk to stock and merchandise, at a low stage of water. It is unsafe for strangers, and the ferry is indispensable to general travel.

Fort C. F. Smith, on the Big Horn River, was built by Brevet Lieutenant-Colonel N. C. Kinney, Captain of the 18th Infantry in 1866, and suffered less from Indian adventures on account of the vicinity of the friendly Crow Indians, and because it was west of the main hunting-ground of the Arapahoes, Cheyennes, and Sioux.[43] It is the last residence of white men until the traveler reaches Bozeman City.

Associated with Captain Kinney in the building of Fort C. F. Smith, and with wonderful vigor and patience resisting the effect

---

[43] This fort, third of the three Colonel Carrington caused to be built, or rebuilt, to guard the Bozeman Trail, was established August 12, 1866 at the Big Horn Crossing of the trail, in present-day Montana, ninety-one miles north of Fort Philip Kearney. Although no official plan of the fort seems to exist, fairly good descriptions by eye-witnesses are contained in Hebard and Brininstool, *The Bozeman Trail*, 135 ff. Abandoned in 1868, in 1910 only the ruined remains of a few of the original adobe structures were to be seen. Two and one-half miles south of the fort the notable Hayfield fight occurred, in which a handful of soldiers and civilians successfully beat off the attack of several hundred of Red Cloud's warriors. A drawing of the fort as it appeared in 1867 is reproduced by Hebard and Brininstool, Vol. II, facing 110.

of wounds and apprehended heart disease, should be mentioned Brevet Major Thomas B. Burrowes.[44] His father is well known as the veteran friend of education in Pennsylvania.

The second distance, before referred to, is divisible as follows:

From Fort C. F. Smith to Dubois Creek,
   a fork of Beauvàis Fork of Big Horn
   River, N. W. by N............... 10 miles.
   This stream is about fifteen feet wide.
      Road good except the crossings of
      two small creeks, and distant from
      the mountains about seven miles.
      The timber is ash and box elder.

[44] Thomas B. Burrowes of Pennsylvania was commissioned a first lieutenant in the Eighteenth U.S. Infantry, May 14, 1861. He was brevetted Major in September, 1864 for gallant and meritorious service in the battle of Jonesboro, Ga. He retired from active service in March, 1879 and died on October 12, 1885.

His father, Thomas Henry Burrowes, is characterized by his biographer as "a politician by choice and an educator by accident." He was active in promoting the "buckshot war" of 1834 in Pennsylvania, from which he retired ingloriously by crawling through a rear window of the State Senate Chamber, to retire "to the more peaceful pursuit of agriculture." Paradoxically enough for such a character, he had a long and moderately distinguished career as an educator, organizing the free school system of Pennsylvania and ending his life as President of the Pennsylvania Agricultural College.

To North Fork of Dubois Creek, N.W. by N............................. 10 miles.

Road crosses small creeks and ravines, and is quite bad. The
stream is narrow, and eight miles
from the mountains. Grass good,
and timber for fuel.

To South Fork of Prior's River, N.W... 8 miles.

Road passes one long cañon, cutting
the divide between Big Horn and
Rocky Ranges, crossing several
creeks, and in places quite rough.
Grass good.

To Ice Water Spring, N.W. by N...... 15 miles.

At four miles is water in a small
branch. At five miles farther is
Millard's Spring, with good grass
and water. This spring rises and
flows from a high, level prairie, four
miles from the base of the mountains, forming a branch of Prior's
River, three feet wide and twelve
inches deep. At six miles farther
comes Ice Water Spring, with good
grass, but no timber, although at
Prior's River, two miles beyond,
the timber is abundant. Road is
in many places quite rocky. Ice
Water Springs rise from a mound
in the prairie, supplying four small
streams which unite in a channel
six feet wide and three feet deep,
flowing with great rapidity.

To Spring Creek, W.N.W. . . . .   8 miles.

Road crosses Prior River and its four miles of beautiful valley, thence up the valley of Spring Creek, or North Fork of Prior's River. Here are many steep bluffs until the road attains the summit of the divide between Prior's River and Clark's Fork. Grass excellent. Only sufficient timber for fuel.

To Clark's Fork, nearly W . . . .   12 miles.

The road is good, and all prairie except two dry creek-crossings, which are not decidedly bad. Clark's Fork is here nearly one hundred yards wide, with a rich valley and abundance of grass and timber.

Total . . . .   63 miles.

The third distance is divisible as follows:

To Rocky Fork . . . .   7 miles.

This stream is forty-five yards wide, about three feet deep, with good ford. Luxuriant timber and grass. Ten miles from the mountains.

To Berdan's Creek—Branch of Rocky Fork . . . .   12 miles.

Rocky Fork is crossed twice. Good camping-grounds are found every three miles. Grass and timber abundant.

To South Fork of Rosebud .... 10 miles.

Three miles up Berdan's Creek. Road rough until the main divide is reached, between this creek and the South Fork of Rosebud. Stream about fifteen feet wide and two feet deep, abounding in beaver dams. Grass good; but only sufficient timber for fuel. Road runs six miles from mountains.

To Rosebud River Camp .... 8 miles.

Down South Fork of Rosebud one mile; thence crossing a divide of three miles. Rosebud is nearly twenty-five yards wide and two and one-half feet deep. Cottonwood and willow timber is plentiful, and grass good. Thence down Rosebud four miles to best camp. About ten miles from the mountains.

To Stillwater, W.S.W. .... 6 miles.

Road crosses the main Rosebud and follows up Stillwater Fork of Rosebud. Road good, timber heavy, and grass good. Stream is about sixty-five yards wide, three feet deep, and quite a rocky ford. About six miles from the mountains.

To Emmil's Fork .... 18 miles.

The road runs W.S.W., to North Fork of the Stillwater. Grass and

timber very heavy, and camping-
grounds every three miles. One divide is crossed before reaching
Emmil's Fork, which here empties
into the Yellowstone River. Emmil's Fork, named from the massacre of Emmil's party, in 1822, is
about twenty feet wide and eighteen inches deep.[45] The Yellowstone is here about one hundred and
twenty yards wide and from three
to five feet deep. The valley is
from six to fifteen miles wide, and
timber is very heavy.

To Big Boulder Creek . . . . 17 miles.

Eight miles up Yellowstone Valley,

---

[45] The massacre of Immell's party occurred in 1823.
Benjamin O'Fallon, reporting it to General William
Clark of St. Louis, stated that he had been a long time
on the river; formerly an officer in the United States
Army. "In some respects he was an extraordinary man.
He was brave, uncommonly large, and of great muscular
strength. When timely apprised of danger, he was a
host in himself." See H. M. Chittenden, *The American
Fur Trade of the Far West*, I, 154. The only U.S. Army
officer of this name was Michael Immel of Pennsylvania,
successively ensign and second lieutenant in the First
U.S. Infantry, 1807–1808. Major Stephen H. Long, who
conducted a U.S. exploring expedition to the Rocky
Mountains in 1819–20, reported the arrival in his camp
of Immell on his return from an expedition to the Sioux.
He reported the occurrence of a volcanic eruption near
the "pseudo volcanoes" on the Missouri, which seems
to indicate that he had been on the Yellowstone.

crossing Lower Cross Creek at five
miles, and Upper or Big Cross
Creek three miles beyond. Road,
grass, and timber good; thence the
road is over level prairie nine miles,
with abundance of grass and timber.

To Yellowstone Ferry . . . . 12 miles.
Road good. Timber is mostly on the
north bank. The ferry is diagonal-
ly across the river, of nearly two
hundred and seventy-five yards.

Total . . . . 90 miles.

The fourth distance is divisible as follows:

Yellowstone Ferry to Warm Spring,
S.W. . . . . 4½ miles.
Up the Yellowstone River, after
crossing, four and a half miles.
Road here bears west toward the
hills, becoming very heavy, and
crossing a succession of small
creeks and ravines.

To Twenty-five Yard River . . . . 10½ miles.
Southwest five miles across the ridge
to the Yellowstone. Road difficult,
crossing sidling hills. Up the valley two miles to foot of "Big Hill."
Across the ridge, with better road,
3½ miles. This river derives its
name from its width. Plenty of
young timber, and grass good.

To Beaver or Pass Creek.............. 17 miles.
    Road runs S.W. by S. Road for ten
    miles very good, until leaving the
    river and entering the pass called
    Flat Head or Clark's Pass. The
    last eight miles crosses a number
    of spring creeks, which flow from
    the snow range. No timber in this
    pass, except small pine and aspen.

To Cold Spring Creek.............. 10 miles.
    Up Beaver or Pass Creek. Road
    very rough. Grass good. Timber
    in abundance, of small varieties of
    pine and aspen.

To Head-waters, Cold Spring Creek.... 5 miles.
    Road crosses the divide to the east
    Branch of Gallatin River. Timber
    largely destroyed by fire several
    years ago.

To Bozeman City................... 4 miles.
    Down the East Gallatin River. Here
    is a successful flour-mill, and a
    small but thrifty village.

    Total.................. 51 miles.

The fifth distance is divisible as follows.
Road adopted in 1866:

To Madison River................. 33 miles.
    Southwest to West Gallatin River
    thirteen miles. Road runs across
    the valley, which is twelve miles,
    and nearly all occupied by farms,

with abundance of grass, and well
watered by small streams from the
mountains. This river is about one
hundred and fifty yards wide, and
from two to two and one-half feet
deep, very swift, with a heavy
growth of cottonwood timber.
Thence, southwest by south, nearly twenty miles across the dividing
ridge to the Madison River. Road
good; grass abundant; but little
timber near the road.

To Meadow Creek . . . . 21 miles.
Road crosses Madison River. This
river is nearly two hundred yards
wide and three feet deep. Thence
up the stream five miles, westward
up a cañon four miles, to main
divide of Hot Spring valley. This
spring boils up vigorously, and
with temperature unpleasant to
the hand. Near are the first quartz
leads. The road is good, but rough,
Thence south, across the divide,
to Meadow Creek, twelve miles.

To Virginia City—by cut-off . . . . 16 miles.
The usual road is twenty-two miles.
                                                            ———————
Total . . . . 70 miles.

Aggregate distances 365 miles.

Appendix 1

THE following extract, from Senate
Document No. 13, 1867, furnishes
that portion relating to the massacre
near Fort Philip Kearney in 1866, being Report of the Special Commission sent to investigate the cause of that disaster.

DISPOSITION AND CONDUCT OF THE INDIANS
ABOUT FORT PHILIP KEARNEY, AND THE
CAUSES OF THE SAME

The main object sought to be secured by
the treaty of Laramie of July, A.D. 1866, was
the opening of a new route to Montana from
Fort Laramie, *via* Bridger's Ferry and the
head-waters of the Powder, Tongue, and Big
Horn Rivers. This country was occupied
by the Oglala and Mineconjou bands of
Sioux Indians and the northern Cheyenne
and Arapahoe tribes, and the mountain
Crows.

The region through which the road was to
pass and does pass is the most attractive and
valuable to Indians. It abounds with game,
flocks of mountain sheep, droves of elk and

deer, and herds of buffalo range through and live in this country, and the Indians with propriety call it their last best hunting-grounds. All these Indians were reluctant to allow the proposed road to pass through these hunting-grounds, but all would reluctantly assent to this for so liberal an equivalent as the government was ready to give. The Indians were required further to stipulate that the government should have the right to establish one or more military posts on this road in their country. All the Indians occupying it refused thus to stipulate, and through the chiefs, headmen, and soldiers protested against the establishment of any military post on their hunting-grounds along that road north of Fort Reno.

While negotiations were going on with Red Cloud and their leading chiefs to induce them to yield to the government the right to peaceably establish these military posts, which right they persistently refused to yield, saying that it was asking too much of their people—asking all they had—for it would drive away all the game, Colonel H. B. Carrington, 18th United States Infantry, with about seven hundred officers and men, arrived at Laramie, en route to their country to establish and occupy military posts along the Montana road, pursuant to General Orders No. 33, Headquarters Department of the Missouri, March 10, 1866, Major-General Pope commanding. The destination and purpose of Colonel Carrington and his command were communicated to their chiefs. They seemed to construe this as a determination on the part of the government to occupy their country by military posts, even without their consent or that of their people, and as soon as practicable withdrew from the council with their adherents, refusing to accept any presents from the Commission, returned to their country, and with a strong force of warriors commenced a vigorous and relentless war against all whites who came into it, both citizens and soldiers.

Quite a large number of Indians, who did not occupy the country along this road, were anxious to make a treaty and remain at peace. Some of this class had for a long time resided near Fort Laramie. Others (Brulès) occupied the White Earth River Valley and the Sand Hills south of that river.

The Commissioners created and appointed several of the leading warriors of these Indians chiefs, viz., Big Mouth, Spotted Tail, Swift Bear, and Two Strikes. A portion of these Indians have remained near Fort Laramie, and a portion of them on the Republican Fork of the Kansas River, and have strictly complied with their treaty stipulations.

The number of Sioux Indians who considered themselves bound by the treaty and have remained at peace is about two thousand, while the Mineconjou and a portion of the Oglala and Brulè bands, the northern Cheyennes and Arapahoes, with a few Sans Arcs, numbering in the aggregate about six hundred lodges, remained in their old country and went to war under the auspices of their old chiefs.

We therefore report that all the Sioux Indians occupying the country about Fort Philip Kearney have been in a state of war against the whites since the 20th day of June, A.D. 1866, and that they have waged and carried on this war for the purpose of defending their ancient possessions and the possessions acquired by them from the Crow Indians by conquest after bloody wars, from invasion and occupation by the whites.

This war has been carried on by the Indians with most extraordinary vigor and unwonted success. During the time from July 26th, the day on which Lieutenant Wands's train was attacked, to the 21st day of December, on which Brevet Lieutenant-Colonel Fetterman, with his command of eighty officers and men, was overpowered and massacred, they killed ninety-one enlisted men and five officers of our army, and killed fifty-eight citizens and wounded twenty more, and captured and drove away three hundred and six oxen and cows, three hundred and four mules, and one hundred and sixty-one horses. During this time they appeared in front of Fort Philip Kearney, making hostile demonstrations and committing hostile acts, fifty-one different times, and attacked nearly every train and person that attempted to pass over the Montana road.

MASSACRE OF BREVET LIEUTENANT-COLONEL FETTERMAN'S PARTY, AND THE CAUSES WHICH LED TO IT

General Orders No. 33, Headquarters Department of Missouri, dated March 10, 1866, directed that two new military posts should be established on this new route to Montana—one "near the base of the Big Horn Mountain," the other "on or near the Upper Yellowstone"—and designated the 2d Battalion of the 18th Infantry to garrison the three posts on this route, and created the Mountain District, Department of the Platte, and directed the colonel of the regiment (Colonel H. B. Carrington) to take post at Fort Reno and command the district, which included all the troops and garrisons on this route.

General Orders No. 7, Headquarters Department of the Platte, June 23, 1866, directed that the 2d Battalion 18th Infantry should take post as follows: Two companies at Fort Reno, on Powder River, two companies about eighty miles nearly north of Reno, on the waters of Powder or Tongue River, which post should be known as Fort Philip Kearney, and two companies at the crossing of the Big Horn River on the same road, and about seventy miles beyond Fort Philip Kearney, to be known as Fort C. F. Smith, and directed that the colonel of the regiment should take post at Fort Philip Kearney, and command the "mountain district."

The orders above referred to were issued with the express understanding, apparently, that this road to Montana was to be opened through the Indian country by compact or treaty with the Indians occupying it, and not by conquest and the exercise of arbitrary power on the part of the government. Hence Colonel Carrington's instructions looked mainly to the duty of selecting and building the two new forts, Philip Kearney and C. F. Smith, and the command assigned was only sufficient for this purpose and properly garrisoning the posts. This command numbered in all about seven hundred men, five hundred of whom were new recruits, and twelve officers, including district commander and staff. The commanding officer, Colonel Carrington, could not and did not fail to see at once, that although his command was entirely sufficient to erect the new forts, build the barracks, warehouses, and stables, and make preparations for winter, and properly garrison his posts, and could protect emigration from the small thieving parties of Indians, it was still entirely inadequate to carry on systematic and aggressive war against a most powerful tribe of Indians, fighting to maintain possession and control of their own country, in addition to those other duties. This officer carried the orders above referred to into effect with promptness and zeal, organizing the mountain district June 28, 1866, establishing Fort Philip Kearney on the 15th of July, and Fort C. F. Smith on the 3d day of August, and as early as the 31st day of July informed General P. St. George Cooke, the department commander, that the status of Indians in that country was one of war, and requested reinforcements sent to him, and two days previously had telegraphed the adjutant-general of the army for Indian auxiliaries, and additional force of his own regiment.

On the 9th of August, General Cooke, commanding department of the Platte, informed Colonel Carrington that Lieutenant-General Sherman ordered the posts in his, Colonel Carrington's district, supported as much as possible, and announced a regiment coming from St. Louis.

No auxiliaries were assigned, and no reinforcements came until November, when company C, 2d United States Cavalry, reached Fort Kearney, sixty strong, armed with Springfield rifles and Star carbines. In December, about ninety recruits joined the battalion in the mountain district, a portion of whom were assigned to a company stationed at Fort Philip Kearney. No other reinforcements were sent to the district. Approved requisitions for ammunition were not answered. The command at Fort C. F. Smith was reduced to ten rounds per man; the command at Fort Philip Kearney to forty-five rounds per man, and the command at Fort Reno to thirty rounds per man. Recruits could not practice any in firing. Little time could be allowed from fatigue duty for drill, and with but twelve officers and three posts little could have been done in drilling recruits, if time could have been allowed.

The result of all this was that the troops were in no condition to fight successful battles with Indians or other foes, and this from no fault of Colonel Carrington; and I am astonished at the zeal with which they fought, and the damage they inflicted, December 21st.

The numerous demonstrations and attacks made by Indians prior to the 6th of December seemed to have been made for the sole purpose of capturing stock, picket posts, and small parties of soldiers who might venture beyond the cover of the garrison, and of annoying and checking the wood train constantly drawing material for the new forts.

On the morning of December 6th the wood train was attacked, a common occurrence, about two miles from the fort, and forced to corral and defend itself. Brevet Lieutenant-Colonel Fetterman, with a command of seventeen mounted infantry and thirty-five cavalry, moved out to relieve the wood train, and drive off the Indians, and Colonel Carrington, with twenty-five mounted infantry, moved out for the purpose of cutting off the Indians from retreat, and destroying them. On this day, at a point on Peno Creek, about five miles from the fort, the Indians, the second time after the fort was established, made a stand and strong resistance, and nearly surrounded Colonel Fetterman's party. The infantry obeyed orders and behaved well. The cavalry, with the exception of ten enlisted men, disobeyed the orders of Colonel Fetterman, and fled with great precipitancy from this portion of the field. As the cavalry retreated, the Indians made a great display and every effort to create a panic with the infantry, but Colonel Fetterman, Lieutenant Wands, and Lieutenant Brown succeeded in keeping this small body of infantry cool, and by reserving their fire for proper range, rescued it from annihilation, and made a junction with Colonel Carrington's party, on the east side of Peno Creek. Lieutenant Bingham, after leaving Colonel Fetterman's party, with Lieutenant Grummond, a sergeant from Colonel Carrington's command, and two men from his own, without the knowledge or orders of any of his superiors, pursued into an ambuscade, more than two miles from the main party, a single Indian who was on foot just in front of their horses, and Lieutenant Bingham and the sergeant were there killed. The results of this day's fighting, although not of a decidedly successful character to the Indians, were such as naturally to induce the belief on their part that by proper management and effort they could overpower and destroy any force that could be sent out from the fort to fight them, and no doubt at this time they resolved to make the effort the first auspicious day, and postponed their proceedings from the new to the full moon. In the mean time everything was quiet about the fort, although they often appeared on the surrounding hills.

On the morning of December 21st the picket at the signal station signaled to the fort that the wood train was attacked by Indians, and corralled, and the escort fighting. This was not far from 11 o'clock A.M., and the train was about two miles from the fort, and moving toward the timber. Almost immediately a few Indian pickets appeared on one or two of the surrounding heights, and a party of about twenty near the Big Piney, where the Montana road crosses the same, within howitzer range of the fort. Shells were thrown among them from the artillery in the fort, and they fled.

The following detail, viz., fifty men and two officers from the four different infantry companies, and twenty-six cavalrymen and one officer, was made by Colonel Carrington. The entire force formed in good order and was placed under command of Brevet Lieutenant-Colonel Fetterman, who received the following orders from Colonel Carrington: "Support the wood train, relieve it, and report to me. Do not engage or pursue Indians at its expense; under no circumstances pursue over Lodge Trail Ridge." These instructions were repeated by Colonel Carrington in a loud voice to the command when in motion and outside the fort, and again delivered in substance through Lieutenant Wands, officer of the day, to Lieutenant Grummond, commanding cavalry detachment, who was requested to communicate them again to Colonel Fetterman.

Colonel Fetterman moved out rapidly to the right of the wood road, for the purpose no doubt of cutting off the retreat of the Indians then attacking the train. As he advanced across the Piney, a few Indians appeared in his front and on his flanks, and continued flitting about him, beyond rifle range, till they disappeared beyond Lodge Trail Ridge. When he was on Lodge Trail Ridge, the picket signaled the fort that the Indians had retreated from the train; the train had broken corral and moved on toward the timber.

The train made the round trip, and was not again disturbed that day.

At about fifteen minutes before 12 o'clock Colonel Fetterman's command had reached the crest of Lodge Trail Ridge, was deployed as skirmishers, and at a halt. Without regard to orders, for reasons that the silence of

Colonel Fetterman now prevents us from giving, he, with the command, in a few moments disappeared, having cleared the ridge, still moving north. Firing at once commenced, and increased in rapidity till, in about fifteen minutes and at about 12 o'clock M., it was a continuous and rapid fire of musketry, plainly audible at the fort. Assistant Surgeon Hines, having been ordered to join Fetterman, found Indians on a part of Lodge Trail Ridge not visible from the fort, and could not reach the force there struggling to preserve its existence. As soon as the firing became rapid Colonel Carrington ordered Captain Ten Eyck, with about seventy-six men, being all the men for duty in the fort, and two wagons with ammunition, to join Colonel Fetterman immediately. He moved out and advanced rapidly toward the point from which the sound of firing proceeded, but did not move by so short a route as he might have done. The sound of firing continued to be heard during his advance, diminishing in rapidity and number of shots till he reached a high summit overlooking the battle-field, at about a quarter before 1 o'clock, when one or two shots closed all sound of conflict.

Whether he could have reached the scene of action by marching over the shortest route as rapidly as possible in time to have relieved Colonel Fetterman's command, I am unable to determine.

Immediately after Captain Ten Eyck moved out, and by orders of Colonel Carrington issued at the same time as the orders detailing that officer to join Colonel Fetterman, the quartermaster's employees, convalescents, and all others in garrison were armed and provided with ammunition and held in readiness to reinforce the troops fighting, or defend the garrison.

Captain Ten Eyck reported, as soon as he reached a summit commanding a view of the battle-field, that the Peno Valley was full of Indians; that he could see nothing of Colonel Fetterman's party, and requested that a howitzer should be sent to him. The howitzer was not sent. The Indians, who at first beckoned him to come down, now commenced retreating, and Captain Ten Eyck, advancing to a point where the Indians had been standing in a circle, found the dead naked bodies of Brevet Lieutenant-Colonel Fetterman, Captain Brown, and about sixty-five of the soldiers of their command. At this point there were no indications of a severe struggle. All the bodies lay in a space not exceeding thirty-five feet in diameter. No empty cartridge shells were about, and there were some full cartridges. A few American horses lay dead a short distance off, all with their heads toward the fort. This spot was by the roadside, and beyond the summit of a hill rising to the east of Peno Creek. The road, after rising this hill, follows this ridge along for about half or three-quarters of a mile, and then descends abruptly to Peno Creek. At about half the distance from where these bodies lay to the point where the road commences to descend to Peno Creek was the dead body of Lieutenant Grummond; and still farther on, at the point where the road commences to descend to Peno Creek, were the dead bodies of the three citizens and four or five of the old, long-tried and experienced soldiers. A great number of empty cartridge shells were on the ground at this point, and more than fifty lying on the ground about one of the dead citizens, who used a Henry rifle. Within a few hundred yards in front of this position ten Indian ponies lay dead, and there were sixty-five pools of dark and clotted blood. No Indian ponies or pools of blood were found at any other point. Our conclusion, therefore, is that the Indians were massed to resist Colonel Fetterman's advance along Peno Creek on both sides of the road; that Colonel Fetterman formed his advanced lines on the summit of the hill overlooking the creek and valley, with a reserve near where the large number of dead bodies lay; that the Indians, in force of from fifteen to eighteen hundred warriors, attacked him vigorously in this position, and were successfully resisted by him for half an hour or more; that the command then being short of ammunition, and seized with panic at this event and the great numerical superiority of the Indians, attempted to retreat toward the fort; that the mountaineers and old soldiers, who had learned that a movement from Indians, in an engagement, was equivalent to death, remained in their first position, and were killed there; that immediately upon the commencement of the retreat the Indians charged upon and surrounded the party, who could not now be formed by their officers, and were immediately killed. Only six men of the whole command were killed by balls, and two of these, Lieutenant-Colonel Fetterman and Captain Brown, no doubt inflicted this death upon themselves, or each other, by their own hands, for both were shot through the left temple, and powder burnt into the skin and flesh about the wound. These officers had also oftentimes asserted that they would not be taken alive by Indians.

In the critical examination we have given this painful and horrible affair we do not find, of the immediate participants, any officer living deserving of censure; and even if evidence justifies it, it would ill become us to speak evil of or censure those dead who sacrificed life struggling to maintain the authority and power of the government and add new luster to our arms and fame.

Of those who have been more remotely connected with the events that led to the massacre, we have endeavored to report so specifically as to enable yourself and the President, who have much official information that we cannot have, to determine where the censure must fall. The difficulty, in a nutshell, was that the commanding officer of the district was furnished no more troops or supplies for this state of war than had been provided and furnished him for a state of profound peace.

In regions where all was peace, as at Laramie in November, twelve companies were stationed; while in regions where all was war, as at Philip Kearney, there were only five companies allowed.

Appendix 2

LIST OF MEN KILLED IN ACTION WITH INDIANS NEAR FORT PHILIP KEARNEY, D. T., ON THE 21ST DAY OF DECEMBER, 1866.

No.	NAMES.	RANK.	COMP'Y.	BATTALION AND REGIMENT.
1.	Augustus Lange....	1st Sergt.	A	2d, 18th Inf.
2.	Hugh Murphy......	Sergt.	"	"
3.	Robert Lennon.....	Corporal.	"	"
4.	William Dule.......	"	"	"
5.	Frederick Acherman.	Private.	"	"
6.	William Betzler.....	"	"	"
7.	Thomas Burke......	"	"	"
8.	Henry Buchanan....	"	"	"
9.	George E. R. Goodall	"	"	"
10.	Michael Harlen.....	"	"	"
11.	Martin Kelley......	"	"	"
12.	Patrick Shannon....	"	"	"
13.	Charles N. Taylor...	"	"	"
14.	Joseph D. Thomas..	"	"	"
15.	David Thorey......	"	"	"
16.	John Timson.......	"	"	"
17.	Albert H. Walter...	"	"	"
18.	John M. Weaver....	"	"	"
19.	Maximilian Dehring.	"	"	"
20.	Francis S. Gordon...	"	"	"
21.	John Woodruff.....	"	"	"
22.	Francis Raymond...	Sergt.	C	"
23.	Patrick Rooney.....	"	"	"
24.	Gustave A. Bauer...	Corporal.	"	"
25.	Patrick Gallagher ..	"	"	"
26.	Henry E. Aarons....	Private	"	"
27.	Michael O'Gara....	"	"	"

314

Appendix

LIST OF MEN KILLED IN ACTION, ETC.
—*Continued*

No.	Names.	Rank.	Comp'y.	Battalion and Regiment.
28.	Jacob Rosenberg....	Private.	C	2d, 18th Inf.
29.	Frank P. Sullivan...	"	"	"
30.	Patrick Smith......	"	"	"
31.	William Morgan....	Sergeant.	E	"
32.	John Quinn........	Corporal.	"	"
33.	George W. Burrell..	Private.	"	"
34.	Timothy Cullinans..	"	"	"
35.	John Maher........	"	"	"
36.	George N. Waterbury.	"	"	"
37.	Alexander Smith....	1st. Sergt.	H	"
38.	Ephraim C. Bissell..	Sergeant.	"	"
39.	George Philip......	Corporal.	"	"
40.	Michael Sharkey....	"	"	"
41.	Frank Karston.....	"	"	"
42.	George Davis.......	Private.	"	"
43.	Perrie F. Doland....	"	"	"
44.	Asa H. Griffin......	"	"	"
45.	Herman Keil.......	"	"	"
46.	James Kean........	"	"	"
47.	Michael Kinney....	"	"	"
48.	Delos Reed........	"	"	"
49.	Thomas M. Madden.	Recruit.	unas'd	"
50.	James Baker.......	Sergeant.	C	2d Cavalry.
51.	James Kelley.......	Corporal.	"	"
52.	Thomas F. Honigan.	"	"	"
53.	Adolph Metzlers....	Bugler.	"	"
54.	John McCarty......	Artificer.	"	"
55.	Thomas Amberson..	Private.	"	"
56.	Thomas Broglin....	"	"	"
57.	William Bugbee....	"	"	"
58.	William Cornog.....	"	"	"
59.	Charles Cuddy.....	"	"	"
60.	Patrick Clancey....	"	"	"

Absaraka

No.	NAMES.	RANK.	COMP'Y.	BATTALION AND REGIMENT.
61.	Harry S. Deming...	Private.	C	2d Cavalry.
62.	Hugh B. Doran.....	"	"	"
63.	Robert Daniel......	"	"	"
64.	Nathan Foreman...	"	"	"
65.	Andrew M. Fitzgerald	"	"	"
66.	Daniel Greene......	"	"	"
67.	Charles Gamford....	"	"	"
68.	John Giller.........	"	"	"
69.	Ferdinand Houser...	"	"	"
70.	Frank Jones........	"	"	"
71.	James B. McGuire..	"	"	"
72.	John McColley.....	"	"	"
73.	George W. Nugent..	"	"	"
74.	Franklin Payne.....	"	"	"
75.	James Ryan........	"	"	"
76.	Oliver Williams.....	"	"	"
77.	John Wheatley.....	Citizen.		
78.	John Fisher........	"		

Enlisted Men 18th U. S. Infantry..............49
  "   "   2d U. S. Cavalry.................27
Citizens.......................................2
                 ——
    Total.............................78

NAMES OF COMMISSIONED OFFICERS OF THE 18TH U. S. INFANTRY KILLED IN THE SAME ACTION

Captain William J. Fetterman, Brevet Lieutenant-Colonel U. S. Army.

Captain Frederick H. Brown.

Lieutenant George W. Grummond.

Appendix

RECAPITULATION

	OFFI-CERS	SER-GEANTS	CORPO-RALS	PRI-VATES	CITI-ZENS	AGGRE-GATION
18th Infantry	3	7	8	34	. .	52
2d Cavalry..	. .	1	2	24	. .	27
Citizens.....	. .	. .	. .	. .	2	2
Total...	3	8	10	58	2	81

Appendix 3

OFFICIAL REPORTS OF COLONEL CARRINGTON
ON THE ACTIONS OF DECEMBER 6 AND 21,
1866.

FORT PHILIP KEARNEY, *December* 6, 1866

Bvt. Maj. HENRY G. LITCHFIELD,
  Acting Assistant Adjutant-General,
    Omaha:

I have the honor to report skirmish with a
body of Indians, numbering in the aggregate
not less than 300 warriors, with results and
casualties. The death of Lieutenant Bingham, Second U. S. Cavalry, is greatly la-
mented by us all, and while his unaccount-
able separation from Brevet Lieutenant-
Colonel Fetterman with full half of his command defeated the movement as originated
and in full success, he paid the penalty of
his life, and whatever the circumstances he
died a soldier.

Sergeant Bowers, Company E, second battalion Eighteenth U. S. Infantry, was killed;
first killing 3 Indians.

He had previously distinguished himself
in several Indian skirmishes, and was a veteran of the regiment, honored in life and

mourned in death. He deserves whatever the Government can grant in honor of his memory.

I inclose rough map indicating the movements, and reference to the map already furnished will greatly assist the general commanding in his judgment of the localities referred to.

The facts are as follows: At 1 o'clock p. m. a messenger reported the wood train attacked about 4 miles west. Simultaneously with this report Indians appeared upon Lodge Trail Ridge, and their pickets rode within 2 miles on the north branch of Piney Creek, evidently to watch the movements of the garrison.

I ordered every horse mounted, placing Brevet Lieutenant-Colonel Fetterman, Eighteenth U. S. Infantry, in command of one company, with Lieutenant Bingham's company of regular cavalry, with orders to take the road, relieve the wood party, and crowd the Indians across Piney Creek, giving him instructions that I would in person take the mounted infantry and endeavor to cut off all retreat.

I left first with 21 mounted infantry, 3 orderlies, and Lieutenant Grummond, as I was familiar with the formation of the country and knew there was no outlet for the attacking force, except across Lodge Trail Ridge or between that ridge and Peno Head, about 9 miles distant from the fort.

Upon reaching the crossing of the creek I found ice formed, but pushed on, having to dismount in 3 feet of water to open the way, my horse being thrown in breaking the ice. Upon clearing the way I pushed on, ascending the eastern slope of Lodge Trail Ridge, making direct for the head of Peno Creek.

The Indian pickets fell back except 3 on the highest ridge. Four miles out 4 Indians appeared in the road to my right. They were pickets, but a party of 32 were in a ravine close by them. At the same time I saw on the hills across the creek over 100 Indians descending to the creek, followed by Lieutenant-Colonel Fetterman's command, which had promptly carried out the original order on the left. Delivering a sharp fire at a small party in my way, who instantly fled, I pushed on at a gallop westward along the ridge. While crossing an intervening ravine the party on the summit of Lodge Trail Ridge disappeared.

Quick firing was now heard on the left, and I could see several large parties operating in the valley of the west fork of Peno Creek and retiring before the advance of Fetterman's command. They seemed to have noticed my appearance and to have returned, but again retired as I advanced.

Upon descending the ridge to take the main valley of Peno and cut off the body operating on the west branch, I found to my surprise 15 cavalry, dismounted and without an officer. I passed through them, ordering them to mount and follow upon the gallop.

Upon turning the point marked "A" upon the map, I was confronted by a large force of Indians, who, retiring before Captain Fetterman's command, attempted to cut off my detachment or stop its advance.

But 6 men turned the point with me, one a young bugler of the Second Cavalry, who told me that Lieutenant Bingham had gone down the road around the hill to the right. This seemed impossible, as he belonged to Captain Fetterman's command. I sounded the recall on his report, but in vain. One of my men fell and his horse on him. The principal chief operating during the day attempted to secure his scalp, but, dismounting, with 1 man to hold horses, and reserving fire, I succeeded in saving the man and holding the position until joined by Fetterman, twenty minutes after. The cavalry that had abandoned him had not followed me, though the distance was short; but the Indians, circling around and yelling, nearly 100 in number, with one saddle emptied by a single shot fired by myself, did not venture to close in. Upon the appearance of this force the Indians broke in every direction. I moved to the right towards Lieutenant Bingham's reported movement, and soon met Lieutenant Grummond with 3 men, hotly pursued by Indians. He informed me that he had met Lieutenant Bingham after descending the ridge, and accompanied him, with the idea that the cavalry were close behind; but that, while chasing a dismounted Indian and cutting him with their sabers, they were surrounded and Lieutenant Bingham was cut off.

After an hour's search we found Lieutenant Bingham's body and that of Sergeant Bowers. The latter was still living, but not scalped. He died before an ambulance arrived from the fort, having been cleft to the brain.

Severe weather and coming night prevented further pursuit, the Indians breaking for the mountains and Tongue River Valley.

My total casualties were: One officer killed, 1 sergeant killed, 1 sergeant and 4 privates wounded. Three horses were killed and 5 wounded. The Indians' loss was not less than 10 killed, besides wounded; and several of their ponies and Indians on foot were seen before dark working down the valley or over the hills.

Reference is had to Brevet Lieutenant-Colonel Fetterman's report also. He knew little of the country, but carried out his instructions promptly. Captain Brown, who accidently joined him, knew the ground, and the result would have been a good fight if he had retained Lieutenant Bingham's command.

By hard riding I reached the point I hoped to attain, the Indians fleeing before me; but by the decease of Lieutenant Bingham all clue is lost to his leaving his commanding officer, or his object. If he left to join my party he neglected to report to me. His sergeant says his horse ran away with him, and that the lieutenant told him he could not hold him.

It is due to the cavalry to say that they were mostly recruits and are all ready to take the next chance.

My regimental quartermaster, Lieut. A. H. Wands, by mistake joined the wrong party, supposing I took the road to the woods, but did good service. Captain Brown, always quick after an Indian skirmish, and whose operations September 25, 1866, deserve public mention, went as volun-

teer and greatly contributed to the success
of Captain Fetterman's movements.

Much was done. The loss of Lieutenant
Bingham makes all seem loss; but the winter
campaign is fairly open and will be met.

I do, however, most earnestly ask for
officers. As Brevet Captain Bisbee leaves,
Captain Brown also, I am to be left again
with 6 officers for 6 companies, including
adjutant and commissary.

Potter, Fenton, and others should come at
once. If Captain Burrowes goes before retiring board and Captain Kinney's resignation
is accepted the upper post will suffer also.

This is all wrong. There is much at stake;
I will take my full share, but 2 officers to a
company is small allowance enough, with mercury at zero and active operations on hand.

I am, very respectfully, your obedient
servant,

HENRY B. CARRINGTON,
Colonel Eighteenth U. S. Infantry,
Commanding Post.

From the 6th to the 19th of December Indians appeared almost daily about the wood
party or within sight of the fort. December
19 the picket on Pilot Hill reported the
train as corralled and threatened by a large
force. I sent Brevet Major Powell with a

detachment to relieve the train. He did his work—pressed the Indians towards Lodge Trail Ridge, but having peremptory orders not to cross it, he returned with the train, reporting the Indians in large force, and that if he had crossed the ridge he never would have come back with his command.

On the morning of the 20th, very early, I had both saw-mills at work upon 3-inch plank, and at 9 o'clock, with 60 infantry and 20 cavalry, and the ordinary train guard, I went myself to the woods to test the animus and force of the Indians, and to build a bridge across Piney Creek, to facilitate the passage of the wagons off Pine Island, and two channels up to the divide, from which the trains moved to and from the fort. Trees were felled for stringers; the bridge, 45 feet long and 16 feet wide, was built; the wagons were loaded, and the train reached the fort at 6 o'clock p. m. without casualty. I saw no Indians and no fresh trail upon the snow which had fallen the night before. December 21, anticipating that Indians might have seen my work, I gave the wood train additional guard, which, with the ax-men (soldiers) and armed teamsters, made not far from 90 men.

The picket on Pilot Hill reported the wood train to be corralled about a mile and a half from the fort. The movement made to support the train will appear from the following official reports:

HEADQUARTERS POST,
Fort Philip Kearney, Dak.,
January 3, 1867.

ASSISTANT ADJUTANT-GENERAL, DEPARTMENT OF THE PLATTE,
Omaha, Nebr.:

SIR: I respectfully state the facts of fight with Indians on the 21st ultimo. This disaster had the effect to confirm my judgment as to the hostility of Indians, and solemnly declares by its roll of dead and the number engaged that my declaration, from my arrival at Laramie, in June, was not idle conjecture, but true.

It also declares that in Indian warfare there must be perfect coolness, steadiness, and judgment. This contest is in their best and almost last hunting-grounds. They can not be whipped or punished by some little dash after a handful, nor by mere resistance of offensive movements. They must be subjected and made to respect and fear the whites.

It also declares with equal plainness that my letter from Fort Laramie as to the absolute failure of the treaty, so far as relates to my command, was true.

It also vindicates every report from my pen and every measure I have taken to secure defensive and tenable posts on this line.

It vindicates my administration of the Mountain District, Department of the Platte, and asserts that the confidence reposed in me by Lieutenant-General Sherman has been fully met.

It vindicates my application so often made for reinforcements, and demonstrates the fact that if I had received those assured to me by telegraph and letter I could have kept up communications and opened a safe route for emigrants next spring.

It proves correct my report of 1,500 lodges of hostile Indians on Tongue River not many hours' ride from the post.

It no less declares that while there has been partial success in impromptu dashes, the Indian, now desperate and bitter, looks upon the rash white man as a sure victim, no less than he does a coward, and that the United States must come to the deliberate resolve to send an army equal to a fight with the Indians of the Northwest.

Better to have the expense at once than to have a lingering, provoking war for years. It must be met, and the time is just now. I respectfully refer to my official reports and correspondence from department headquarters for verification of the foregoing propositions, and proceed to the details of Fetterman's massacre.

On the morning of the 21st ultimo at about 11 o'clock a. m. my picket on Pilot Hill reported the wood train corralled and threatened by Indians on Sullivant Hills, a mile and a half from the fort. A few shots were heard; Indians also appeared in the brush at the crossing of Pinery by the Virginia City road. Upon tendering to Brevet Major Powell the command of Company C, Second U. S. Cavalry, then without an officer, but which he had been drilling, Brevet Lieutenant-Colonel Fetterman claimed by rank to go out. I acquiesced, giving him the men of his own company that were for duty and a portion of Company C, Second Battalion, Eighteenth U. S. Infantry.

Lieut. G. W. Grummond, who had commanded the mounted infantry, requested to take out the cavalry. He did so. In the previous skirmish Lieutenant Grummond was barely saved from the disaster that befell Lieutenant Bingham by timely aid.

Brevet Lieutenant-Colonel Fetterman also was admonished, as well as myself, that we were fighting brave and desperate enemies who sought to make up by cunning and deceit all the advantage which the white man gains by intelligence and better arms.

My instructions were therefore peremptory and explicit. I knew the ambition of each to win honor, but being unprepared for large aggressive action through want of force (now fully demonstrated), I looked to continuance of timber supplies to prepare for more troops as the one practicable duty. Hence two days before Major Powell, sent out to cover the train under similar circumstances, simply did that duty when he could have had a fight to any extent.

The day before, viz., the 20th ultimo, I went myself to the Pinery and built a bridge of 45 feet span to expedite the passage of wagons from the woods into open ground.

Hence my instruction to Brevet Lieutenant-Colonel Fetterman, viz., "Support the wood train, relieve it, and report to me. Do not engage or pursue Indians at its expense. Under no circumstances pursue over the ridge, viz., Lodge Trail Ridge, as per map in your possession."

To Lieutenant Grummond I gave orders to report to Brevet Lieutenant-Colonel Fetterman, implicitly obey orders, and not leave him.

Before the command left I instructed Lieut. A. H. Wands, my regimental quartermaster and acting adjutant, to repeat these orders. He did so. Fearing still that the spirit of ambition might override prudence (as my refusal to permit 60 mounted men and 40 citizens to go for several days down Tongue River Valley after villages had been unfavorably regarded by Brevet Lieutenant-Colonel Fetterman and Captain Brown), I crossed the parade and from a sentry platform halted the cavalry and again repeated my precise orders.

I knew that the Indians had for several days returned, each time with increased numbers, to feel our strength and decoy detachments to their sacrifice, and believed to foil their purpose was actual victory until reinforcement should arrive and my preparations were complete. I was right. Just as the command left, 5 Indians reappeared at the crossing. The glass revealed others in the thicket, having the apparent object of determining the watchfulness of the garrison or cutting off any small party that should move out. A case-shot dismounted 1 and developed nearly 30 more, who broke for the hills and ravines to the north.

In half an hour the picket reported that the wood train had broken corral and moved on to the Pinery. No report came from the detachment. It was composed of 81 officers and men, including 2 citizens, all well armed, the cavalry having new carbines, while the detachment of infantry was of choice men, the pride of their companies.

At 12 o'clock firing was heard toward Peno Creek, beyond Lodge Trail Ridge. A few shots were followed by constant shots, not to be counted. Captain Ten Eyck was immediately dispatched with infantry and the remaining cavalry and 2 wagons and orders to join Colonel Fetterman at all hazards.

The men moved promptly and on the run, but within little more than half an hour from the first shot, and just as the supporting party reached the hill overlooking the scene of action, all firing ceased.

Captain Ten Eyck sent a mounted orderly back with the report that he could see and hear nothing of Fetterman, but that a body of Indians on the road below him were challenging him to come down, while larger bodies were in all the valleys for several miles around. Moving cautiously forward with the wagons—evidently supposed by the enemy to be guns, as mounted men were in advance—he rescued from the spot where the enemy had been nearest 49 bodies, including those of Brevet Lieutenant-Colonel Fetterman and Capt. F. H. Brown. The latter went out without my consent or knowledge, fearless to fight Indians with any adverse odds, and determined to kill one at least before joining his company.

Captain Ten Eyck fell back slowly, but not pressed by the enemy, reaching the fort without loss. The following morning, finding general doubt as to the success of an attempt to recover other bodies, but believing that failure to rescue them would dishearten the command and encourage the Indians, who are so particular in this regard, I took 80 men and went to the scene of action, leaving a picket to advise me of any movement in the rear and to keep signal communication with the garrison. The scene of action told its story. The road on the little ridge where the final stand took place was strewn with arrowheads, scalp poles, and broken shafts of spears. The arrows that were spent harmlessly from all direction show that the command was suddenly overwhelmed, surrounded, and cut off while in retreat. Not an officer or man survived. A few bodies were found at the north end of the divide, over which the road runs, just below Lodge Trail Ridge.

Nearly all were heaped near four rocks at the point nearest the fort, these rocks, inclosing a space about 6 feet square, having been the last refuge for defense. Here were also a few unexpended rounds of Spencer cartridges.

Fetterman and Brown had each a revolver shot in the left temple. As Brown always declared he would reserve a shot for himself as a last resort, so I am convinced that these two brave men fell each by the other's hand rather than undergo the slow torture inflicted upon others.

Lieutenant Grummond's body was on the road between the two extremes with a few others. This was not far from 5 miles from the fort and nearly as far from the wood train. Neither its own guard nor the detachment could by any possibility have helped each other, and the train was incidentally saved by the fierceness of the fight in the brave but rash impulse of pursuit.

The officers who fell believed that no Indian force could overwhelm that number of troops well held in hand.

Their terrible massacres bore marks of great valor, and has demonstrated the force and character of the foe; but no valor could have saved them.

Pools of blood on the road and sloping sides of the narrow divide showed where Indians bled fatally, but their bodies were carried off. I counted 65 such pools in the space of an acre, and 3 within 10 feet of Lieutenant Grummond's body.

Eleven American horses and 9 Indian ponies were on the road or near the line of bodies; others crippled were in the valleys. At the northwest or farther point, between two rocks and apparently where the command first fell back from the valley, realizing their danger, I found citizen James S. Wheatley and Isaac Fisher, of Blue Springs, Nebr., who with "Henry rifles" felt invincible, but fell, one having 105 arrows in his naked body. The widow and family of Wheatley are here. The cartridge-shells about him told how well they fought.

Before closing this report, I wish to say that every man—officer, soldier, or citizen—received burial with such record as to identify each. Fetterman, Brown, and Grummond lie in one grave. The remainder also share one tomb, buried as they fought, together, but the cases in which they were laid are duly placed and numbered.

I asked the general commanding to give my report, in absence of division commander, an access to the eye and ear of the general-in-chief. The department commander must have more troops, and I declare this my judgment solemnly and for the general public good, without one spark of personal ambition other than to do my duty daily as it comes, and whether I seem to speak too plainly or not, ever with the purpose to declare the whole truth, and with proper respect to my superior officers, who are entitled to the facts as to scenes remote from their own immediate notice.

I was asked to send all the bad news; I do it so far as I can. I give some of the facts as to my men, whose bodies I found just at dark, resolved to bring all in, viz.: Mutilations: Eyes torn out and laid on the rocks; noses cut off; ears cut off; chins hewn off; teeth chopped out; joints of fingers; brains taken out and placed on rocks with other members of the body; entrails taken out and exposed; hands cut off; feet cut off; arms taken out from sockets; private parts severed and indecently placed on the person; eyes, ears, mouth, and arms penetrated with spear-heads, sticks, and arrows; ribs slashed to separation with knives; skulls severed in every form, from chin to crown; muscles of calves, thighs, stomach, breast, back, arms, and cheek taken out.

Punctures upon every sensitive part of the body, even to the soles of the feet and palms of the hand.

All this only approximates to the whole truth.

Every medical officer was faithfully aided by a large force of men, and all were not buried until Wednesday after the fight.

The great real fact is that these Indians take alive when possible, and slowly torture. It is the opinion of D. S. M. Horton, post surgeon, that not more than six were killed by balls. Of course the whole arrows, hundreds of which were removed from naked bodies, were all used after removal of the clothing.

I have said enough. It is a hard but absolute duty. In the establishment of this post I designed to put it where it fell the heaviest upon the Indian and, therefore, the better for the emigrant. My duty will be done when I leave, as ordered to my new regiment headquarters, Fort Caspar.

I submit herewith list of casualties, marked A. I shall also, as soon as practicable, make full report for the year 1866 of operations in the establishment of this new line.

I am, very respectfully, your obedient servant,

HENRY B. CARRINGTON,
Colonel Eighteenth Infantry, Commanding.

Index

Index

ABSARAKA, intertribal warfare over, xx, 4–5; history, xxix–xxxviii; description, 3–11; fitness of name, 8, 10; geographical survey, 12–21; climate and resources, 22–29. See also Indians and Gen. Carrington.

Adair, Lieut. John I., activities, 111, 118–19, 127, 146, 186, 205, 272.

Agriculture, resources of Absaraka, 22–24.

Almstedt, Major Henry, celebrates Fourth of July, 112; gift of vegetables, 204.

American Museum, P. T. Barnum conducts, 263.

Ammunition, paucity of supply, 42, 84, 142, 246.

Arapahoe Indians, warfare over Absaraka, xx, 7; attack Julesburg, 50; Treaty of 1866 with, 82, 128; hostile to whites, 152.

Army, separations, 56–57, 205; removals, 203; hospitality, 266, 269, 271–72, 274–75.

Arnold, Capt. Wilbur F., activities, 225, 232, 259–60.

Arrison, Henry, killed, 138.

Arrows, as weapons, 214–16.

Ash Hollow, battle, 38.

Augur, Gen. C. C., 270, 274.

BAD lands, 20.

Bailey, Capt. ——, characterized, 159; party attacked, 184; guides Carringtons, 258–70.

Band, of Eighteenth Regiment, 39, 44, 55, 126, 183, 246.

Barnum, P. T., 263.

Barnes, Sergeant ——, fisherman, 79–80; flagstaff maker, 176; poet, 176, 180.

Beating, of soldiers, prohibited, 124–25, 206.

Beauvais, G. P. ——, rancher, 62–63.

339

Index

Beckwourth, James, activities, 151–52, 226; career, 152–53.

Bené (Beni, Benoit), Jules, career, 49–50.

Bent's Fort, built, 4.

Big Horn Mountains, as boundary of Crows, 3; characterized, 15–17; appearance, 101.

Big Horn River, home of Crows, 3; Sioux occupy, 5; valley described, 20; Fort C. F. Smith established, 113, 144; crossed, 287–88.

Big Mouth, 288.

Big Piney River. See Piney Forks.

Bingham, Lieut. Horatio S., killed, xxx–xxxi, 222–27, 306, 318–24.

Bisbee, Lieut. Wm, H., activities, 52, 205, 324.

Bissell, Lieut. ——, killed, 243.

Black Foot, Crow Chief, 150.

Blackfoot Indians, allies of Sioux, 4.

Black Hills, Cheyennes abandon, 4; gold discovered xxv, 28; new post planned, 42; road via planned, 102.

Black Horse, attends council, 7–8, 127–36; followers beaten, 139–40; illness, 187; peace advocate, 212.

Blacksnakes, 265.

Blood Indians, hostile to whites, 152.

Bonner, T. D. biographer of Beckwourth, 153.

Botsford, ——, 164.

Bows, Indian, 215–16.

Bowers, Sergeant C. R., killed, 225–26, 318–19, 322.

Bowman, Lieut. ——, escorts Carringtons, 257–67.

Bozeman, John M., opens trail, xxii; career, 104–105.

Bozeman Road, origin, xxii, controversy over, xxiv–xxv, 81, 298–300; rivals, 14; forts established on, 30–31. See also General Carrington, Indians, and Fetterman Massacre.

Brannan, ——, as guide, 12, 156; gives warning, 95; killed, 159.

Brent, Lieut. Thomas L., 275.

340

Index

341

Index

Index

Index

Index

Index

Index

Index

Index

Piegan Indians, hostile to whites, 152.

Pilot Hill, described, 170; picket attacked, 184, 186.

Pine timber, abundance, 19–20, 29. See also Pinery.

Pine Island, picnic party, 164–65.

Pinery, besieged, 148; described, 161–63. See also Wood trains.

Piney Forks, described, 19, 169; cascades 191; cattle raided, 196; bridge built, 325, 329.

Platte Bridge. See Fort Caspar.

Platte River, characterized, 45; crossed, 51–54, 273; Old California Crossing, 48, 63. See also North Platte.

Postlewait, Joseph, killed, 145.

Pope, Gen. John B., orders occupation of Absaraka, xxiv, 34, 299; career, 34.

Potter, Adjutant Carroll H., accompanies Carringtons, 270–72.

Potter, Mrs., hospitality, 274.

Powder River, Gen. Connor invades, xxii, 12, 35; Cheyennes occupy, 4–7; Sioux occupy, 5–7; described, 16–18; as white deadline, xxv, 89, 118, 134; Gen. Carrington occupies, 103–257. See also Crazy Woman's Fork, Piney Forks, and Clear Fork.

Powell, Major James, defends trains, 161, 324–25; in Fetterman Massacre, 230, 328–29.

Pretty Bear, attends council, 127–36.

Proctor, Capt. ——, 112, 266.

Pumpkin Buttes, 102, 168.

Pumpkin Creek, 72.

QUIVERS, Indian, 217.

RANCHES, described, 59–69.

Rattlesnakes, 46, 115–16.

Recreations, regimental party, 54–56; at Fort Philip Kearney, 164–70, 190, 205; discarded, 244; flagstaff celebration, 175–82; games of Indian children, 219.

Red Arm, attends council, 7–8, 127–36.

Red Cloud, leader in Indian war, xxiv–xxv, 88, 95, 134, 151–53, 212; campaign against planned, 245–47; career, 88–89.

Index

351

Index

Index

Index